DON QUIXOTE
AND CATHOLICISM

Purdue Studies in Romance Literatures

Editorial Board

Íñigo Sánchez Llama, Series Editors
Elena Coda
Paul B. Dixon
Patricia Hart

Deborah Houk Schocket
Gwen Kirkpatrick
Allen G. Wood

Howard Mancing, Consulting Editor
Floyd Merrell, Consulting Editor
Joyce L. Detzner, Production Editor

Associate Editors

French
Jeanette Beer
Paul Benhamou
Willard Bohn
Thomas Broden
Gerard J. Brault
Mary Ann Caws
Glyn P. Norton
Allan H. Pasco
Gerald Prince
Roseann Runte
Ursula Tidd

Italian
Fiora A. Bassanese
Peter Carravetta
Benjamin Lawton
Franco Masciandaro
Anthony Julian Tamburri

Luso-Brazilian
Fred M. Clark
Marta Peixoto
Ricardo da Silveira Lobo Sternberg

Spanish and Spanish American
Catherine Connor
Ivy A. Corfis
Frederick A. de Armas
Edward Friedman
Charles Ganelin
David T. Gies
Roberto González Echevarría
David K. Herzberger
Emily Hicks
Djelal Kadir
Amy Kaminsky
Lucille Kerr
Howard Mancing
Floyd Merrell
Alberto Moreiras
Randolph D. Pope
Elżbieta Skłodowska
Marcia Stephenson
Mario Valdés

 volume 79

DON QUIXOTE AND CATHOLICISM

Rereading Cervantine Spirituality

Michael J. McGrath

Purdue University Press
West Lafayette, Indiana

Copyright ©2020 by Purdue University. All rights reserved.

♾ The paper used in this book meets the minimum requirements of American National Standard for Information Sciences—Permanence of Paper for Printed Library Materials, ANSI Z39.48-1992.

Printed in the United States of America
Template for interior design by Anita Noble;
template for cover by Heidi Branham.
Cover image:
Allegory of the Battle of Lepanto (1572)
Paolo Veronese (1528–88)
Wikipedia Commons

Cataloging-in-Publication Data on file at the Library of Congress
Paperback ISBN: 978-1-55753-899-4
Epub ISBN: 978-1-55753-900-7
ePDF ISBN: 978-1-55753-901-4

*This book is dedicated with much love to
my mother Virginia McGrath,
to my brother Kevin,
and the memory of my father David T. McGrath.*

Contents

ix Acknowledgments
1 Introduction
7 **Chapter One**
   Miguel de Cervantes and Early Modern Catholicism
35 **Chapter Two**
   The Hermeneutics of Cervantine Spirituality
57 **Chapter Three**
   Don Quixote and Moral Theology
      What a Knight and His Squire Can Teach
      Us About Cervantes's Catholicism
83 **Chapter Four**
   Tilting at the Truth
      Don Quixote's Spiritual Journey
      as a Contemplative in Action
111 **Chapter Five**
   The Anthropological Vision of *Don Quixote*
123 **Chapter Six**
   From La Mancha to Manresa
      Sancho Panza's Incarnational Spirituality
139 Conclusion
141 Notes
171 Bibliography
185 Index

Acknowledgments

When I first read *Don Quixote* as an undergraduate student at Georgia Southern University, I had no idea that it would become as large a part of my life as it is now. While I was an M.A. student at Middlebury College and a Ph.D. student at the University of Kentucky, I had the opportunity to study *Don Quixote* under the guidance of two of the most influential scholars of the novel: Dr. Alberto Sánchez (Middlebury College) and Dr. John Jay Allen (University of Kentucky). Alberto and Jay ignited my passion for *Don Quixote* and Miguel de Cervantes. On a more personal note, their intellectual acumen was only surpassed by their kindness as human beings.

When I was elected to serve on the Executive Board of the Cervantes Society of America (CSA), I had the opportunity to present my research at the Society's annual Cervantes symposium. Earlier versions of the material in this book were subject to the scrutiny of the attendees and presenters, whose knowledge of the novel, Golden Age Spain, and literature in general inspired me to consider *Don Quixote* from new perspectives. I am grateful for their comments, questions, and encouragement. In addition, I am thankful for the reports I received from the anonymous readers of my manuscript. Many thanks, as well, to Joyce Detzner, who is the Production Editor for the Purdue Studies in Romance Literatures series, for her support and guidance.

I wish to acknowledge with gratitude the semester sabbatical Georgia Southern University granted me to conduct research for this book. I would also like to thank Antonio Cortijo, editor of *ehumanista*, and the editors of Iberoamericana Vervuert Publishing for permission to reprint material from the chapters titled "*Don Quixote* and Moral Theology: What a Knight and His Squire Can Teach Us About Cervantes's Catholicism" and "From La Mancha to Manresa: Sancho Panza's Incarnational Spirituality."

As my life unfolded before my eyes, the word "quixotic" was no longer an abstract literary term. It had become a guiding principle of my life. Consequently, I began to view personal experiences, accomplishments, and failures through the lens of Miguel de Cervantes's masterpiece *Don Quixote*. It is a novel that transcends time and space because, as I soon discovered, it is a blueprint for humanity. I am grateful to the many people in my life whose friendship always inspires me to dream the impossible dream.

Introduction

In this study I offer an interpretation of *Don Quixote* that is often readily dismissed. Four hundred years since its publication, Miguel de Cervantes's masterpiece continues to inspire and to challenge the reader. How to interpret a novel like *Don Quixote*, however, presents a formidable challenge because one aspect of its genius is its interpretative malleability. Hispanist Michael Gerli compares reading *Don Quixote* to peeling an onion: "one laughs and cries and is astonished as one advances from the dry exterior mantle and discovers multiple translucent layers of rich discourse built one upon another—all of them genetically connected, yet all separate, all distinct, and all with their own bite and texture. All of Cervantes's texts, it seems, point to multiple references as they produce and multiply resonances and significations—confirm, deny, or equivocate" (Gerli 3–4). British author Sarah Fielding, in the novel *The Cry* (1754), warns the reader not to limit his or her interpretation of the novel only to the knight's amusing adventures:

> To travel through a whole work only to laugh at the chief companion allotted us, is an insupportable burthen. And we should imagine that the reading of that incomparable piece of humor left us by Cervantes, can give but little pleasure to those persons who can extract no other entertainment or emolument from it than laughing at Don Quixote's reveries, and sympathizing in the malicious joy [of his tormentors] ... That strong and beautiful representation of human nature, exhibited in Don Quixote's madness in one point, and extraordinary good sense in every other, is indeed very much thrown away on such readers as consider him only as the object of their mirth. (qtd. in Gerli 13)

Introduction

Cervantes's writing style, often described as "writing between the lines," a technique writers utilize to avoid persecution because of their heterodox ideology, challenges the reader to consider more than what appears on the page. Political philosopher Leo Strauss describes this style of writing as "a peculiar type of literature, in which the truth about all crucial things is presented exclusively between the lines" (25). Naturally, the irony and ambiguity of this style of expression engenders in each reader a subjective interpretation. This process is further complicated, however, if the author's writing style is purposefully ambiguous, as is Cervantes's in *Don Quixote*. In the prologue to *Don Quixote*, for example, Cervantes addresses his relationship with the knight-errant:

> Pero yo, que, aunque parezco padre, soy padrastro de *don Quijote*, no quiero irme con la corriente del uso, ni suplicarte casi con las lágrimas en los ojos, como otros hacen, lector carísimo, que perdones o disimules las faltas que en este mi hijo vieres, y ni eres su pariente ni su amigo, y tienes tu alma en tu cuerpo y tu libre albedrío como el más pintado, y estás en tu casa, donde eres señor della, como el rey de sus alcabalas, y sabes lo que comúnmente se dice, que debajo de mi manto, al rey mato. Todo lo cual te esenta y hace libre de todo respeto y obligación, y así puedes decir de la historia todo aquello que te pareciere, sin temor que te calumnien por el mal ni te premien por el bien que dijeres della. (95–96)

The moment Cervantes grants the reader permission to interpret the novel according to his or her subjective reality, he creates a dynamic in which the reader shares authorial responsibility. Two Hispanists who understand the relationship between author and protagonist differently, for example, are Tom Lathrop and Howard Mancing. Lathrop suggests that the "I" who claims to be the knight's step-father is only a fictional representation, i.e., a character of the real Cervantes: "This person—this character—is not Miguel de Cervantes from the title page (that's the real one), but rather a fictional representation of Cervantes, a character created by Cervantes as another element in his fiction" (*Don Quixote* xviii). Howard Mancing posits another interpretation: "No one, to my knowledge, doubts that the ['I'] of the prologue is anyone other than the person referred to on the title page ... Miguel de Cervantes" (*The Chivalric World* 192). Spanish author and philosopher Miguel de Unamuno (1864–1936) provides yet

Introduction

another example of how this passage from the prologue to Part I can be interpreted.[1] He not only distances the author from his protagonist, but he removes Cervantes altogether from the creation of his character:

> No cabe duda sino que en *El ingenioso hidalgo Don Quijote de la Mancha* que compuso Miguel de Cervantes Saavedra se mostró éste muy por encima de lo que podríamos esperar de él juzgándole por sus otras obras; se sobrepujó con mucho á sí mismo. Por lo cual es de creer que el historiador arábigo Cide Hamete Benengeli no es puro recurso literario, sino que encubre una profunda verdad, cual es la de que esa historia se la dictó á Cervantes otro que llevaba dentro de sí, y al que ni antes ni después de haberla escrito trató una vez más; un espíritu que en las profundidades de su alma habitaba. (226)

Philosopher Costica Bradatan describes this phenomenon as a "transfer of reality" in which "the imagined character comes to appear as being more real and authentic than the author who imagined him" (456).

As the author of the written text, Cervantes guides the reader from beginning to end, but his literary style cultivates an experience by which the reader can assign his or her own meaning to the novel:

> From the first days in the eighteenth century when Don Quixote ceased to be regarded as a mere satire against romances of chivalry, students of the novel have tended to join one of two critical schools, depending on their interpretation of the role played by the knight. A "soft" school regards Don Quixote as the hero as well as the protagonist of the novel … On the mild side, this view underlines the persistent and invincible sublimity of Don Quixote's motivation and contrasts it with the pedestrian character of the novel's sane folk. On the extreme side, it establishes an analogy with Christ. (Mandel 154)

While critics who subscribe to the "extreme side" of Don Quixote's role within the novel may or may not agree that there exists an analogical relationship between the knight and Jesus, they do acknowledge the subtle, and not so subtle, manifestations of the novel's underlying religious identity. Many Hispanists, including Carlos Fuentes, Américo Castro, Marcel Bataillon, and Alban Forcione, assert, to varying degrees, that Cervantes was a Christian

Introduction

humanist whose Erasmian influence permeates the religious identity of the novel. Other critics, namely Helmut Hatzfeld and José Antonio López Calle, read the novel's religious elements as representative of Tridentine Catholicism. More recently, Ken Colston and Sean Fitzpatrick do not question the novel's Catholic ideology. Forcione offers a cogent explanation for the diversity of opinions:

> Neither the view of Cervantes as orthodox spokesman for Tridentine ideology nor as freethinking, iconoclastic pioneer of the Enlightenment does justice to the vitality and incisiveness that characterize his engagement with religious subjects in his literary works. Cervantes's religious consciousness is profoundly undoctrinaire; it is alive with a complex ferment of spiritual and secular tendencies, and it can comfortably manifest itself at the opposite extremes of irreverent burlesque of the mental habits of the devout and hymns informed by the lofty spirituality of the most religious of his contemporaries.[2] (Forcione 353–54)

The reader's engagement with Catholicism in *Don Quixote* is not unique, however, with respect to Cervantes's *oeuvre*, nor is the author's subtle criticism of it. Michael Armstrong-Roche notes the ostensible Catholic orthodoxy of *Los trabajos de Persiles y Sigismunda* (1617): "For many readers, therefore, few matters would appear to be so clear-cut as the religious allegiances of *Persiles*. Its chaste heroes Persiles and Sigismunda travel as pilgrims to Rome, ostensibly for instruction in the faith, and readers more than once are treated to creeds and paeans to Rome's status as seat of the Catholic Church" (114). The protagonists' marriage in Rome and subsequent procreation of offspring, for example, are in accord with the Council of Trent's decree on the unitive and procreative dimensions of marriage: "During this council, a concept of the 'social responsibility' of love and marriage was also introduced for the first time ... the consequence of post-Tridentine love is the happy ending that closes the book, with the promise of an offspring that will make the couple's life happier upon their return to their kingdom, and expand throughout the northern lands the gospel of God and submission to the Roman Catholic Church" (López Alemany 213). Monipodio's den of thieves in the *Novela ejemplar Rinconete and Cortadillo* is an example of the duality of Cervantes's perspective on Catholicism

(Johnson, *Cervantes and the Material World* 42). In general, the practices, which include a novitiate year, prayer in front of a statue of the Virgin Mary, recitation of the Holy Rosary, and votive Masses are in opposition to Erasmian spirituality. In addition, Stanislav Zimic observes Cervantes's satiric depiction of Erasmus's *Colloquies* (1518) in *Rinconete and Cortadillo*: "Lo que aquí nos preocupa, sobre todo, es destacar la típica perspectiva irónica de los *Coloquios* erasmianos y, en general, de la literatura satírico-moral de inspiración erasmiana" (138–39n). The same venue is also home to characters, however, whose beliefs, including the sale of indulgences and false piety, are reminiscent of Cervantes's exaggeration of Catholicism and the Catholic Church in *Don Quixote*.

Historian David Hannay observed in 1898, "There is a difficulty in speaking of *Don Quixote*. One has to come after Fielding and Scott, Heine, Thackeray, and Sainte-Beauve. ... These are great names, and it may seem after they have spoken there is nothing left to say" (152). More than one hundred years later, Hannay's list of "great names" now includes Américo Castro, Marcel Bataillon, Carlos Fuentes, Miguel de Unamuno, and the names of many other scholars whose innovative and sagacious research inspired me to undertake this study. The authors and texts I cite, as well as my arguments and interpretations, are mediated by my religious sensibility. Consequently, I propose that my study represents one way of interpreting *Don Quixote* and a complement to other approaches. It is my assertion that the religiosity and spirituality of Cervantes's masterpiece illustrate that *Don Quixote* is inseparable from the teachings of Catholic orthodoxy. Furthermore, I argue that Cervantes's spirituality is as diverse as early modern Catholicism. I do not believe that the novel is primarily a religious or even a serious text, and I consider my arguments through the lens of Cervantine irony, satire, and multiperspectivism.[3] As a Roman Catholic who is a Hispanist, I propose to reclaim Cervantes's Catholicity from the interpretive tradition that ascribes a predominantly Erasmian reading of the novel.

Chapter One

Miguel de Cervantes and Early Modern Catholicism

Miguel de Cervantes was born in Alcalá de Henares, a university town about twenty miles from Madrid, in 1547. While his exact date of birth is unknown, it is believed that he was born on September 29, which is the Feast of Saint Michael, and baptized on October 9 in the Iglesia de Santa María la Mayor:

> Domingo, nueve días del mes de octubre, año del Señor de mill e quinientos e quarenta e siete años, fue baptizado Miguel, hijo de Rodrigo Cervantes e su mujer doña Leonor. Baptizóle el reverendo señor Bartolomé Serrano, cura de Nuestra Señora. Testigos, Baltasar Vázquez, Sacristán, e yo, que le bapticé e firme de mi nombre. Bachiller Serrano.[1] (Fernández Álvarez 24–25)

The decision of Cervantes's parents to have him baptized under the patronage of St. Michael, the archangel whose first responsibility is to combat Satan, provides insight into his family's religiosity.[2] Cervantes's sister Luisa (1546–1620) was prioress of the Carmelite Convent of the Imagen in Alcalá de Henares on three different occasions. In addition to Luisa, Cervantes's sisters Andrea (1544–1609) and Magdalena (1553–1611), as well as his wife Catalina de Salazar (1565–1626), were members of the Third Order of St. Francis.[3] In 1609, Cervantes joined the Brotherhood of the Slaves of the Most Holy Sacrament, a confraternity whose members included Lope de Vega (1562–1635) and Francisco de Quevedo (1580–1645). Cervantes biographer and noted Hispanist Jean Canavaggio postulates that Cervantes was a faithful and obedient member who followed the Order's strict rules "to the letter" (Canavaggio 236).[4]

Cervantes's paternal grandfather, Juan de Cervantes (ca. 1477–1556), who was an esteemed scholar and lawyer in Spain, worked

Chapter One

in Alcalá de Henares from 1509–12, and the author's father, Rodrigo, was born there in 1509 (d. 1585). The powerful religious reformer Cardinal Francisco Jiménez de Cisneros (1436–1517) founded the University of Alcalá de Henares in the same year, and soon thereafter the city became one of the most prominent cities of learning in Renaissance Europe. In addition to its world-famous university, Alcalá de Henares was also the home to more than twenty convents, two major seminaries, five monasteries, and three parish churches. In his book *Spanish Cities*, Richard Kagan comments on Anton van den Wyngaerde's (1525–71) drawings of Alcalá de Henares from 1565: "By minimizing his references to secular life, Wyngaerde seems to be suggesting that the city of Alcalá de Henares was dedicated to the study of theology and to the service of the Catholic Church, two of the university's avowed goals" (Canavaggio 236). The young Cervantes did not live many years in Alcalá de Henares before his father Rodrigo's itinerant lifestyle, a result of his economic and legal difficulties, moved the Cervantes family to Córdoba, where Juan de Cervantes still lived, in 1553. In this same year, the city of Córdoba opened its first Jesuit school, Santa Catalina.

The influence of Juan de Cervantes, who served Córdoba as its mayor and chief magistrate, made it possible for his grandson to attend Santa Catalina, whose students belonged to aristocratic families. Jesuit schools during Cervantes's day focused heavily on grammar and rhetoric. Cervantes and his family lived in Córdoba for only three years. The death of Juan de Cervantes motivated Cervantes's father to seek the security offered by another family member, Andrés (1518–93), who was Rodrigo's brother and the mayor of Cabra, a village forty miles from Córdoba. The Cervantes family remained in Cabra, although information about their stay there is scant, until 1564, the year in which Rodrigo's name appears on a real estate document in Seville.

In 1563, Cervantes continued his Jesuit education at the Colegio San Hermenegildo (Seville). One of his teachers was Father Pedro Pablo Acevedo (1522–73), who had been Cervantes's teacher at the Colegio de Santa Catalina in Córdoba. Father Acevedo was a playwright who established the norms, including staging and music, of Jesuit school drama. He incorporated drama into his classes as a teaching aid, and this manner of instruction must have sparked the young Cervantes's passion for drama, a genre in which he would not earn the recognition he aspired to achieve.[5] Years later, Cervantes would write about his time as a Jesuit school student in *El coloquio de los perros*:

> No sé qué tiene la virtud, que, con alcanzárseme a mí tan poco, o nada della, luego recibí gusto de ver el amor, el término, la solicitud y la industria con que aquellos benditos padres y maestros enseñaban a aquellos niños, enderezando las tiernas varas de su juventud, por que no torciesen ni tomasen mal siniestro en el camino de la virtud, que justamente con las letras les mostraban. Consideraba cómo los reñían con suavidad, los castigaban con misericordia, los animaban con ejemplos, los incitaban con premios y los sobrellevaban con cordura, y, finalmente, como les pintaban la fealdad y horror de los vicios y les dibujaban la hermosura de las virtudes, para que, aborrecidos ellos y amadas ellas, consiguiesen el fin para que fueron criados. (Cervantes, *Novelas* 316)

Rodrigo de Cervantes moved his family to Madrid in 1566. During this time, Cervantes was a disciple of the Catholic priest Juan López de Hoyos (1511–83), who was an admirer of the Christian humanist Desiderius Erasmus (1466–1536) and the director of the Estudio Público de Humanidades de la Villa de Madrid, where Cervantes studied for several months.[6]

Cervantes's literary accomplishments during the time he was a student of the Estudio Público de Humanidades de la Villa de Madrid included a sonnet that he dedicated to Queen Isabel de Valois (1545–68), who was the wife of King Philip II (1556–98), as well as four poems in honor of the Queen upon her death a year later. López de Hoyos published the poems Cervantes wrote shortly after the Queen's death. Cervantes's lack of critical acclaim as a poet, however, did not discourage him from writing poetry. In fact, Cervantes's masterpiece *Don Quixote* contains forty-five poems that appear in a variety of formats.

In his biography of Cervantes, *No Ordinary Man: The Life and Times of Miguel de Cervantes*, Donald McCrory relates that a royal warrant dated September 15, 1569 authorized the arrest of Cervantes for wounding another man in a duel. The victim was Antonio de Sigura, and the punishment, as dictated by a panel of judges that consisted of four jurists (Salazar, Ortiz, Hernán Velázquez and Álvaro García de Toledo), called for Cervantes's right hand to be cut off (Fernández Álvarez 57). Aware of the

Chapter One

punishment he was facing, Cervantes fled Madrid for Seville, where he remained a short time before he moved to Rome to work in the household of Cardinal Giulio Acquaviva (1546–74).[7] Cervantes's tenure in the household of Cardinal Acquaviva provided him with an insightful education in Catholicism and its traditions and rituals:

> Not yet twenty-three, Cervantes's time in an ambitious prelate's household in Rome, the centre of the universal Church, would have shown him the power of a culture where ceremony ruled supreme; a world of patronage, faction, and worship. It was also his entry into the world of a Christian prince being educated for high office. This granted, his sojourn in Rome would have been much more valuable than generally credited. He would have seen aspects of courtly and ecclesiastical life as well as the functioning of the diplomatic process; no prince of the Church was free from the machinery of statecraft and political intrigue. The history of alliances, truces, secret affinities and clandestine negotiations which involved the Papal States and other states at the time prove this. Aware of these or not, while working for Acquaviva he was soon to hear rumours of the growing conflict between Venice and Turkey; it was the talk of the town. (McCrory 51)

In addition, the brief time he spent in Italy afforded Cervantes the opportunity to learn about Italian literature, references to which appear frequently throughout *Don Quixote*. The *novella* of *El curioso impertinente*, as well as other interpolated stories in *Don Quixote*, are based upon Italian models.[8]

Cervantes enlisted in the army in 1570 as a harquebusier and supported the Holy League, which consisted of soldiers from Spain, Italy, and Malta, in its battles against the Turkish Muslims. Cervantes fought valiantly in the Battle of Lepanto (Greece, 1571), the naval campaign during which he lost use of his left hand as a result of a serious wound. In spite of a serious illness that afflicted him, Cervantes refused to abandon the Battle of Lepanto. Cervantes biographer Manuel Fernández Álvarez describes the author's military service and the pride with which Cervantes would remember this time in his life:

> Una batalla en la que Cervantes participa heroicamente—y aquí el término heroico adquiere toda su grandeza—, hasta el

> punto de que le faltaría poco para perecer en la contienda …
> pero de la que guardaría un recuerdo emocionado, como algo
> grandioso de lo que estaría profundamente orgulloso toda su
> vida. (Fernández Álvarez 88)

The Christian fleet consisted of more than 200 galleys and Cervantes, as well as his brother Rodrigo, served on *La Marquesa*. The Holy League's victory did not come without a price. In all, it suffered nearly 13,000 casualties and lost 50 galleys. The number of Ottoman casualties and prisoners, however, numbered over 28,000, and the Ottomans lost 210 ships, 130 of which the Holy League captured.

Cervantes's participation in the Battle of Lepanto was, arguably, the defining moment of his life. In the prologue to Part II of *Don Quixote* (1615), he praises Spain's participation in the Battle of Lepanto and writes proudly about the crippling injury he received to his left hand:

> Lo que no he podido dejar de sentir es que me note de viejo y
> de manco, como si hubiera sido en mi mano haber detenido
> el tiempo, que no pasase por mí, o si mi manquedad hubiera
> nacido en alguna taberna, sino en la más alta ocasión que vieron
> los siglos pasados, los presentes, ni esperan ver los venideros.
> Si mis heridas no resplandecen en los ojos de quien las miras,
> son estimadas, a lo menos, en la estimación de los que saben
> dónde se cobraron; que el soldado más bien parece muerto en
> la batalla que libre en la fuga; y es esto en mí de manera, que si
> ahora me propusieran y facilitaran un imposible, quisiera antes
> haberme hallado en aquella facción prodigiosa que sano ahora
> de mis heridas sin haberme hallado en ella. Las que el soldado
> muestra en el rostro y en los pechos, estrellas son que guían a
> los demás al cielo de la honra, y al de desear la justa alabanza.[9]
> (25–26)

Cervantes's dedicated service to the Holy League is even more admirable, considering that the years in which he served were difficult ones. In addition to the crippling injury to Cervantes's left hand, Barbary pirates, under the leadership of Arnaut Mamí (d. 1600) and his lieutenant Dalí Mamí, captured *El Sol*, the ship on which Cervantes and his brother were returning to Spain in 1575.[10] The pirates took Cervantes to Algiers, where he remained for five years as a prisoner. His captivity, as María Antonia Garcés notes, was by no means an anomaly for sixteenth-century

Chapter One

Spaniards: "From the massive campaigns led by the ransomer monks to raise funds for the rescue of captives, to the processions held when these ransomed men and women returned home, to the chains and shackles hung in churches and public buildings to signify liberation, the cruel reality of captivity in Barbary was ever present for the Spaniards" (*Cervantes in Algiers* 172).[11] When Dalí Mamí saw that Cervantes had letters of commendation from Don Juan de Austria (1547–78), who was King Philip II's half-brother, and Gonzalo Fernández de Córdoba (1520–78), who was the third Duke of Sessa (Italy), for his military service, he increased the price of the ransom, believing that Cervantes was an important soldier. Cervantes describes his experience as a prisoner in *El capitán cautivo*, another one of the interpolated stories that appears in *Don Quixote*.

Cervantes's captivity in Algiers must have been transformational with respect to his spirituality. When he arrived there, he discovered a multicultural and multilingual city that attracted a heterogeneous population of people: Turks, Arabs, Berbers, Christian captives, Jews, exiled *moriscos*, and converts to Islam from different parts of the world (Garcés, *An Early Modern Dialogue with Islam* 2).[12] His captivity would later inform his literature. In the biographical drama *El trato de Argel*, which Cervantes wrote shortly after he returned to Spain, for example, the captive Saavedra tries to persuade another prisoner not to convert to Islam:

> Si tú supieses, Pedro, a dó se extiende
> la perfección de nuestra ley cristiana,
> verías cómo en ella se nos manda
> que un pecado mortal no se cometa,
> aunque se interesase en cometerle
> la universal salud del mundo.
> Pues ¿cómo quieres tú, por verte libre
> de libertad del cuerpo, echar mil hierro[s]
> al alma miserable, desdichada,
> cometiendo un pecado tan inorme
> como es negar a Cristo y a su Iglesia? (*Teatro completo* 905–06)

Islam continued to be anathema to Cervantes after he returned to Spain, and he expressed his anti-Muslim sentiment, at times disdainful and confrontational, numerous times in his literature.[13] Cervantes's years of captivity, however, also provided him with a new perspective on Muslim-Catholic relations and of his own faith: "Placed in that context, Cervantes's dealings with Moors and renegades, his stirring defense of the Catholic faith, are illuminated with a new light, one that makes him more accessible, more human, and—in a word—more real" (Canavaggio 91).

Evidence of Cervantes's enlightened attitude toward Muslim-Catholic relations is *El capitán cautivo*, whose protagonists are Zoraida, a Muslim who is a convert to Catholicism, and Captain Ruy Pérez de Viedma, a Christian who is a prisoner in Algiers. Zoraida, who adopts the name María because of her devotion to the Virgin Mary, arranges for Ruy Pérez to escape but on the condition that he take her to Spain, where she hopes to be baptized a Catholic and to marry the captive captain. Their prospective marriage, more than an act of love, fulfills the religious beliefs of Catholicism and assumes a mystical dimension because Zoraida, or María, and Ruy Pérez also desire to grow closer to God.

Before they can marry, however, Zoraida must be baptized a Catholic, and only then is she able marry in the Catholic Church.[14] The sincerity of Zoraida's intentions is open to debate. Francisco Márquez Villanueva postulates that Zoraida's desire to convert to Catholicism and to marry Ruy Pérez is pure chicanery, motivated by a longing to be free. Franco Meregalli affirms that Zoraida genuinely loves Ruy Pérez but that she wishes to convert to Catholicism because it is the religion of the man she loves. Ciriaco Morón Arroyo, however, disputes Villanueva's and Meregalli's interpretations completely. Morón Arroyo reads the episode through a strictly theological lens, informed by a Thomistic explanation of the characters' words and actions. He believes the theological underpinnings of the episode are apparent from its beginning when Luscinda asks if Zoraida is baptized. Morón Arroyo notes that Cervantes would have chosen different words if the meaning of the episode were not intended to be interpreted within the context of Catholic doctrine.

While Cervantes was a prisoner, he refused to convert to Islam, and even though he was living in an environment hostile to Christians, he remained steadfast in his faith. According to witnesses, he lived "as a good Christian, zealous for God's good name, confessing and taking communion when Christians customarily do so; and if he occasionally had dealings with Moors and renegades, he always defended the Holy Catholic faith, and

Chapter One

he strengthened and inspired many not to become Moors or renegades" (Canavaggio 82). Antonio de Sosa, who wrote about his experiences as a captive in *Topografía e historia general de Argel* (1612), and, specifically, the time he spent with Cervantes, testified that Cervantes also wrote poetry about Christ and the Virgin Mary while a prisoner (McCrory 78).

Cervantes married Catalina de Salazar y Palacios, who was from the town of Esquivias (Toledo), after he returned to Spain in 1580.[15] Shortly thereafter, he began his literary career. In addition to writing plays at this time, Cervantes published the first, and only, part of the pastoral romance *La Galatea* (1585). While this novel did not earn Cervantes the recognition he had hoped, he included this genre in *Don Quixote*, which contains several pastoral narrations, including the episodes of Marcela and Grisóstomo (Part I, Chapters X–XIV) and the false Arcadia (Part II, Chapter LVIII).

Cervantes worked as a royal commissary from 1587–94 in Andalusia, during which time he traveled frequently from town to town. One of his duties as a royal commissary included gathering corn, wheat, olive oil, and other supplies for the Spanish Armada, which waged an unsuccessful war with England in 1588. In fact, Cervantes's first commission was to requisition wheat for the armada in the town of Écija. The townspeople, however, were not willing to provide wheat or any provisions until they received payment for previous requisitions. Cervantes, with unshakable determination, seized whatever wheat he could find from the granaries of landowners, among whom were prebendary canons. In response to Cervantes's affront to the Church, the vicar general of Seville excommunicated him.[16] Two months later, in December of 1587, the Church excommunicated Cervantes once again after he imprisoned a recalcitrant sacristan in the town of Castro del Río (Córdoba). After successfully appealing both edicts of excommunication, Cervantes returned to full communion with the Church. In 1592, while Cervantes was in Castro del Río, he had to defend himself once again, but this time the civil authorities levied charges against him. Francisco Moscoso, the chief magistrate of Écija, issued a warrant for Cervantes's arrest that falsely charged him with the illegal sale of wheat. In spite of his protestations of innocence, however, he was imprisoned for several days. Cervantes was able to go free after Pedro Isuzna, who was the commissary general, cleared his name. The years Cervantes lived in southern Spain provided him with further knowledge of its people and its geography, which he writes about in future literary endeavors, namely *Don Quixote* and the *Novelas ejemplares*.

Cervantes began to work as a tax collector in 1594, but three years later Cervantes fell victim to Simón Freire de Lima, a crooked banker in Seville who absconded with all of the money Cervantes had deposited with him. Unable to repay the money, Cervantes was sent to Seville's royal prison, where he resided for more than a year with prisoners of the same ilk as criminals of Monipodio's den of thieves in the exemplary story *Rinconete and Cortadillo*. In spite of his personal setbacks, Cervantes continued to write. It is believed that he began his masterpiece *El ingenioso hidalgo don Quijote de la Mancha* while in jail.

Cervantes spent time in Madrid, Esquivias, and Toledo from 1597–1604. In 1604 Cervantes and his family moved to Valladolid, the city where King Philip III (1598–1621) moved his royal court in 1601. Cervantes lived the last ten years of his life, however, in Madrid. During this time, Cervantes published his best known literary accomplishments: *Novelas ejemplares, El viaje del Parnaso* (1614), *Segunda parte del ingenioso caballero don Quijote de la Mancha* (1615), *Ocho comedias y ocho entremeses, nunca representados* (1615), and *Los trabajos de Persiles y Sigismunda* (1617).

Before Cervantes died on April 23, 1616, he requested that ten Masses be celebrated for the repose of his soul and that his burial place be inside the walls of Madrid's Convent of the Discalced Trinitarians.[17] Francisco Pérez, who was an almoner of the Trinitarian monastery, administered extreme unction to the author, who acknowledges receiving it in the prologue to *Persiles*, on April 18.[18] Cervantes reveals his belief in the afterlife, also in the prologue to *Persiles*: "¡Adiós, gracias; adios, donaires; adios, regocijados amigos; que yo me voy muriendo, y deseando veros presto contentos en la otra vida" (36).

Dutch historian Johan Huizinga and German philosopher Ernst Cassirer assert that the humanist spirit of the Middle Ages intensified in the Renaissance, fostering a new secular and non-secular individualism in which self-reflection, meditation, and the potential for human achievement manifested itself not only in material practices and productions, such as art and politics,

Chapter One

but also in theory and form.[19] Cassirer believes that the mystical theologian Nicholas Cusanus (1401–64) exemplifies "the full consciousness and spiritual essence" of Renaissance humanism:

> Cusanus is the only thinker of the period to look at all of the fundamental problems from the point of view of *one* principle in which he masters them all. His thought knows no barriers that separate disciplines. In keeping with the medieval ideal of the whole, it includes the totality of the spiritual and physical cosmos. He is both a speculative theologian and a speculative mathematician; he is as interested in statics and in general theories of movement as he is in questions of astronomy and cosmography; he is as concerned with problems of church history as he is with problems of political history, history of law, and general history. ... We can apply to Cusanus' thought the antithesis *complicatio* and *explicatio*, which he uses to illuminate the relationship of God to the world and of the world to the human mind. (Cassirer 7; author's italics)

The religious movement *Devotio Moderna*, for example, which began in the late-fourteenth century, was the impetus for other methods of prayer, notably *Ejercitatorio de la vida espiritual* (1500), by the Benedictine Spanish mystic García de Cisneros (1455–1510), and St. Ignatius of Loyola's *Ejercicios espirituales* (1522–24), that personified Renaissance Christian Humanism.[20] The new individualism of the Renaissance also motivated the devout, who now included the elite of society, to attend confession on a regular basis, which, according to Jesuit historian Robert Bireley, "facilitated a private conversation between priest and penitent and encouraged the use of the sacrament for individual spiritual direction and the application of moral norms to individual cases—that is, casuistry" (230). In addition to the repentance of sins to receive absolution from the priest, who sits *in persona Christi*, general confession was another expression of this new individualism. This type of confession considers all the sins a person has committed at the time of confession, and the goal is to gain greater self-knowledge and to live a more devout life.

Self-flagellation was another manifestation of devotion in early modern Spanish culture. Before the establishment of flagellant brotherhoods in the sixteenth century, self-flagellation was usually in response to Marian visions or during times of crises. By 1575, according to William A. Christian, Jr., there were thousands of flagellant brothers, known as "Blood Brothers," who participated in processions, especially on Holy Thursday and Good Friday (185). The four flagellant brotherhoods in Toledo, for example, consisted of members who numbered six hundred to two thousand. The following description of the activities of Cuenca's True Cross brotherhood in 1578 provides insight into the practice of self-flagellation:

> There is another brotherhood of the holy True Cross, in which there are more than five hundred brothers of candle [*hacha*] and discipline, with a few women. On the night of Holy Thursday a procession is held and the brothers go out, those of candles with their candles lit, and those of discipline flagellating themselves and shedding much blood. Clergy and monks who are in town go in the procession. It is very devout, and well-supplied with wax. They say sixty masses for each brother who dies. (Christian, Jr. 189)

Penitential culture was most prevalent in southern Spain, especially in Córdoba and Seville, where Cervantes attended Jesuit schools.

In 1576, the residents of Chillón (Ciudad Real) organized a procession during a time of crisis, which included flagellation, hopeful that their devotion would be rewarded:

> In April 1576 we witnessed a great drought in this town, and after many processions were made to the chapels on the outskirts—Saint Sebastian, Saint Catherine, and Saint Bridget, which are near the town—and considering the dryness of the township, and that everything was being ruined as it was already April, almost all the people of the town decided to go [to the shrine of Our Lady of the Castle] in procession one morning, including a great number of men, women, and children and some brothers of the Holy True Cross who went flagellating themselves. All of these people, together with the clergy, left the town under calm skies [*con gran serenidad*]. And [at the shrine] they celebrated mass and preached and then left to return to the town. And it pleased Our Lord through the intercession of this Holy Lady Saint His Mother to send so much rain that everyone got wet and had to return very quickly because the roads turned to rivers. As a result all of the townspeople held it certain that this grace and many others in remedy of the needs of this town had been done through the intercession of this Holy Lady. (Christian, Jr. 64)

Chapter One

In Part I, Chapter LII, Don Quixote and Sancho encounter a similar procession, whose participants pray for an end to a drought. In addition to the procession to a holy shrine, there are also prayers and flagellations. In Part II of *Don Quixote*, however, Cervantes portrays the act of self-flagellation differently. In order to disenchant Dulcinea, Sancho must flagellate himself three thousand three hundred times. Once the squire realizes that he cannot avoid the self-flagellation, he resolves to "salir de la deuda lo más presto que sea posible, porque goce el mundo de la hermosura de la señora Dulcinea del Toboso, pues, según parece al revés de lo que pensaba, en efecto es Hermosa" (333). Sancho's use of the word *deuda* alludes to the Sacrament of Confession, which was "the centerpiece of the Postridentine program of religious reform and reeducation" (O'Banion 21).[21] Penitents who self-flagellate do so for the expiation of their sins. They repay their "debt" to God and to society. Any sin, but especially a mortal sin, requires the debt of sinfulness to be repaid, either eternal, when the sinner does not seek absolution, or temporal, when the sinner receives absolution through the Sacrament of Confession:

> If anyone says that satisfaction for sins, as to their temporal punishment, is in no way made to God through the merits of Christ by the punishments inflicted by Him and patiently borne, or by those imposed by the priest, or even those voluntarily undertaken, as by fasts, prayers, almsgiving or other works of piety, and that therefore the best penance is merely a new life, let him be anathema.[22] (*The Canons and Decrees of the Council of Trent* 140)

In Part II, Chapter LXXI, Don Quixote offers to pay Sancho, who has not yet completed his "penance," for each of the three thousand three hundred lashes. In addition, the knight volunteers to keep count of them with his rosary, which David Quint describes as an agreement that "smacks of religious parody, of a donor paying monastics for prayers to be said in order to free the dead from purgatorial time" (159). In order to mitigate the temporal punishment for a sin, the priest may ask the penitent to pray the rosary, an act of devotion that includes the recitation of the Hail Mary for each of the fifty beads that begin and end with one of the four sets of mysteries.[23] In this scene, the rosary may be read as a sacramental that the knight uses to help Sancho complete his act of "penance." I discuss at length the rosary in *Don Quixote* in the chapter titled, "Tilting at the Truth: Don Quixote's Spiritual Journey as a Contemplative in Action."

It is within this environment that Erasmus, an ordained priest who in spite of his condemnation of beliefs and practices that he considered to be superstitious or corrupt remained Catholic his entire life, propagated Christian Humanism, whose core principle was *philosophia Christi*, or "philosophy of Christ," which he defines in *Sileni Alcibiades* (1515):

> For it seems that Sileni were small images divided in half, and so constructed that they could be opened out and displayed; when closed they represented some ridiculous, ugly flute-player, but when opened they suddenly revealed the figure of a god, so that the amusing reception would show off the art of the carver. (Phillips 77)

Erasmus considered Jesus to be the quintessential *silenus*:

> If you look on the face only of the Silenus-image, what could be lower or more contemptible, measured by popular standards? Obscure and poverty-stricken parents, a humble home; poor himself, he has a few poor men for disciples, chosen not from king's palaces, not from the learned seats of the Pharisees or the schools of the Philosophers, but from the customs-house and the fishermen's nets ... In such humility, what grandeur! In such poverty, what riches! In such weakness, what immeasurable strength! In such shame, what glory! In such labours, what utter peace! (Phillips 79–80)

Christian Humanism exalts the individual worth and personal dignity of the common man, who, created *in imagine Dei*, is called to unite his life with the teachings of Jesus through the pursuit of knowledge, especially Latin and Greek texts and patristic literature; civic humanism, which consists of an active political life that promotes self-realization vis-à-vis a collective concern for the common good; and an intimate and deeply personal relationship with Jesus, as opposed to the opulent public displays of piety, such as ceremonies, parades and processions that permeated early modern Spanish society.[24] Erasmus expounds on the *philosophia Christi* in *Enchiridion militis Christiani* (1501):

Chapter One

> It was plainly set forth, at least for all Latinate readers, in the *Enchiridion Militis Christiani*, the "Handbook [or, better, Dagger] of a Christian Warrior," where the subject is the *imitatio Christi* and the emphasis is on the inwardness of true religion ... The true way of piety is in following Christ. He is the "sole archetype, from which if anyone swerve by even a nail's breadth he goes astray and deviates from the way." Christ's "philosophy" is for Christians nothing other than the meaning of Christ himself, "no empty voice," but, on the contrary, simplicity, patience, purity; in short, whatever he himself taught. (Reardon 34–35)

In the *Oration on the Dignity of Man* (1486), Italian Christian Humanist and Platonist Pico della Mirandola (1463–94) argues that the dignity of a human being is his or her potential to ascend the Great Chain of Being, the hierarchical order of the universe where God is at the top, Man is in the middle, and inanimate objects are at the bottom:

> The nature of all creatures is defined and restricted within laws which We have laid down; you, by contrast, impeded by no such restrictions, may, by your own free will, to whose custody We have assigned you, trace for yourself the lineaments of your own nature. I have placed you at the very center of the world, so that from that vantage point you may with greater ease glance round about you on all that the world contains. We have made you a creature neither of heaven nor of earth, neither mortal or immortal, in order that you may, as the free and proud shaper of your own being, fashion yourself in the form you may prefer. It will be in your power to descend to the lower, brutish forms of life; you will be able, through your own decision, to rise again to the superior order whose life is divine. (Mirandola 7–8)

The English philosopher John Locke (1632–1704) was a Christian Humanist who asserted that happiness is the product of a person's relationship with God: "Every man has an immortal soul, capable of eternal happiness or misery, whose happiness depending upon his believing and doing those things in this life which are necessary to the obtaining of God's favor and are prescribed by God to that end" (46). I address Christian Humanism within the context of Sancho's governorship in Chapter 3.

While there is no concrete evidence that Cervantes ever read any of Erasmus's literature, it is reasonable to conclude based on his relationship with López de Hoyos and the popularity of Erasmus's doctrines in Spain at the time that Cervantes was familiar with Erasmus's writings. Perhaps the most important critic on Erasmus and Cervantes is Forcione, who has written prolifically about Erasmus' influence in Cervantes's literature, especially the *Novelas ejemplares* (1613): "Cervantes's collection of exemplary tales ... is perhaps Spain's most imposing tribute to the breadth of vision and generosity of spirit inspiring the Christian Humanist movement and distinguishing its enduring literary products" (21). Specifically, Forcione cites the Christian Humanist literary characteristics of the *Novelas ejemplares*:

> *The Novelas ejemplares* stand as one of the fullest literary realizations of the characteristic nonlinear discourse of the great humanist writers of the sixteenth century, who turned to dialectic, ironic, and paradoxical modes of exposition in their efforts to explore the complexities of truth, to provoke their readers' collaboration in that exploration, and to revitalize perceptions blunted by the tyranny of familiarity and appearance. (28–29)

Not all critics agree, however, with Forcione. Joseph Ricapito rejects outright any Erasmian influence in the *Novelas ejemplares*, reasoning that Cervantes's literature is more a product of the spirituality of the Counter-Reformation than of the earlier Christian Humanism, which was more prevalent in Spain during the first half of the sixteenth century: "Although he sustains his theory with much erudition, it strikes me that the Erasmian influence Forcione discusses appears in Spain much earlier than the seventeenth century ... Cervantes's is a different spiritual atmosphere from the sixteenth century, when Erasmus's writings and thought flourished in Spain" (Ricapito 7). Ricapito subscribes to Américo Castro's "two Cervantes" theory: a public persona and a private one (6).

In spite of Eramus's disdain for the immorality and extreme ritualistic practices of the pre-Tridentine Catholic Church, his writings soon became popular in Renaissance Spain, and his supporters included King Charles I (1516–56); King Philip II (1556–98), who read Erasmus's complete works as a child; Alonso

Chapter One

Manrique de Lara (1476–1538), who was Inquisitor General from 1523–38; and Alonso de Fonseca (1475–1534), who was the Archbishop of Toledo (Rawlings 29). In 1522, Cardinal Francisco Jiménez de Cisneros invited Erasmus to be one of several distinguished Spanish and foreign scholars who contributed to the *Complutensian Polyglot Bible*, which is a six-volume critical edition of the Scriptures that contains parallel text in Hebrew, Latin Vulgate, Greek, and Aramaic (Tovar Foncillas 65).[25] Marcel Bataillon notes that several of Spain's most well-known religious figures, including Fray Luis de León (1527–91), Fray Luis de Granada (1505–88), and Fray Diego de Estella (1524–78) were also followers of Erasmus:

> Hombres apegados a todo lo exterior de la religión, pero que no temen denunciar el sofocamiento de lo interior por lo exterior; hombres, en definitiva, que tienen profundo parentesco con Erasmo y que difieren sobre todo de él por su adhesión más resuelta a los dogmas y a los ritos fundamentales del catolicismo. (Bataillon 785)

As Erasmus's influence spread throughout Spain, however, conservative Catholics, including several of Spain's most well-known theologians, as well as Franciscans and Dominicans, who opposed Erasmus's anti-monastic views, protested Christian Humanism.[26] The strength of the anti-Erasmian movement, which began in earnest in the 1530s and included support from the Inquisition, weakened Erasmus's authority considerably.[27]

The same time Erasmus's influence was spreading throughout Spain, two saints whose spirituality permeated Spanish society during Cervantes's formative years were St. Teresa of Avila and St. Ignatius of Loyola. The life of Teresa of Avila (1515–82), a mystic whom Pope Paul VI (1963–78) declared a Doctor of the Church in 1970, exemplified Catholic spirituality.[28] She underwent a conversion in 1554 after reading St. Augustine, and in 1562 she was responsible for changing the atmosphere of her convent, which had become more of a place for gossip than for worship.[29] As a result of the reforms introduced by Teresa, the convent became a place more conducive to prayer and spiritual growth. In addition, she founded convents throughout Spain, in spite of the restriction that prohibited nuns from being seen in public. The basis of Teresa's spirituality was a contemplative encounter with God. Unlike Ignatius, who believed that God "pulls us out" to all things on earth, Teresa's spirituality is based upon mastering the inner world. The inner journey to wholeness is but a stepping stone to the mystical union with God; the degree to which we know and love God is proportionate to the depth of our self-knowledge.

In *El castillo interior* (1588), Teresa provides many examples of her belief that images are the primary experience of the journey to a mystical union with God. The soul is a crystal that contains many dwelling places. In order to enter the first dwelling place, however, a person must practice prayer and reflection. Humility, Teresa asserts, is necessary to pass from one place to the next, and she compares this virtue to a bee that is always making honey. When the bee stops working, "todo va perdido" (Sicari 43). The visually symbolic in *Don Quixote*, which I address later in this chapter, is evocative of Teresian spirituality.[30]

Ignatius was born in 1491 at Loyola castle in Guipúzcoa, Spain. At the age of sixteen he became a page to the treasurer of the kingdom of Castile. As a result of the time he spent at the court, he developed an affinity for women, an addiction to gambling, and a keen interest in weaponry, especially swords. When Ignatius was thirty years old, he fought for Spain against the French, who had attacked Pamplona. A cannonball wounded one of Ignatius's legs and completely broke the other. The French admired Ignatius's courage so much, they returned him to his home at the castle of Loyola instead of sending him to a prison.[31] When Ignatius was not able to find any books of chivalry in the castle, his sister-in-law Magdalena gave him Ludolph of Saxony's *The Life of Christ* and Jacobus de Voraigne's *Golden Legend*, also known as *Flos Sanctorum*.[32] Soon after, he realized that his goals of fame and glory as a soldier did not provide him with the inner peace and fulfillment he experienced while reading these books. Ignatius writes about his conversion in the *Ejercicios espirituales* (1522–24), which he describes as:

> Todo modo de examinar la consciencia, de meditar, de contemplar, de orar vocal y mental, y de otras espirituales operaciones, segun que adelante se dirá: porque asi como el pasear, caminar, y correr son exercicios corporales, por la mesma manera todo

Chapter One

> modo de preparar, y disponer el ánima para quitar de sí todas las afecciones desordenadas, y, después de quitadas, para buscar, y hallar la voluntad de Dios en la disposición de su vida, para la salud del ánima. (1)

Inspired by his conversion, Ignatius traveled to Jerusalem in 1522.[33] First, however, he wanted to make a pilgrimage to the shrine of Our Lady of Montserrat. Along the way, Ignatius visited the Franciscan sanctuary of Our Lady of Aránzazu, where he commended his pilgrimage to the Holy Land to the Virgin Mary.[34] The next day, Ignatius departed the sanctuary and continued his pilgrimage to Montserrat.

While travelling to Montserrat, Ignatius engaged in a conversation with a Moor, who informed him that he did not believe in the perpetual virginity of the Virgin Mary. Ignatius countered the Moor's belief with several arguments, but his efforts were futile. After the Moor departed, Ignatius, feeling troubled and angry that he had not defended the Virgin's honor, vowed to punish the Moor for his blasphemy. Ignatius's determination to restore the Virgin's honor by means of violence began to waver, however, as he considered his new vocation in life. When Ignatius was approaching a crossroads that consisted of a highway road and a village road, which was the one that would lead him to the Moor, he thought even more about what God wanted him to do. Undecided about which road to follow, he gave free rein to his mule, trusting that God's will would be apparent based on which road the mule chose to follow.[35] When the mule walked toward the highway road and away from the village road, Ignatius accepted the mule's choice as the will of God.

When Ignatius arrived to Montserrat, he made a general confession and prayed all night at the base of the altar dedicated to the Our Lady of Montserrat. The next day, he left his sword and knife at the altar, gave away all of his fine clothes to a poor man, and dressed himself in worn clothes and sandals. Ignatius's next stop was a cave outside of the town of Manresa, where he spent nearly ten months in prayer.

Ignatius studied philosophy at the University of Alcalá de Henares and later at the University of Salamanca from 1526–27, but the authorities of the Inquisition suspected him of being an *alumbrado*, an accusation that hindered his academic progress.[36]

Consequently, Ignatius traveled to Paris in 1528, and he remained there as a student of the University of Paris until 1535. After being ordained a priest in 1537, Ignatius went to Rome, where he met with Pope Paul III, who invited Ignatius to teach Scripture and theology. In 1540, Pope Paul III promulgated *Regimini militantis Ecclesiae*, the papal bull that granted the Society of Jesus official status within the Catholic Church. The members elected Ignatius as the Society's first Superior General in 1541, and by the time of his death in 1556, there were more than 1,000 Jesuits in Europe and Latin America.[37] The Catholic Church celebrates Ignatius's feast day on July 31, the day Pope Gregory XV (1621–23) canonized him in 1622.[38]

The quixotic nature of Ignatius's life has not escaped the attention of readers over the centuries.[39] The first critic to undertake a comparative study of Ignatius and Don Quixote was the Swiss theologian Jean Leclerc, who, in 1688, published his research in *Bibliothèque universelle et historique*. In 1736, French priest Pierre Quesnel published a two-volume satire of Ignatius titled *Histoire de l'Admirable Dom Inigo de Guipuscoa, Chevalier de la Vierge, et Fondateur de la Monarchie des Inighistes*.[40] Quesnel, who was also a journalist, employed poetic license in writing about the events of Ignatius's life, which he portrays as quixotic:

> My present undertaking is to write the history of a Spanish gentleman, who proposing to copy the wonderful achievements of the heroes of the legend, quitted a military life to dedicate himself to the service of the Virgin Mary, and after having vowed himself her knight, in this quality traversed a great part of the world, rendering himself as famous by his extravagances in spiritual knight-errantry, as his illustrious countryman Don Quixote was afterwards in temporal. (1)

In *Dictionnaire philosophique* (1764), Voltaire, who was an Enlightenment writer and philosopher, couches his harsh critique of Ignatius's fervent religiosity in the context of Don Quixote's madness:

> If you are desirous of obtaining a great name, of becoming the founder of a sect or establishment, be completely mad; but be sure that your madness corresponds with the

Chapter One

> turn and temper of your age. Have in your madness reason enough to guide your extravagances; and forget not to be excessively opinionated and obstinate. It is certainly possible that you may get hanged; but if you escape hanging, you will have altars erected to you.
>
> In real truth, was there ever a fitter subject for the Petites-Maisons, or Bedlam, than Ignatius, or St. Inigo the Biscayan, for that was his true name? His head became deranged in consequence of his reading the "Golden Legend"; as Don Quixote's was, afterwards, by reading the romances of chivalry. (Voltaire 256)

In 1777, Rev. John Bowle, an English scholar who published an annotated edition of *Don Quixote* in 1781, asserted his belief that Cervantes did indeed base the character of Don Quixote on Ignatius in a letter to Rev. Thomas Percy, Bishop of Dromore (Ireland):

> Amidst the uncertainty of guesses, if I am not peremptory and dogmatical, you will with your wonted candour receive my reveries and conjecture, that Ignacio Loyola might have been pitched upon by the author, as a person worthy of distinguished notice from him. In a word, it has been justly remarked of him by a late French writer, that he was as famous in his spiritual knight errantry, as his illustrious countryman Don Quijote was in his quest of adventures. (136)

An anonymous author in 1836, however, disagrees with the notion that *Don Quixote* is a satire of Ignatius and the Jesuits:

> But the Spanish critics are not alone in such wild fancies, an Englishman has even surpassed them in absurdity. We allude to the Rev. Mr. Bowles [sic], who gravely contends that the whole book is a covert satire on the Jesuits, and their founder, Ignatius de Loyola. It will be sufficient to observe, that if the book does contain such a satire, it has been so carefully hid that it was reserved for a foreigner to detect it. ("Cervantes and His Writings" 350)

In 1854, the journal *Notes and Queries* was the forum for disparate opinions. An author, identified only by the initials J. B. P., postulated that *Don Quixote* is most definitely a satire of Ignatius and the Jesuits. Later that same year, W. B. MacCabe offered a strong rebuttal, concluding, "J. B. P., like many others, cries out 'Jesuit' where there is 'no Jesuit'" (408).

The author who has perhaps written most extensively about the similarities between Ignatius and Don Quixote, however, is Unamuno. In *Vida de Don Quijote y Sancho* (1905), he cites numerous events in Ignatius's life that are nearly identical to the life and adventures of Don Quixote.[41] Unamuno's comparisons not only support the supposition that Cervantes based Don Quixote on the life of the saint, but their unmistakable similarities also blur the line that separates reality and fiction: "For Unamuno there doesn't seem to be any significant difference between the life of St. Ignatius as drawn in Rivadeneira's biography, and that of Don Quixote, as narrated by Cervantes" (Vandebosch 22).

A constitutive element of the spiritualities of Teresa and Ignatius, who share the belief that prayer should be meditative and contemplative, is mental imagery. Teresa does not use images to convey her thoughts; instead, her thoughts convey the meanings of the images and the experience. For example, the interior castle is a symbol of wholeness in God, and there are seven mansions, or dwelling places, that the soul must pass through in order to reach the center where God dwells. In the *Spiritual Exercises*, Ignatius instructs the retreatant to imagine himself or herself at a scene from the life of Jesus and to contemplate on it and its significance to the life of the retreatant. For example, the First Contemplation, which occurs on the first day of the second week, is dedicated to contemplating the Incarnation.[42] The spiritual director instructs the exercitant to visualize people and events associated with the Incarnation in order to see them, to listen to them, and to observe what they are doing. The first Contemplation concludes with a colloquy in which the exercitant contemplates what to say to the people in the scene, who are the Three Divine Persons and the Virgin Mary, and to ask them for favors that will cultivate spiritual growth. Unlike Martin Luther, who believed that the sense of hearing and not sight defined a true Christian, and Erasmus, who espoused that authentic Christianity is a spiritual and not a visible worship of God, Cervantes demonstrates in *Don Quixote* a proclivity toward the visually symbolic, aligning himself with the Catholic Church and the visually symbolic elements of its faith (altars, images, rosary beads, statues, etc.).

Chapter One

While imaginative contemplation fostered a transformational theological experience, the visually symbolic in Cervantes manifested itself in a more concrete way. The publication of Andrea Alciato's *Emblematum Liber* in 1531 gave birth to a new genre of visual symbolism that quickly spread all over Europe. The publication of Juan de Horozco's *Emblemas morales* (1589), the first book of emblems published in Spain, formalized the symbiotic relationship between visual and literary culture as a medium of understanding "the way in which certain encounters or events compel us to transcend our mundane existence and to contemplate what appears to be a higher, more universal— more *real*—experience of meaning and being" (B. Nelson 3).[43] An emblem consists of a motto, an illustration, and text, often didactic, whose message appears as an allegory in the illustration.[44]

Studies of visual symbolism in Cervantes's prose began to surface on a regular basis in 1975 with the publication of Karl-Ludwig Selig's "The Battle of the Sheep: *Don Quixote* I, xviii" (1975). Since Selig's publication, a number of academics, including Edward C. Riley, Marissa C. Álvarez, E. C. Graf, and Christopher Weimer, have addressed the visually symbolic in Cervantes's literature (see Works Cited). The most influential scholar, however, is Frederick A. de Armas, who reads Cervantes's prose as ekphrastic texts. His seminal studies *Cervantes, Raphael and the Classics* (1998) and *Quixotic Frescoes: Cervantes and Italian Renaissance Art* (2006) focus on the different ways in which Cervantes depicts Italian art and architecture. Ekphrasis and pictorial allusion, de Armas asserts, is more difficult to uncover because of Cervantes's authorial style: "It is as if we have to look beneath writings and rewritings to discover the remnants of an Italian fresco, oil painting, or sculpture. The text is thus exhibited as a site for archaeological reconstruction where remnants from the past (scattered objects and figures from early modern art and its antique models) can be discovered beneath a sixteenth-century Spanish ideological and physical landscape" (*Quixotic Frescoes* xiii). De Armas, nevertheless, approaches the emblematics of *Don Quixote* by using memory markers that the narrators place in the text or the knight imagines to reveal the hidden images of Italian art and architecture in the novel.

In his article, Selig compares the episode of the battle of the sheep and the image of Alciato's Emblem 176 titled the "Insani

Gladius."[45] The visual symbolism of this episode, Álvarez points out, provides insight into Don Quixote's temperament (152).[46] The narrator's description of the knight's disposition when he attacks Alifanfarón de la Trapobana and his army illustrates the resolve he displays in other episodes, such as the attack on the windmills: "Esto diciendo, se entró por medio del escuadrón de las ovejas, y comenzó de alanceallas, con tanto coraje y denuedo como si de veras alanceara a sus mortales enemigos" (264). The didactic text that accompanies Alciato's Emblem 176, "Insani Gladius," speaks to the consequences that befall a person who is unable to control his or her anger: "Fury does not know how to confront its enemies: its blows / fall wide and, lacking any plan, it rushes to its ruin." This same episode from Part I, Chapter XVIII also provides the reader with an example of the knight's paradoxical character: "Como eso puede desparecer y contrahacer aquel ladrón del sabio mi enemigo. Sábete, Sancho, que es muy fácil cosa a los tales hacernos parecer lo que quieren, y este maligno que me persigue, envidioso de la gloria que vio que yo había de alcanzar desta batalla, ha vuelto los escuadrones de enemigos en manadas de ovejas" (265). I elaborate on the knight's temperament vis-à-vis the condition of the moral act in the chapter titled "*Don Quixote* and Moral Theology: What a Knight and His Squire Can Teach Us About Cervantes's Catholicism."

The first Jesuits had a profound impact on Catholicism during Cervantes's lifetime. Pope Paul III appointed Diego Laínez (1512–65) and Peter Faber (1506–46) to teach theology at the University of Rome. The Pope also appointed Laínez, Faber, Alfonso Salmerón (1515–85), and Claude Le Jay (1504–52) as theologians to the Council of Trent (1545–63). Pope Paul III designated Faber as his *peritus*, or expert, who, because of this title, exercised a great deal of authority at the Council of Trent. In spite of the high profile positions these first Jesuits occupied, they did not seek to reform the Church, heeding the words of Ignatius, who remarked, "Where there are different factions and sects, members of the Society will not oppose either party but show love for both" (O'Malley, *The First Jesuits* 285). It was inevitable that they would engender some degree of controversy, however, due to the nature of the authority granted to them by Pope Paul III. The accusations of heresy leveled against the Jesuits by some Catholic leaders, including Bishop Eustace du Bellay (1551–63) of Paris

Chapter One

and the faculty of theology at the University of Paris, reflected more a general distrust of the Society than any position espoused by the Jesuits who held teaching positions or who participated in the Council of Trent. A letter from the faculty of theology at the University of Paris in 1554 reads in part:

> This new society claiming for itself alone the unusual title of the name of Jesus admits anybody quite without restraint or discrimination, however criminal, illegitimate, and shameful they be. It has no difference from secular priests in its outward garb, in tonsure, in saying privately the canonical hours or in singing them publicly in church, nor in observing cloister, silence, in its choice of foods and days, in fasting and in its various laws and ceremonies which distinguish and preserve the status of Religious ... [This Society] seems to violate the uprightness of the monastic life and weaken the zealous, pious, and very necessary exercise of virtues, abstinence and austerity; indeed it provides an opportunity to freely desert the other Religious Orders and detracts from proper obedience and subjection to bishops; it unjustly deprives both civil and ecclesiastical lords of their rights; it brings on trouble for both the [civil and ecclesiastical] community and jealousies and various schisms. (*Jesuit Writings of the Early Modern Period* 244)

In spite of these attacks, which Ignatius perceived to be more hostile toward the papal bulls that established the legitimacy of the Society of Jesus than against the beliefs and practices of the Society itself, the Jesuits remained steadfast in their mission. In order to counter the efforts to discredit the Society, Ignatius enlisted the assistance of several notable supporters of the Society, including kings, dukes, university representatives, and bishops throughout Europe. The accusations and efforts to delegitimize the Society emboldened the Jesuits to remain faithful to their founding principles and to establish a stronger bond with the papacy, which continued to support Ignatius and the members of the Society.

The mission of the earliest Jesuit schools founded in Europe was to educate the young men who would later serve the Society of Jesus as priests. The first school opened in Gandía, Spain in 1545. In 1548, however, a Jesuit school that admitted all students, including those who did not wish to join the Society of Jesus, was founded in Messina, Italy; this school became the prototype of subsequent Jesuit schools. The pedagogical approach of the Jesuit schools that Cervantes attended in Córdoba and Seville was based on the Parisian method, a methodology practiced at the University of Paris, where Ignatius earned a Master's degree in philosophy and lived with Peter Faber and Francis Xavier (1506–52), with whom Ignatius would establish the Society of Jesus in 1540.[47] Ignatius first learned about the Parisian method, however, at the University of Alcalá de Henares during the brief time he was a student there.

In spite of the Jesuits' indifference to scholasticism and humanism, if not total rejection in some cases, several books of piety, including the writings of Catherine of Siena (1347–80), *Vita Christi* by Ludolph the Carthusian (1374), and Giovanni de Caulibus's Pseudo-Bonaventuran devotional text *Meditationes vitae Christi* (1300), influenced their theology and spirituality. The book that had the most impact on the Jesuits was, however, Thomas à Kempis's *The Imitation of Christ* (1418–27). Even though *The Imitation of Christ* did not espouse all of the Jesuits' beliefs, most notably the importance of ministry, the Jesuits, as John O'Malley notes, still relied on it for guidance and inspiration:

> In the *Imitation* they found in fact a great deal that was supportive and that confirmed certain directions they had taken; the book contained at least in embryonic form some of the first Jesuits' great themes. It encouraged frequent confession and Communion, though without defining what "frequent" meant. It encouraged daily examination of conscience. The whole of Book Three was entitled "The Book of Consolation" and emphasized the significance of the presence and absence of inner devotion—rudiments of ideas elaborately and systematically articulated in the "Rules of the Discernment of Spirits" in the *Exercises*. (*The First Jesuits* 265)

Thomas à Kempis's discussion of the interior life must have been especially inspirational to the Jesuits, who believed that ministry cannot be efficacious unless a person is properly disposed to performing it.

During Cervantes's lifetime, Catholicism embodied many of the features that defined the Renaissance in Spain. The conservative Christian culture of this time did not succumb, however, to the Baroque obsession of novelty, espoused by individuals who believed that only a radical transformation of economic and social institutions would improve their quality of life. José Antonio Maravall argues that the intransigence of the people who governed these institutions was foundational to their survival:

> Una crisis económica, social, con repercusiones de toda índole, que el hombre del Barroco vive, lleno de inquietud por las desfavorables novedades que el tiempo pueda traer. Es un estado de ánimo particularmente en España. ... De expectativas así, el hombre del XVII, y muy especialmente el español no espera nada bueno (nos referimos, claro está, a los integrados en el sistema). Consecuentemente, para ellos, en la política, en la religión, en la filosofía, en la moral, se trata de cerrar el paso a toda novedad, precisamente porque, aun no queriéndola, se presenta traída por el desorden de los tiempos. ... Nada de novedad, repitámoslo, en cuanto afecte al orden político-social. (455–57)

The control exerted by the Inquisition since the late fifteenth century and the Catholic Monarchs' campaign to consolidate their power formed the foundation of a society whose religious identity became, nominally, more entrenched in Catholicism with the doctrinal and dogmatic mandates from the Council of Trent, especially those that address the Eucharist, and, specifically, the public adoration of the Body of Christ:

> The holy council declares, moreover, that the custom that this sublime and venerable sacrament be celebrated with special veneration and solemnity every year on a fixed festival day, and that it be borne reverently and with honor in processions through the streets and public places, was very piously and religiously introduced into the Church of God. For it is most reasonable that some days be set aside as holy on which all Christians may with special and unusual demonstration testify that their minds are grateful to and mindful of their common Lord and Redeemer for so ineffable and truly divine a favor whereby the victory and triumph of His death are shown forth.[48] (*The Canons and Decrees of the Council of Trent* 110)

Due in large part to the Council of Trent's dogmatic decrees, popular religious culture in early modern Spain encompassed society, as devotion extended beyond individual parishes to city-wide celebrations that included religious processions, especially Corpus Christi, and the veneration of saints' days. These celebrations, whose nature was part-sacred and part-profane, were so plentiful that in late sixteenth-century Castile, "up to one day in every four was devoted to a religious feast" (Rawlings 94).[49] In accord with the Renaissance's spirit of renewal, there was a revival of the writings of the Church Fathers and St. Thomas Aquinas (1225–74), whose influence on Cervantes I discuss in this study.[50] In addition, devotional literature by St. John of the Cross (1542–91), Fray Luis de León, St. Ignatius of Loyola (1491–1556), Fray Luis de Granada, and Fray Alonso de Madrid (1485–1570), among many others, further defined Spain's Catholic identity.

The novel's polyphonic composition engenders different readings, but it does not necessarily exclude an interpretation that can be substantiated by historical and literary evidence. The skepticism about Cervantes's Catholic faith, and, specifically, how he manifests it in *Don Quixote* should be challenged. The preponderance of scholarship that focuses on Erasmus's influence on Cervantes minimizes or discounts entirely the presence of serious and devout Roman Catholicism in the novel.[51] While it may be convenient to dismiss the abundant references to Catholicism, and, specifically to the teachings of Ignatius, as exclusively a source of satire or a dimension of daily life in seventeenth-century Spain, I think doing so would ignore another example of Cervantes's genius and deprive the reader of a mystical experience.

Chapter Two

The Hermeneutics of Cervantine Spirituality

The crux of the debate surrounding the religious ideology of *Don Quixote* centers on Ignatian spirituality and Christian Humanism, although the historical and cultural factors of Cervantes's day cannot be discounted: "The broader history of Spanish Catholicism should be seen not merely in the spiritual life of the clergy and laity or in the general expression of their religious culture but also in the interaction with national institutions and society throughout this period" (Payne xiii). The presence of Islam, Judaism, and pockets of Protestantism (one in Seville and one in Valladolid; Payne 46), therefore, threatened not only the integrity of Spain's identity as a Catholic stalwart but also had sociopolitical repercussions.[1] It is against this complicated background that Cervantes writes his masterpiece, and any attempt to understand how the novel may be interpreted as a manual of Cervantine spirituality should consider the different faiths and, especially, the different manifestations of Catholicism, including local practices, processions, flagellant brotherhoods, monastic orders, and confraternities, in Spain during Cervantes's lifetime. In this chapter, I discuss the hermeneutics of Cervantine spirituality in order to contextualize this study.

The relationship between the Jesuits and Erasmus was a complicated one. According to Ribadeneira, Ignatius began to read Erasmus's *Enchiridion militis Christiani* while he was a student in Barcelona. Ribadeneira reports in his biography that Ignatius "observed that the reading of that book chilled the spirit of God in him and gradually extinguished the ardor of devotion" (Olin 116–18). Ignatian scholar John C. Olin, however, refutes Ribadeneira's account based on three reasons. First, Olin believes that a young Ignatius would not have been versed well enough in Latin to read Erasmus, affirming that it would be more plausible that he read the *Enchiridion* as a student at the University of Alcalá

Chapter Two

de Henares. Second, Olin posits that the first pages, especially the references to a courtier and a soldier who wishes to change his life, must have appealed to Ignatius, who underwent a similar conversion after he sustained the injury in the war against the French that required him to convalesce for many months, during which time he read the books about Jesus and the lives of saints that inspired him to seek a more meaningful relationship with Jesus. Third, Olin asserts that the Fourth Rule of the *Enchiridion*, in which Erasmus addresses the need to subordinate all things to God, would have captivated Ignatius, who manifests this philosophy in the "Principle and Foundation" of the *Spiritual Exercises*:

> El hombre es creado para alabar, hacer reverencia y servir á Dios nuestro Señor, y mediante esto salvar su ánima: y las otras cosas sobre la haz de la tierra son creadas para el hombre, y para que le ayuden en la prosecucion del fin para que es creado. De donde se sigue, que el hombre tanto ha de usar dellas, quanto le ayudan para su fin: y tanto debe quitarse dellas, quanto para ello lo impiden; por lo qual es menester hacernos indiferentes á todas las cosas creadas en todo lo que es concedido á nuestro libre albedrío, y no le esta prohibido: en tal manera, que no queramos de nuestra parte mas salud que enfermedad, riqueza que pobreza, honor que deshonor, vida larga que corta, y por consiguiente en todo lo demas; solamente deseando y eligiendo lo que mas nos conduce para el fin que somos criados. (Loyola, *Ejercicios* 16–17)

Another connection that Olin makes between Ignatius and Erasmus is Fr. John Helyar's manuscript of Ignatius's *Spiritual Exercises*, which is the oldest extant copy. Before Helyar left England to travel to Paris in 1534, he was a disciple of Vives. Helyar studied the *Spiritual Exercises* in Paris, most likely under the tutelage of Ignatius or Peter Faber. Olin cites Helyar's manuscript as evidence that "the spirit of Ignatius is not the antithesis of the spirit of Vives and Erasmus":

> Here was a method, a way of personal reform, quite different from the external practices and accessory devotions the humanists so frequently deplored. But regardless of how we may note the points of resemblance between the two spiritualities, the very existence of Helyar's manuscript affords concrete evidence of a certain compatibility. (Olin 125)

Bataillon also comments on this spiritual kinship, noting, in particular, the Erasmists' affinity for a contemplative prayer similar to the *Spiritual Exercises*:

> Erasmo mismo da su aprobación a una práctica ... que consiste en dividir en "horas" la historia de la muerte del Señor para que los niños se acostumbren a conmemorar cada día algún momento de ella con acción de gracias. Y se apresura a añadir que reemplazar esas por las de la Virgen "no es, desde luego, una invención impía, pero, si se permite confesar la verdad, es cambiar el vino en agua." ¿Quién sabe si la meditación ignaciana no pareció primero a los erasmistas como una reacción utilísima contra la invasión de la devoción mariana. (Bataillon 590)

Later in life, however, Ignatius viewed Erasmus, and, specifically, the controversy surrounding his beliefs, as a detriment to the spiritual formation of the Jesuits. Olin, however, attributes Ignatius's increasing repudiation of Erasmus's literature to a widespread disenchantment with Erasmus and his beliefs. By the 1530s, Erasmus's influence in Spain began to wane considerably as the Catholic Church, and especially traditional Catholicism, became more entrenched during the Counter Reformation.

Another opinion of Erasmus appears in the preface to Peter Canisius's edition of *The Letters of St. Jerome* (1562), which Canisius wrote in order to correct Erasmus's edition of St. Jerome's letters (1516). In addition to exhorting Erasmus to limit his scholarship to less theological endeavors, Canisius writes that Erasmus should "either have left sacred studies entirely alone or else have shown himself less supercilious in his judgments on the writings of the Fathers. As soon as he begins to play the theologian he becomes unduly self-confident and arrogant" (O'Malley, *The First Jesuits* 263). In the same preface, Canisius continues his acerbic attack on Erasmus:

> For, in fact, after Erasmus began to play the theologian, he was overly self-confident and claimed too much for himself. Often more fascinated with words than with things, he comported himself like a stern Aristarchus. ... Certainly there was no lack of eggs for Luther to hatch.[2] Erasmus the monk attacked the monks, and, hardly a serious philosopher, he treated the scholastic doctors almost as if they were idiots. Then, motivated by I know not what spirit, he practically wanted to pursue only a

Pyrrhonic theology with respect to the teachings of the Church. But while he found fault with and assailed others, he nevertheless constantly made excuses for himself and vehemently fought on his own behalf. Consequently, he was not interested in deferring to anybody. At length it came to pass that none of his enemies toppled the authority of Erasmus's name more fiercely than the founder himself and that now he possesses about as much influence among the impious as he does among the devout. (Pabel 147)

Jesuit historian O'Malley points out that the Jesuits' critique of Erasmus, however, did not reach the level of vitriol hurled at him by more conservative Catholic enemies, who described the Christian humanist as "infamous heretic," "son of the devil," "captain of apostasy," "evil spirit," and "rabid dog" (*The First Jesuits* 262).

The two scholars whose research has most informed this disputation are Castro, *El pensamiento de Cervantes* (1972), and Bataillon, *Erasmo y España* (1966). Castro, who, subsequent to the publication of *El pensamiento de Cervantes* in 1924, dedicated the rest of his life to studying Cervantine spirituality, finally acquiescing the publication of the revised edition of *El pensamiento de Cervantes* in 1972, a short time before his death, asserted in the first edition: "sin Erasmo, Cervantes no habría sido como fue." Forcione notes Castro's evolution: "However, more important among Cervantists was the emphatic change of direction that marked Castro's own thinking in the twenty years that followed the publication of *El pensamiento de Cervantes*" (Forcione 10). Bataillon and Castro believe that Erasmus's influence is more measured and by no means absolute. Bataillon posits that even if Cervantes did not read any of Erasmus's publications, he would have been familiar with Erasmus due to the prevalence of his beliefs in Spain:

Por lo tanto, podemos, si así lo queremos, suponer que leyó a Erasmo, o bien que respire lo esencial de sus enseñanzas en las lecciones de López de Hoyos, en la conversación de todos los buenos ingenios de las generaciones anteriores a la suya. La incertidumbre no es muy grave. Si nos inclinamos por la segunda hipótesis, ello se debe a que todas nuestras investigaciones demuestran que la España de Carlos V estuvo impregnada

> de erasmismo, que las tendencias literarias de Cervantes son las de un ingenio formado por el humanismo erasmizante, y que sin embargo su ironía, su humor, suenan a algo completamente nuevo. Ni el *Elogio de la locura*, ni los *Coloquios*, ni los *Diálogos* de los Valdés, ni el *Viaje de Turquía* dejan presentir esa fantasía que, en el *Quijote* o en el *Coloquio de los perros*, hace su juego en las fronteras de lo real y de lo inventado, de lo razonable y de lo arbitrario. (Bataillon 801)

Due to the declining interest of Erasmus's writings during Cervantes's lifetime, Bataillon also believes that Cervantes "puede ser considerado, con el mismo derecho, el último heredero del espíritu erasmiano en la literatura española, pese a la profunda diferencia de tono que separa su obra de la de Erasmo" (Bataillon 795, 798).[3] Castro affirms Erasmus's influence on Cervantes, but he also admits that Cervantes's spirituality and beliefs were also in accord with the teachings of the Catholic Church:

> En Cervantes, visto en conexión con el momento en que vive, hallaremos reflejos de ese complicado espíritu en lo que atañe al pensamiento religioso. Católico, sí, hemos de repetirlo; pero en la forma en que lo eran otros hombres de genio, preocupados de novedades. Su cristianismo, según veremos, recuerda, en ocasiones, más a Erasmo que a Trento.[4] (*El pensamiento* 256)

The source of Castro's ambiguity, according to Eric Ziolkowski, is his "contention that the *Quixote*'s author was a skilled dissembler who professed allegiance to the Catholic faith and its institutions while disguising constant barbs against the church and the traditional order under the foolishness of the knight's antics" (25).[5] Castro, however, still views Cervantes's portrayal of the clergy as anticlerical, a stance he attributes to Erasmus's influence.[6]

Some scholars, like Mexican novelist Carlos Fuentes, opine that there exists a preponderance of evidence to suggest that Erasmus's influence is more evident than Ignatius's: "The influence of Erasmian thought on Cervantes can be clearly perceived in three themes common to the philosopher and the novelist: the duality of truth, the illusion of appearances, and the praise of folly" (Fuentes 52–53). In the prefatory letter to *The Praise of Folly* (1511) that Erasmus wrote to his close friend Thomas More, for example, the theologian addresses possible criticism of

Chapter Two

his book in terms reminiscent of Cervantes's writing style in *Don Quixote*: "But perhaps there will not be wanting some wranglers that may cavil and charge me, partly that these toys are lighter than may become a divine, and partly more biting than may beseem the modesty of a Christian, and consequently exclaim that I remember the ancient comedy, or another Lucian, and snarl at everything" (*The Praise of Folly* 2). Critics, including Bataillon and Antonio Vilanova, hypothesized that Cervantes's source for *The Praise of Folly* might have been either its Spanish translation, Jerónimo de Mondragón's *Censura de la locura humana y excelencias della* (1598), or the Italian humanist Faustino Perisauli's *De Triumpho Stultitiae* (ca. 1499).

In 2012, Hispanists Jorge Ledo and Harm den Boer of the University of Basel discovered the only extant early modern Spanish translation of *The Praise of Folly*. They believe the manuscript dates to the early seventeenth century: "In conclusion, holding exclusively to the codicological data gathered, it could be conjectured that the manuscript of the *Moria* was copied during the seventeenth century in France" (Erasmus, Moria *de Erasmo de Roterodamo* 18). Ledo and den Boer posit, however, a lexical analysis of the text raises the possibility that the Spanish translation dates to the late sixteenth century. With respect to Mondragón's treatise, Ledo and den Boer believe the influence of *The Praise of Folly* is negligible: "In his edition of 1958, Antonio Vilanova points out some parallels—mostly sentences or ideas, rarely paragraphs or longer passages. ... Therefore, it is difficult to support Vilanova's view of the work as a *rifacimiento* of Erasmus's *Encomium* which was responsible for transmitting the main ideas of the work to Baroque writers, especially Miguel de Cervantes" (Erasmus, Moria *de Erasmo de Roterodamo* 3n10). Even if Cervantes had read the Spanish translation of *The Praise of Folly*, the assertion that Erasmus's treatise was the true source of *Don Quixote*, as Vilanova contends, is difficult to prove, and likely more so since Ledo and den Boer's discovery.[7] While there is no evidence that Cervantes read *De Triumpho Stultitiae*, it is reasonable to assume that he was familiar with Italian literature during his sojourn in Italy: "Furthermore, MC (Miguel de Cervantes) lived and traveled abroad, especially in Italy, and may well have gained much of his familiarity with humanist thought by reading some works directly in Italian" (Mancing, *The Cervantes*

Encyclopedia, Vol. 1 380). The earliest Spanish adaptation of *The Praise of Folly* is Hernán López de Yanguas's poem *Triunfos de Locura* (1521). Ledo and den Boer, however, believe *Triunfos de Locura* is more similar to Jean Thenaud's *L'Eloge de la Folie*, the first French translation of *The Praise of Folly*, which appears in the Franciscan theologian's encyclopedic allegory *Triumphe des vertus* (1517): "It would be difficult to explain López de Yanguas's knowledge of Thenaud's text, only transmitted in manuscript and addressed to a very concrete audience. Instead, it is easier to regard both works as moralizing recreations of *The Praise of Folly*, through a shared medieval framework of tradition" (Erasmus, Moria *de Erasmo de Roterodamo* 4).

Hispanist Paul M. Descouzis provides convincing evidence that several of the Council of Trent's decrees are exemplified in Cervantes's masterpiece. The four causes of Justification that are the source of twelve parallels when the knight is near death lead Descouzis to conclude: "Doce paralelos con doce decretos del Concilio de Trento son demasiados paralelos para considerarlos como una mera 'coincidencia'" (*Cervantes II* 25–26). The Council of Trent's decree on Marriage stipulates that a marriage is not valid if the man and woman do not express mutual consent to wed.[8] Descouzis notes that Marcela's uncle vows not to give her hand in marriage without her consent: "Mas él, que a las derechas es buen cristiano, aunque quisiera casarla luego, así como la vía de edad, no quiso hacerlo sin su consentimiento, sin tener ojo a la ganancia y granjería que le ofrecía el tener la hacienda de la moza dilatando su casamiento" (204). Descouzis also notes a correlation between the Council's decree on Penance, for example, and the captive's description of his experiences in Navarino and La Goleta in Part I, Chapter XXXIX ("Reflejos del Concilio de Trento" 480).[9] As the captive relates his story, he alludes to two concepts that are foundational to the decree on Penance: Divine origin and moral-theological causality. While the captive was in Navarino, he believed that the Holy League's armada missed an opportunity to defeat the Turkish fleet in the port. He justifies the armada's failure to capitalize on the situation in terms reminiscent of the Council's decree on Penance: "Pero el cielo lo ordenó de otra manera, no por culpa ni descuido del general que a los nuestros regía, sino por los pecados de la cristiandad, y porque quiere y permite Dios que tengamos siempre verdugos que nos castiguen" (Descouzis 527).

With respect to the decree on Contrition, Descouzis postulates that the bandit Roque Guinart illustrates "contrición imperfecta, o atrición" in Part II, Chapter LX ("Reflejos del Concilio de Trento" 481).[10] In the episode in which Guinart and his highwaymen encounter the aristocrat Doña Guiomar de Quiñones and her travelling party, he cites his intention not to harm soldiers or any woman as the reason he decides to return the six hundred *escudos* he intended to steal. Furthermore, Descouzis observes, Guinart recognizes the morally corrupt nature of his lifestyle, yet he believes, like the penitent who finds redemption in God, in a hopeful future: "Pero Dios es servido de que, aunque me veo en la mitad del laberinto de mis confusiones, no pierdo la esperanza de salir dél a puerto seguro" (535). Joaquín Casalduero notes that Roque Guinart personifies Counter-Reformation Catholicism: "la vida del hombre según la concibe el catolicismo de la Contrarreforma: un laberinto, la esperanza, el puerto seguro" (*Sentido y forma* 355).

José Antonio López Calle refutes categorically Castro's humanistic exegesis of Cervantes's religious ideology, arguing that he exaggerates Cervantes's Erasmian influence. In addition, he discounts the assessments of Fuentes, Bataillon, and anyone else who believes that Cervantes was a disciple of Erasmus:

> Por nuestra parte, afirmamos que en Cervantes no hay huella alguna de erasmismo, ni patente ni latente, en el cuadro que del cristianismo nos pinta en el *Quijote* y que, por tanto, no hay razón alguna seria para considerar que su visión del cristianismo sea de carácter erasmista, sino, muy al contrario, contamos con razones poderosas para descartarlo. En lo que sigue nos proponemos examinar críticamente y refutar las razones aducidas en pro del erasmismo del gran libro, apuntalar el carácter católico ortodoxo del cristianismo cervantino, así como resaltar los varios aspectos en que el pensamiento de Cervantes es diametralmente opuesto al de Erasmo, aspectos que los exegetas del *Quijote* en clave erasmista suelen omitir en sus escritos. (López Calle 2)

One example of López Calle's defense of Cervantes's Catholic orthodoxy is his treatment of ceremonies in *Don Quixote*. In Part I, Chapter XIX, for example, Don Quixote and Sancho believe they see a large group of phantoms and monsters approaching them, only to discover that the "phantoms and monsters" are participants in a religious procession that consists of "veinte encamisados, todos a caballo, con sus hachas encendidas en las manos, detrás de los cuales venía una litera cubierta de luto, a la cual seguían otros seis de a caballo, enlutados hasta los pies de las mulas; que bien vieron que no eran caballos en el sosiego con que caminaban" (271). Cervantes does not satirize the procession itself or its purpose. Instead, his knight mistakes the procession's participants for something they are not, similar to the windmills, which Don Quixote believes are giants.[11]

Another ceremony that Castro believes exhibits Erasmian influence that López Calle takes issue with is the cult of saints. The detail with which Cervantes describes the cult of saints is representative of Spaniards' devotion to saints.[12] During Cervantes's lifetime, both Philip II and Philip III collected saints' relics and believed in their curative powers. Philip III, for example, recovered from a deadly fever after the relics of St. Isidore (ca. 1080–1130), the patron saint of Madrid, had been placed at his bedside. In Part II, Chapter VIII, Sancho describes the fame achieved by the saints:

> Pues esta fama, estas gracias, estas prerrogativas, como llaman a esto —respondió Sancho— tienen los cuerpos y las reliquias de los santos que, con aprobación y licencia de nuestra santa madre Iglesia, tienen lámparas, velas, mortajas, muletas, pinturas, cabelleras, ojos, piernas, con que aumentan la devoción y engrandecen su cristiana fama; los cuerpos de los santos o sus reliquias llevan los reyes sobre sus hombros, besan los pedazos de sus huesos, adoran y enriquecen con ellos sus oratorios y sus más preciados Altares. (95)

In the same conversation, Sancho continues to defend his belief that the fame attributed to sainthood is more important than the fame achieved by any other profession, including knight-errantry. In defense of his observation, Sancho cites the canonization of two friars:

> —Quiero decir —dijo Sancho— que nos demos a ser santos, y alcanzaremos más brevemente la buena fama que pretendemos; y advierta, señor, que ayer o antes de ayer que, según ha poco se puede decir desta manera, canonizaron o beatificaron dos frailecitos descalzos, cuyas cadenas de hierro con que ceñían y atormentaban sus cuerpos se tiene ahora a gran ventura el besarlas y tocarlas, y están en más veneración que está, según

> dije, la espada de Roldán en la armería del Rey nuestro señor, que Dios guarde. Así que, señor mío, más vale ser humilde frailecito, de cualquier orden que sea, que valiente y andante caballero; más alcanzan con Dios dos docenas de diciplinas que dos mil lanzadas, ora las den a gigantes, ora a vestiglos o a endriagos. (95)

While Erasmus would no doubt view this type of ceremony as a total repudiation of the presence of Jesus Christ, López Calle notes that Sancho describes it in order to convince Don Quixote that the fame achieved by a saint is more significant than the fame achieved by a knight-errant: "si la alusión fuera burlesca o irónica, entonces el argumento de Sancho no tendría mucho sentido, pues en tal caso uno de los efectos más importantes de la manifestación de la fama de los santos quedaría invalidado" (López Calle 6). Don Quixote's response reflects Cervantes's admiration of monastic life, but the knight's words also exhibit the Catholic soteriology that everyone, regardless of profession, is called to holiness: "—Todo eso es así —respondió don Quijote—; pero no todos podemos ser frailes, y muchos son los caminos por donde lleva Dios a los suyos al cielo: religión es la caballería; caballeros santos hay en la gloria" (II, 95).[13] The comparison of chivalry to a religious order is more meaningful in Cervantes's day because of the reform of the religious orders that began with Cardinal Cisneros (Francisco Jiménez de Cisneros; 1436–1517) and the Council of Trent reaffirmed in Session XXV (1563).

López Calle also challenges Castro's belief that Don Quixote's comments about the statues of St. George, St. Martin of Tours, St. James the Great, and St. Paul in Part II, Chapter LVIII exemplify Cervantes's Erasmian influence. Castro suggests that Don Quixote's reverent tone when he talks about St. Paul, who was Erasmus's favorite saint and theologian, illustrates Cervantes's predilection for the Dutch humanist.[14] López Calle disagrees strongly, however, with Castro's assessment: "es don Quijote el que habla y habla muy en serio, como antes lo ha hecho igualmente sobre san Jorge y san Martín, pero prescindimos del tratamiento de éstos, porque Castro está empeñado en establecer una especie de contienda entre Santiago y san Pablo, de la que el primero sale malparado por Cervantes y el segundo especialmente ensalzado" (López Calle 7).[15] This episode, which I refer to again in Chapter 4, is a bellwether of Don Quixote's spiritual evolution.

López Calle also denies that Cervantes exhibits the same degree of anticlericalism as Erasmus, subscribing more to Bataillon's belief that Cervantes manifests an attitude of "anticlericalismo de *fabliaux*, pero no de anticlericalismo erasmista" (Ziolkowski 3).[16] In Part I, Chapter XIX, for example, Don Quixote and Sancho stop to eat the large amount of food the squire plundered from the pack mules that belong to the clergy who escort the dead body from Baeza to Segovia. The narrator interjects an example of Cervantes's "anticlericalism of *fabliaux*" into the description of the scene: "tendidos sobre la verde yerba, con la salsa de su hambre, almorzaron, comieron, merendaron y cenaron a un mesmo punto, satisfaciendo sus estómagos con más de una fiambrera que los señores clérigos del difunto (que pocas veces se dejan mal pasar) en la acémila de su repuesto traían" (276). López Calle and Enrique Moreno Baez consider Cervantes's comment about the clergy's comfortable lifestyle innocent humor. In addition, Moreno Baez notes that the seemingly anticlerical tone of the phrase is not unique to Cervantes: "No reflejaría el *Quijote* todas las facetas del alma española si no contuviera un par de esos chistes anticlericales que tanto abundan en nuestra literatura de todos los tiempos" (Moreno Baez 64). One of the more seemingly anticlerical allusions occurs in Part I, Chapter XXI when Don Quixote attacks the barber whose basin the knight believes is Mambrino's helmet. After the barber abandons his donkey, Sancho exchanges the trappings for Dapple's: "Y luego, habilitado con aquella licencia, hizo *mutatio caparum*, y puso su jumento a las mil lindezas, dejándole mejorado en tercio y quinto" (297). Casalduero negates the anticlerical tone of the *mutatio caparum*: "La vitalidad eclesiástica de la Contrarreforma no tenía por qué temer esas burlas. Lo importante creo que es darse cuenta de que la acción de cambiar es la que hace pensar en la ceremonia cardenalicia. Para mí, eso es todo" (*Sentido y forma* 117).

Furthermore, López Calle believes that Cervantes's "critique" of the clergy is in the same vein as the critical observations of other influential Catholics concerning the state of the Catholic Church in the sixteenth century, namely St. Teresa of Avila.[17] Cervantes's seemingly anticlerical writings cannot be accepted on face value, I posit, especially since he might have been one of a number of recognized Catholics who, like Teresa, did not agree with certain practices of a small percentage of the clergy.[18]

Chapter Two

Hispanist and theologian Mariano Delgado does not subscribe to the belief that Cervantes was a "criptoerasmista" either (222). He challenges Bataillon's assertion that the character who personifies Cervantes's religious ideology is Don Diego de Miranda, whom Don Quixote names Knight of the Green Coat because of the color of his overcoat (Part II, Chapter XVI):

> Oigo misa cada día; reparto de mis bienes con los pobres, sin hacer alarde de las buenas obras, por no dar entrada en mi corazón a la hipocresía y vanagloria, enemigos que blandamente se apoderan del corazón más recatado; procuro poner en paz los que sé que están desavenidos; soy devoto de Nuestra Señora y confío siempre en la misericordia infinita de Dios Nuestro Señor.[19] (157)

Bataillon's assessment is predicated, however, on a semantic alteration of the text: "reemplacemos la misa de cada día por la misa del domingo, pasemos por alto la devoción a Nuestra Señora—que, por lo demás, no impide a Don Diego poner toda su confianza en la misericordia divina—: este cuadro de una vida sencilla, holgada, piadosa y benefactora, sin sombra de fariseísmo, aparecerá rigurosamente conforme al ideal erasmiano" (*Erasmo y España* 793). Delgado questions how Bataillon or anyone, for that matter, knows that Cervantes's portrait of Don Diego is based on Erasmus's Christian Humanism:

> Una crítica literaria que no toma en serio al autor, sino que le hace decir lo que en realidad queremos escuchar, no se puede tomar en serio. ¿Cómo podemos saber que Cervantes en el retrato de la piedad del caballero del Verde Gabán pensaba en el ideal erasmista y no en el ideal de la reforma tridentina que a finales del siglo XVI imprimía su sello en la sociedad española? (224)

Delgado affirms his argument by noting that the hypothesis surrounding Cervantes's Erasmian discipleship vis-à-vis *Don Quixote* was a product of the nineteenth and twentieth centuries:

> El punto débil de considerar a Cervantes como anticlerical y criptoerasmista en las diferentes variantes consiste, como ha resaltado certeramente nuestro amigo José Jiménez Lozano, premio Cervantes 2002, en que dicha tesis se les ha ocurrido

> a los intelectuales de los siglos XIX y XX, pero no a los contemporáneos del mismo Cervantes, ni siquiera a los censores inquisitoriales de su obra que estaban más cerca que nosotros del erasmismo español y podían juzgarlo mejor.[20] (224)

Francisco Márquez Villanueva, however, concurs with Bataillon:

> La más simple consideración de estos personajes de los *Colloquia* muestra, respecto a don Diego de Miranda, una obvia coincidencia de ideología básica (la vida *prudente*), a la vez que multitud de ideas y temas intercambiables (anonimato, amistad, convites, piedad, matrimonio, bienestar económico, etc.). Pero tan importante o más resulta asimismo la identidad de fórmula literaria: la pieza oratoria en que se autorretrata un estilo de vida, lección de moral y no de psicología, ejercicio académico y jamás un trasunto de realidad humana. El caballero del encuentro en el camino, cuando aún no es personaje novelístico, se sentiría como en su propia casa entre las páginas de Erasmo. (*Personajes y temas del* Quijote 105)

Erasmus's ambivalence toward daily Mass, however, problematizes Márquez Villanueva's assertion that Don Diego is a character the Dutch Humanist would create. Erasmus assailed what he believed to be Catholicism's superstitious practices, such as pilgrimages, statues, and daily Mass when they are not a source of *metanoia*:

> He found society, and especially religious life, full of practices, ceremonies, traditions and conceptions, from which the Spirit seemed to have departed. He does not reject them offhand and altogether: what revolts him is that they are so often performed without understanding and right feeling. But to his mind, highly susceptible to the foolish and ridiculous things, all that sphere of ceremony and tradition displays itself as a useless, nay, a hurtful scene of human stupidity and selfishness. (Huizinga, *Erasmus* 100–01)

In the *Colloquy* titled "The Whole Duty of Youth" (1522), Erasmus expresses his sentiments about daily Mass in the conversation that takes place between Gaspar, a sixteen-year-old, and the eponymous Erasmus:

> *Erasmus*: You reason very well, if only what you say is certain.
> *Gaspar*: Do you ask anything more certain than the assurance of the Gospel?

> *Erasmus*: To do that is wrong. But some people don't think they're Christians unless they hear mass, as they call it, every day.
> *Gaspar*: I don't condemn their custom, of course, especially when they have plenty of leisure or are persons who spend the whole day in worldly occupations. I simply disapprove of those who persuade themselves superstitiously that the day will be unlucky unless they begin it with mass and go straight from divine service to trade or moneymaking or court where, if their business succeeds—whether by hook or crook—they attribute the success to mass. (*The Collected Works* 95)

Don Diego de Miranda's attendance at daily Mass is emblematic of the Council of Trent's decree that the faithful should receive daily Communion whenever they attend Mass: "The holy council wishes indeed that at each mass the faithful who are present should communicate, not only in spiritual desire but also by the sacramental partaking of the Eucharist" (*The Canons and Decrees of the Council of Trent* 147).[21] Erasmus, on the other hand, had reservations about the superstition ascribed to the efficacy of the Eucharist: "I do not see what an imperceptible body really should be able to effect, nor what value it would have if it could be perceived" (Enno Van Gelder 156). Furthermore, speaking of the Body of Christ, he asks, "How can the same body be present simultaneously in so many and such small substances and in so many pieces" (Enno Van Gelder 156). It is no wonder that Erasmus stated that the Eucharist was an "incomprehensible mystery" (Enno Van Gelder 156).

Descouzis describes the Knight of the Green Coat as an "arquetipo del cristiano de la Contrarreforma Española" (*Cervantes I* 124). Alessandro Martinengo characterizes the Knight of the Green Coat as a "cavaliere della Controriforma" (212). Helmut Hatzfeld interprets Don Diego de Miranda's introduction to Don Quixote and Sancho as evidence that the Knight of the Green Coat "es justamente el tipo de la piedad de la Contrarreforma, la piedad de las buenas obras" (135). Don Diego's lifestyle exemplifies a Tridentine mentality. He attends Mass daily, and while he is not an ascetic, he shares his wealth with the poor and performs charitable works. In addition, he is a devotee of the Virgin Mary and places all of his trust in Jesus.[22] In *Don Quixote*, Cervantes illustrates that the Tridentine lifestyle of devotion is not the only way to cultivate a greater awareness of God in everyday life.

Hatzfeld not only asserts the presence of a traditional Catholic ideology in *Don Quixote*, he also believes that Jesuit theology and spirituality were an integral component of the Counter Reformation: "Aquel espíritu ascético-moral y estrictamente eclesiástico del catolicismo, tal como se instituye en los *Ejercicios espirituales* de San Ignacio, por una parte y en los cánones de Trento por otra" (133). Hatzfeld cites numerous examples from the novel that support his belief, including many that are in accord with Ignatian spirituality. One such example is the word *conciencia* (*conscience*), which, according to Hatzfeld, appears twenty-seven times "en típica fraseología ignaciana" (140). Hatzfeld notes that Cervantes's use of the word *conciencia* is similar to Ignatius's concept of it as it appears in the *Spiritual Exercises*:

> Antes de todas las meditaciones propone Ignacio una exacta investigación del estado de la conciencia, un examen particular y un examen general, que deben ser realizados con gran frecuencia y a base de gráficos sinópticos. Se recomienda un culto a la conciencia, emparentado con lo que hoy se llama psicoanálisis. No es, pues, maravilla que la conciencia haya sido un tirano de la sociedad de la Contrarreforma. (140)

In addition to the word *conciencia*, Hatzfeld cites many other examples, including Sacred Scripture, the numerous appearances of the word *católico*, and dogmatic formulations, that support his assertion that "más fuertemente aún que en las demás tierras católicas influye en España la Contrarreforma, no tan sólo en la literatura religiosa, sino en la profana" (150).

There are episodes in the novel that may appear to exhibit Erasmus's influence on Cervantes. Erasmus wrote pejoratively of the hypocrisy of the clergy whose rituals and ceremonies he believed distracted from Jesus's message. In addition, in *The Praise of Folly* Erasmus singles out the clergy of the Catholic Church as the focus of a particularly sharp criticism of religious life:

> Whereas on the contrary, these jolly fellows say they have sufficiently discharged their offices if they but anyhow mumble over a few odd prayers, which, so help me, Hercules! I wonder if any god either hear or understand, since they do neither themselves, especially when they thunder them out in that manner they are wont. But this they have in common with

those of the heathens, that they are vigilant enough to the harvest of their profit, nor is there any of them that is not better read in those laws than the Scripture.[23] (71–72)

In Part II, Chapter XXXII, Cervantes illustrates Erasmus's critique that members of the clergy are not what they appear to be. After the Duke and Duchess's chaplain insults Don Quixote, the knight exalts his profession as the more noble and honorable one:

> Unos van por el ancho campo de la ambición soberbia; otros, por el de la adulación servil y baja; otros, por el de la hipocresía engañosa, y algunos, por el de la verdadera religión; pero yo, inclinado de mi estrella, voy por la angosta senda de la caballería andante, por cuyo ejercicio desprecio la hacienda, pero no la honra. (296–97)

It should come as no surprise that the knight considers his profession as superior to all others because of the books of chivalry that inspired him to become Don Quixote. Not as apparent, however, is the inference that knight errantry is a religion. Huizinga notes that religion and chivalry cannot be separated:

> The conception of chivalry as a sublime form of secular life might be defined as an aesthetic ideal assuming the appearance of an ethical ideal. Heroic fancy and romantic sentiment form its basis. But medieval thought did not permit ideal forms of noble life, independent of religion. For this reason, piety and virtue have to be the essence of a knight's life. Chivalry, however, will always fall short of this ethical function. Its earthly origin draws it down. (*The Waning of the Middle Ages* 58)

The authors of chivalric literature modeled their stories on monasticism, which was one of the cornerstones of the first orders of chivalry in the middle and late Middle Ages. The French soldier and author Phillipe de Mézières (1327–1405) composed the statutes for the Order of the Passion of Christ, which he hoped would unite Christendom in their war against the Turks. Cervantes's ironic appropriation of the order of knighthood tradition becomes apparent in Part I, Chapter III when the innkeeper knights Don Quixote:

> Advertido y medroso desto el castellano, trujo luego un libro donde asentaba la paja y cebada que daba a los harrieros, y

Hermeneutics

> con un cabo de vela que le traía un muchacho, y con las dos ya dichas doncellas, se vino adonde don Quijote estaba, al cual mandó hincar de rodillas; y, leyendo en su manual (como que decía alguna devota oración), en mitad de la leyenda alzó la mano y diole sobre el cuello un buen golpe, y tras él, con su mesma espada, un gentil espaldaraza (siempre murmurando entre dientes, como que rezaba). Hecho esto, mandó a una de aquellas damas que le ciñese la espada, la cual lo hizo con mucha desenvoltura y discreción, porque no fue menester poca para no reventar de risa a cada punto de las ceremonias; pero las proezas que ya habían visto del novel caballero les tenían la risa a raya. (133)

Don Quixote employs two words that have religious connotations, *profesar* and *profesión*. The *Diccionario de Autoridades* (1726–39) defines the verb *profesar* as "exercer alguna cosa, con inclinación voluntaria, y continuación en ella" and "Se toma regularmente por obligarse por toda la vida, en alguna Religión, haciendo solemnemente los tres votos de pobreza, obediencia y castidad." In Part II, Chapter VIII, while Don Quixote and Sancho travel to El Toboso, Don Quixote recognizes that he and Sancho practice Catholicism, and, in addition, speaks about his *profession* of knight errant as a force against the Seven Deadly Sins:

> Así, ¡oh Sancho!, que nuestras obras no han de salir del límite que nos tiene puesto la religión cristiana, que profesamos. Hemos de matar en los gigantes a la *soberbia*; a la *envidia*, en la generosidad y buen pecho; a la *ira*, en el reposado continente y quietud del ánimo; a la *gula* y al sueño, en el poco comer que comemos y en el mucho velar que velamos; a la [lujuria] y *lascivia*, en la lealtad que guardamos a las que hemos hecho señoras de nuestros pensamientos; a la *pereza*, con andar por todas las partes del mundo, buscando las ocasiones que nos puedan hacer y hagan, sobre cristianos, famosos caballeros. Ves aquí, Sancho, los medios por donde se alcanzan los estremos de alabanzas que consigo trae la buena fama.[24] (93–94; emphasis added)

The behavior and values that the knight espouses represent, arguably, ways in which a person could grow closer to God. On the surface, Cervantes's stance may be understood as anticlerical, yet it also conceals the Ignatian belief of "finding God in all things," because the knight and his squire are righteous, or at least try to be, in their behavior. Allen notes that this passage exemplifies the irony of Don Quixote's character: "The disparity between the struggle against pride, seen as external, and the struggle against the other vices through *self*-purification highlights precisely the object of the systematic irony directed against Don Quixote up to this point" (*Don Quixote: Hero or Fool?* 166). Furthermore, in the same episode with the chaplain in Part II, Chapter XXXII, Don Quixote states, "caballero soy y caballero he de morir si place al Altísimo" (296). In the end, however, Don Quixote, now Alonso Quijano, does not die a knight.

In *The Praise of Folly*, Erasmus also expresses particularly harsh criticism of monks and monasteries. Erasmus's critique is based on his experience as a professed monk who entered the monastery in 1487 shortly after the death of his parents and at the insistence of his guardians. During the nearly six years in which Erasmus lived in the monastery, the repetitive and simple lifestyle failed to inspire him and contributed to his animosity toward monastic life:

> And yet, like pleasant fellows, with all this vileness, ignorance, rudeness, and impudence, they represent to us, for so they call it, the lives of the apostles. Yet what is more pleasant than that is they do all things by the rules and, as it were, a kind of mathematics, the least swerving from which were a crime beyond forgiveness—as how many knots their shoes must be tied with, of which color everything is, what distinction of habits, of what stuff made, how many straws broad their girdles and of what fashion, how many bushels wide their cowl, how many fingers wide their hair, and how many hours sleep. (*The Praise of Folly* 65)

Cervantes addresses monks and monastic life, but his measured tone contrasts greatly with Erasmus's acerbic description. In Part I, Chapter XIII, Don Quixote and Sancho meet shepherds who are travelling to Grisóstomo's funeral, and one of the shepherds, Vivaldo, who recognizes that Don Quixote is not sane, engages the knight by suggesting that the profession of knight-errantry seems to be more challenging than the life of a Carthusian monk:

> Así, que somos ministros de Dios en la tierra, y brazos por quien se ejecuta en ello su justicia. Y como las cosas de la guerra y las a ellas tocantes y concernientes no se pueden poner en ejecución sino sudando, afanando y trabajando, síguese que aquellos que la profesan tienen, sin duda, mayor

trabajo que aquellos que en sosegada paz y reposo están rogando a Dios favorezca a los que poco pueden.²⁵ (211)

In citing this episode, López Calle writes that "Don Quijote se nos manifiesta aquí como un ortodoxo católico y contrario a la doctrina de Erasmo" (4). Furthermore, Cervantes seems to imply that God needs all of his "ministers" on earth to serve Him.

The hermeneutic of skepticism surrounding Cervantes's religiosity is by no means limited to Catholicism and Christian Humanism. Hispanist Jesús G. Maestro presents a markedly different understanding of Cervantes's religiosity, one that does not postulate either an Ignatian or an Erasmian reading of the novel. Instead, he describes Cervantes as a Catholic atheist, a person who does not believe in God but who recognizes the Catholicity of the environment in which he or she lives. Furthermore, Maestro compares Cervantes's atheism to philosopher Baruch Spinoza's rationalism:

> Más que leer a Cervantes como un rescoldo cálido de Erasmo, pacifista e idealista del religioso Renacimiento, habría que empezar a leerlo como un ardiente heterodoxo que preludia las líneas de un pensamiento mucho más crítico, afín a filósofos tan particulares como Spinoza, al que los credos más fundamentalistas del siglo XVII—dada su capacidad crítica—repudiaron insoportablemente. Cervantes tiene más en común con el pensamiento de Baruch Spinoza que con el de Erasmo de Rotterdam. (*Las ascuas del Imperio* 226)

Maestro expounds on this comparison, labelling Cervantes's religious referents as devoid of content: "Cervantes no es soluble en agua bendita" ("Cervantes y la religión" 28).

Scholars who believe that Cervantes was a *converso* cite his crypto-judaism as a source of his skepticism toward the Catholic faith. Castro and Márquez Villanueva were the first critics to propose that Cervantes was a *converso*.²⁶ Daniel Eisenberg states emphatically that Cervantes, however, was a *converso*, although his only evidence is what Cervantes writes and does not write in his literature. For example, Eisenberg cites the paucity of information Cervantes provides about Rome near the end of *Persiles*, concluding that Cervantes was bothered by the opulence of the capital of Catholicism ("La actitud de Cervantes" 68). The literary evidence that Eisenberg provides as the foundation of his case, however, merits consideration of the crypto-judaism question surrounding Cervantes's life. In the same article, Eisenberg acknowledges that there is no genealogical or historical documentation in support of his thesis. Furthermore, one of the critics he cites who discards entirely the possibility that Cervantes was a New Christian is Jean Canavaggio, whom Eisenberg describes as the most authoritative biographer of Cervantes today. Michael McGaha asserts his belief that Cervantes's literature provides the best evidence that he was a *converso*, especially with respect to one drama: "I find it unbelievable that anyone other than a *cristiano nuevo* could have written the 'Entremés del retablo de las maravillas,' for example" ("Is There A Hidden Jewish Meaning" 174). *El retablo de las maravillas* is one of the interludes in *Ocho comedias y ocho entremeses, nunca representados* (1615). Before the performance of this one-act drama begins, Chanfalla announces to the spectators, who consist of the town's mayor and other municipal authorities, the play is only visible to those who are of Old Christian lineage. Each spectator, fearful of being stigmatized as a New Christian, reacts as if they actually see what the two swindlers Chanfalla and Chirinos only narrate. Even if Cervantes did have *converso* lineage, it would not necessarily make him anti-Catholic or a skeptic of the faith. St. Teresa of Avila and St. John of the Cross, two of the most influential figures in Christianity, had proven *converso* lineage.

Ken Colston, who is the author of many articles about the Renaissance, and, specifically, Shakespeare and Christianity, offers a new perspective on Cervantes's Catholic faith. In the November 2012 issue of the *New Oxford Review*, an online journal, Colston describes what transpired at a National Endowment for the Humanities Summer Seminar for School Teachers on *Don Quixote*:

> It was delightful to sit at a table and simply read a classic text with high-school teachers and college professors from all over the country. I was appalled, however, by the ruling assumptions about Catholicism, and about Cervantes, held by nearly everyone in the room, including several practicing Catholics. Cervantes's criticisms of the Church, it was understood, meant that he was "opposed to all organized religion." The "Catholics" of his time were the people who persecuted and exiled Spain's Jewish and Moorish minorities, indexed and burned progressive and scientific books, executed heretics, and kept women on constant house arrest. The sole purpose of the Holy Office

was to torture innocent freethinkers, not to save souls and order the commonwealth. The usual Jacobin prejudices against Christian thought were trotted out—that it is irrational, mired in superstition, opposed to progress and science; that it is inhumane, hypocritical, intolerant, and generally out of step with enlightened contemporary academic research. Cervantes's Gospel leanings were turned against the Church herself: That he and his hero showed sympathy for the poor, women, prisoners, writers, and Moors was considered a statement against the Church hierarchy, not a dramatic rendering of the corporal and spiritual works of mercy. In any case, nothing could really be said for sure about Cervantes's thought because he was a master of disguises, everywhere and nowhere in his text, like an underground writer during the Soviet period.

Given the secular nature of the modern academy, this anachronistic reading is not surprising, despite the fact that Spanish culture has been traditionally and robustly Roman Catholic. All manner of critical approaches to Cervantes, from feminist to deconstructionist to Freudian to reader-response, appear in publications about him, save the one most consistent with his time, place, and person: The one that asserts that the substantially documented biographical facts of his life do establish that he was a practicing and—during the period of his *floreat*—an ardent Roman Catholic, and that therefore the reader is entitled to presume that the Catholic faith in his pages was sincerely even if not uncritically held by the man who actually wrote them. And if one reads his works, one can see that the "oppressive" religious authorities of his time gave the artist at least as much latitude as, say, today's secular media elites give men and women of faith who dare to speak in the public squares. (Colston n.p.)

Colston's sociohistorical interpretation challenges the prevailing hermeneutic of Cervantes's Catholic faith in *cervantismo* today and encourages an inclusive, not exclusive, reading of *Don Quixote*. The complex philosophical, theological, and cultural currents of Cervantes's day, however, cannot be overlooked.

In a recent article (March 21, 2016) titled "Don Quixote and the Via Dolorosa" in *Crisis*, an online magazine that serves as "A Voice for the Faithful Catholic Laity," Sean Fitzpatrick compares the knight's adventures to the Catholic's Lenten journey, where "the spirit is strong but the flesh is weak." Fitzpatrick, in particular, emphasizes the novel's Christological dimension: "The novel takes up its cross, chapter after chapter, and follows after

Chapter Two

Christ. Chapter after chapter, the Knight of the Sorrowful Face falls, and, chapter after chapter, he gets up again and continues on. It is a book that plays out with all the pain and poignancy, all the humanity and humor, that composes the chivalric call of the Christian life." He describes Christianity as a "Chivalric religion" that remains vibrant long after the end of knighthood. Furthermore, Fitzpatrick defines "quixotic" in the context of the Catholic's Lenten journey: "Being 'quixotic' does not mean being quaint or charming or naïve. It means suffering rejection while, at the same time, rejoicing in the joy of the journey, even if it is up a *via dolorosa*" *(*Fitzpatrick n.p.; author's italics).

Fitzpatrick, like Colston, recognizes that Don Quixote is more than a nominal Christian knight, whose efforts to sustain his anachronistic chivalric identity may be viewed as analogous to the Christian's struggle with his or her faith. The compassionate reader may even experience personally Don Quixote's idealistic endeavors and suffer along with him when they fail to materialize because, after all, the reader finds in the novel a reflection of the guiding principles of his or her own life: "Like those readers evoked within the text, each of us brings to our experience of reading everything that we have become already, along with more or less acknowledged desires and our more or less clearly formulated projects. Like the readers within the text, each of us comes to define himself or perceive who he is according to the way he reads *Don Quixote*" (Johnson, Don Quixote 100).

The polylithic religious milieu of Cervantes's time, as well as the events that transpired in his life, exposed the author to different ideologies. It is no wonder then that there exist a number of interpretations of the novel's religious ideology. The universal and timeless appeal of *Don Quixote*, however, has distanced its hero from its author and its author from his own life and the time in which he lived. My analysis of Cervantes's nuanced treatment of Catholicism in *Don Quixote* is based on a reading that returns Cervantes's hero to Cervantes's text and Cervantes to the events that most shaped his life.[27]

Chapter Three

Don Quixote and Moral Theology
What a Knight and His Squire Can Teach Us About Cervantes's Catholicism

The foundation of the Roman Catholic tradition of moral theology is the Sacrament of Confession, the origin of which can be traced back to the teachings of Jesus. In John 20:23, Jesus authorizes the Apostles to forgive sins in His name: "Whose sins you forgive are forgiven them, and whose sins you retain are retained."[1] The Sacrament of Confession, which is also known as Penance and Reconciliation, dates to the first centuries of the Catholic Church. The writings of St. Clement of Rome, St. Ignatius of Antioch, and St. Justin Martyr, among others, speak to the need to confess sins and to reconcile with the Church (Fastiggi 23). The faithful confessed their sins in public, with the members of the church as witnesses, until the late fourth century, when the Church appointed priests to meet with penitents privately. By the year 1000, the Sacrament of Confession resembled in form (absolution) and matter (contrition, confession, and satisfaction) its present state: the priest, in private with the penitent, imparted absolution for the remission of sins and assigned penance as a means of purification from temporal punishment.

The evolution of moral theology as an academic discipline during Cervantes's lifetime was gradual. The moral dilemmas faced by the Spanish explorers in the New World represented a new theological challenge for Renaissance Spaniards. Unlike the *moriscos* who remained in Spain after the Reconquest, the natives of the New World were open to conversion. The manner in which they underwent conversion, however, raised the ire of Catholic clergy, especially, among many others, the Dominican theologians Francisco de Vitoria, O.P. (1483–1546) and Antonio Montesinos, O.P. (1475–1540), who, in a homily from 1511, said, "Decid ¿con qué derecho y con qué justicia tenéis en tan cruel y horrible servidumbre aquestos indios?" (Casas xi; Alonso

Lasheras 31). Vitoria, however, was perhaps more responsible for the prominent place of moral theology in sixteenth-century Spain than any other Catholic theologian. As a professor of theology at the University of Salamanca, he was well-known because of his lectures on moral theology and its place in politics, economics, and international law: "si hemos mostrado que el poder público viene establecido por el derecho natural, y el derecho natural tiene a Dios por autor, es evidente que el poder público procede de Dios y no se basa ni en un pacto de los hombres ni en cualquier derecho positivo" (Cordero Pando 23).[2] Vitoria, whose students and secretaries published the notes from his lectures at the University of Salamanca between 1527 and 1540, applied Thomistic principles, which Cervantes would later incorporate into *Don Quixote*, to the philosophical foundation of a variety of social, political, and ecclesiastical subjects, including civil authority, murder, marriage, and relations with the Native Americans in the New World.

In response to the proclamations of Martin Luther (1483–1546), John Calvin (1509–64), and Ulrich Zwingli (1484–1531), the Council of Trent (Session XIV; 1551) reaffirmed the Sacrament of Confession in a compilation of the Church's teaching about the sacrament that dates back nearly four hundred years. O'Malley observes that the Council's decree on Penance, which consists of nine chapters and fifteen canons, is unique: "No doctrinal decree of the council had up to this point betrayed such a strong imprint of medieval Scholastic theology and canon law (*Trent* 152). The Council of Trent's focus on the Catholic Church's teachings about the Sacrament of Confession and personal discipline defined the manner in which the Church interpreted moral theology: "Broadly speaking, the decrees of that council dealing with the sacrament of confession obliged Catholic theologians to analyze moral questions through the enumeration of sins according to their number, species, and circumstances" (Gallagher 374). Without any formal training, priests were not prepared to judge these moral questions. Consequently, the Council of Trent issued a decree that diocesan seminaries be established to train seminarians and local clergy to be ministers of the Sacrament of Confession. The Catholic Church instituted its first seminary soon after the conclusion of the Council of Trent, and the curriculum, while it prepared seminarians to assume different ministerial roles (father, teacher, and physician), focused on the judicial nature of the Sacrament of Confession (Curran 27).[3] It is against this background that moral theology developed as a new theological genre. The Jesuits's curriculum of study, *Ratio studiorum,* included classes on human acts, law, sins, conscience, and sacraments (Curran 21). Juan Azor (1535–1603), a Jesuit professor of philosophy and theology canonized the manuals of moral theology when he published *Instituciones morales* (1600, 1606, 1611), a three-volume study he based on the material he covered in his classes. Post-Tridentine seminarians focused specifically on two areas related to moral theology: how to hear confessions and how to cultivate a Christian conscience.

In order to gain insight into what Don Quixote and Sancho Panza can illuminate for us about Cervantes's Catholicism, it is helpful to focus first on the end of the novel.[4] In Part II, Chapter LXXIV, Don Quixote is on his deathbed, where he evaluates the life he has lived.[5] In the Prologue to Part II, Cervantes informs the reader that Don Quixote will die at the end of Part II: "te doy a don Quijote dilatado, y, finalmente, muerto y sepultado, porque ninguno se atreva a levantarle nuevos testimonios, pues bastan los pasados" (28). Ostensibly, Don Quixote's death may be attributed to Cervantes's wish that another author will not appropriate the knight like Avellaneda did in his spurious Part II of the novel. Don Quixote's death also provides Cervantes, however, with one final opportunity, which I would argue is the most important because of its implications, to manifest his Catholic faith. Whether the reader accepts this proposition or not depends on how he or she interprets the consequences of the knight's actions. Cesáreo Bandera, for example, describes the knight's adventures, however, as an "existential failure":

> Don Quixote will end his mad adventures without his madness having produced a single benefit to anybody: not a single *entuerto* straightened, not a single injustice eliminated; not a single widow or orphan remedied. The sterility of Don Quixote's madness is total. But this Cervantine intention gradually dawns on us, interestingly, as Cervantes's compassion becomes clearer also by the moment. It is not out of cruelty that Cervantes destroys the last remaining hope that Don Quixote may have accomplished something through his madness.

> This final realization is something like a purgation, intended
> to cleanse Don Quixote (and the reader) of any remaining
> knightly nostalgia. The moment is getting closer for his cure
> and his death. (*The Humble Story* 217–18n)

He bases his assertion on the premise that Don Quixote filters the success of his adventures through the eyes of Amadís of Gaul, the literary knight-errant whom Don Quixote aspires to imitate. Bandera, in response to Luis Rosales, writes, "The critic seems to forget that it was Don Quixote himself who provoked those failures. I do not know what the Christian meaning could be of refusing to, or being incapable of, learning from one's own experience" (215n). Rosales, on the other hand, considers Don Quixote's failures to be the basis of his religious epiphany at the end of the novel: "Don Quijote fracasa en todas sus empresas, y el fracaso, como hemos visto y seguiremos viendo, es inherente al quijotismo. Vivir es fracasar. Todo lo humano se verifica en el fracaso. La historia de don Quijote nos enseña—golpes, violencias, burlas, humillaciones—que el fracaso es inherente al destino del hombre, pero que el heroísmo se demuestra en la manera de aceptar su lección. ... Desde el punto de vista de la moral cristiana, sus continuas derrotas implican el perfeccionamiento de su virtud" (Rosales 866). Bandera understands Don Quixote's "existential failure" as a means to an end that provides the reader with acute insight into Cervantes's relationship with his protagonist:

> ... in the profoundly Christian eyes of Cervantes, a world of
> deceiving appearances is only a prologue to some primitive,
> violent confusion, and original chaos—a world from which
> Christ is completely absent. ... In the final analysis, what
> Cervantes sees behind the ultimate consequences of madness
> looks very much like the original, the spontaneous, sacrificial
> crisis postulated by mimetic theory, but without the possibility
> any longer of the old sacralized victim that would put an end
> to it. Therefore, the only hope for that kind of madness is the
> new victim, the one that puts an end to the old victimizing,
> "scapegoating" process—in other words, Christ. (*A Refuge of
> Lies* 139–40)

Bandera also notes that Cervantes believes that there is only one cure for Don Quixote's madness: "... he believes in the possibility of a spiritual cure for a disease that is fundamentally of a spiritual character, a disease of the soul rather than a disease of the body" (*Refuge* 140). Melveena McKendrick's assertion that Cervantes wrote the prologue to Part II after he finished the novel also suggests that Cervantes's contemplation of his own mortality also could have determined Don Quixote's fate.[6]

Don Quixote expresses regret that he did not dedicate his life to reading books about the lives of saints, proclaiming: "ya soy enemigo de Amadís de Gaula y de toda la infinita caterva de su linaje; ya me son odiosas todas las historias profanas del andante caballería; ya conozco mi necedad y el peligro en que me pusieron haberlas leído; ya, por misericordia de Dios, escarmentando en cabeza propia, las abomino" (634). He distances himself from the material world, represented by those "detestables libros de las caballería" (633), and embraces the ethereal journey that awaits him, symbolized by books "que sean luz del alma" (633). Then, Don Quixote, at this point known as Alonso Quijano el Bueno, asks everyone to leave his room, except for the priest, who hears his confession.[7] Allen attributes the irony of events that culminate with Don Quixote's epiphany to General Comic Irony, which Norman Knox defines as "the appearance of disaster resolves itself into the reality of good fortune" (53). Allen also notes that Divine Providence achieves its ends through General Comic Irony, remarking about Don Quixote's journey from "confident unawareness" to self-awareness: "He never suffers for his virtues, but ... he is brought through suffering to recognize and repent of his faults. This victory over himself is heroic" (*Don Quixote* 191).[8] Cervantes's portrayal of Providence brings to mind St. Thomas Aquinas's philosophy: "For in God Himself there can be nothing ordered towards an end, since He is the last end. This type of order in things towards an end is therefore in God called providence" (Q.22, A.1). In Part II, Chapter LXVI, as Don Quixote and Sancho leave Barcelona, the knight tells his squire: "Lo que te sé decir es que no hay fortuna en el mundo, ni las cosas que en él suceden, buenas o malas que sean, vienen acaso, sino por particular providencia de los cielos, y de aquí viene lo que suele decirse: que cada uno es artífice de su ventura" (580). Cervantes will further illustrate his knowledge of Thomistic philosophy when Don Quixote speaks about God's relationship to time (Part II, Chapter XXV) and peace (Part I, Chapter XXXVII).

Chapter Three

Don Quixote's confession is one of the three Sacraments, in addition to Anointing of the Sick and Eucharist, the faithful, including Cervantes himself, receive at the end of life. Cervantes's portrayal of Don Quixote's death illustrates the impact the Council of Trent had on how to live but also how to die: "En el Barroco tridentino, el moribundo está con su conciencia, con la continua presencia de su vida; la muerte personificada como tal ha desaparecido; en su lugar tenemos al cura, la confesión, todos los sacramentos" (Casalduero, *Sentido y forma* 399). The Sacrament of the Eucharist, which is the Sacrament of Christ's Passover, is the last of the three Sacraments to be administered before death because it prepares a person to "pass over" to eternal life with God.[9] The ordinary minister of the Sacraments of Confession and Anointing the Sick is a priest.[10] The outbreak of the bubonic plague, or "Black Death," which was responsible for the death of millions of Europeans in the Middle Ages, however, made it impossible for a priest to administer these Sacraments to every person who succumbed to this disease:

> Moreover, there were a few whose bodies were accompanied to church by more than ten or twelve of their neighbors, nor were they carried on the shoulders of their honored and esteemed fellow citizens, but by a band of gravediggers, come up from the lower classes, who insisted on being called sextons and performed their services for a fee. They would shoulder the bier and quick-march it off, not to the church that the dead man had chosen before his demise, but in most cases, to the one closest by. They would walk behind four or six clergymen who carried just a few candles—and sometimes none at all—and who did not trouble themselves with lengthy, solemn burial services, but instead, with the aid of those sextons, dumped the corpse as quickly as they could into whatever empty grave they found. (Boccaccio 10)

In response to this sacramental crisis, the Catholic Church produced a manual in Latin that prepared Catholics and Protestants for death. The first *ars moriendi*, or *The Art of Dying*, publication appeared in 1415, and it included an illustrated version for the illiterate.[11] In addition to offering comfort for the dying, the manual suggested five practices to cultivate a lifestyle that would lead to a good death: reflect on mortality; examination of conscience, reconciliation, and forgiveness;

reading and contemplating the Scriptures; liturgy and prayer; and acts of compassion, especially comforting the dying (Derowitsch 39).

In Part II, Chapter XXIV, Don Quixote advises the page, who is eager to begin his military service, not to think about any adversities that might befall him, the worst of which, he says, is death. A good death, however, is a fortunate occurrence: "que el peor de todos es la muerte, y como ésta sea buena, el mejor de todos es el morir" (237). Julius Caesar, the knight continues, when asked to name the best death, answered one that was unexpected and sudden. Don Quixote's assessment of Caesar's response provides insight into the knight's concept of a good death: "y aunque respondió como gentil y ajeno del conocimiento del verdadero Dios, con todo eso, dijo bien, para ahorrarse del sentimiento humano" (237). Don Quixote believes that a good death for a pagan is quick and peaceful. Then, he expresses ambivalence toward how a person dies and death in general: "que puesto caso que os maten en la primera facción y refriega, o ya de un tiro de artillería, o volado de una mina, ¿qué importa? Todo es morir, y acabóse la obra" (237). I believe that Don Quixote's apparent indifference to death is not representative of his beliefs, but rather illustrates a pagan's view of it. In other words, Cervantes's definition of a good death subverts neither paganism nor Catholicism. Instead, he seems to suggest that a good death is not exclusive to Catholicism. Furthermore, Don Quixote qualifies his remark about Caesar's paganism when he asserts that Caesar "dijo bien, para ahorrarse del sentimiento humano." The knight alludes to the Catholic doctrine of redemptive suffering, which the Catholic Church teaches is a trial that God allows for the purpose of self-purification and sanctification. The pagan, however, is unable to find any redemption in suffering, and, therefore, the pain, which transforms the body into a raging inferno because it is not directed toward a higher good, is not ameliorated in any way.

Don Quixote initially seeks to attain the earthly fame and glory of the knights about whom he reads. As a contemplative in action whose relationship with God becomes more intimate as a result of the different adventures, however, Don Quixote expresses his belief that heavenly glory is greater because it is not fleeting. In Part II, Chapter VIII, during his discourse about how different people achieved fame, the knight tells Sancho:

> Todas estas y otras grandes y diferentes hazañas son, fueron y serán obras de la fama, que los mortales desean como premios y parte de la inmortalidad que sus famosos hechos merecen, puesto que los cristianos, católicos y andantes caballeros más habemos de atender a la gloria de los siglos venideros, que es eterna en las regiones etéreas y celestes, que a la vanidad de la fama que en este presente y acabable siglo se alcanza; la cual fama, por mucho que dure, en fin se ha de acabar con el mesmo mundo, que tiene su fin señalado. (93)

The knight addresses the state of Sancho's soul once again in Part II, Chapter XLII when he gives Sancho advice on how to be a good governor: "Esto que hasta aquí te he dicho son documentos que han de adornar tu alma" (379). Rachel Schmidt notes that the phrases "adorn your soul" and "light of my soul" evoke the *ars moriendi* literary genre: "Dicha frase, adornar el alma, hace eco de la metáfora de alumbrar el alma que predomina en el *ars moriendi* medieval, a la vez que asocia este discurso con los libros que sean 'de luz del alma' que Alonso Quijano se propone leer al morirse él mismo" ("The Performance and Hermeneutics of Death in the Last Chapter of *Don Quijote*" 122). Specifically, Don Quixote advises Sancho to love, to obey and to respect God, and to act in a virtuous manner:

> Mira, Sancho: si tomas por medio a la virtud, y te precias de hacer hechos virtuosos, no hay para qué tener envidia a los que tienen de príncipes y señores; porque la sangre se hereda y la virtud se aquista y la virtud vale por sí sola lo que la sangre no vale. (377)

Don Quixote advises Sancho to govern with moral rectitude because of his new state in life. Cervantes challenges the societal belief that only the nobility is capable of virtuous behavior because of their inherited titles. Don Quixote's assertion that virtue is acquired reaffirms Sancho's inherent dignity as a person, which is one of the pillars of Catholic social teaching, and subverts the ideology that socioeconomic class, and not behavior, is the measure of a person's virtue.[12] Within the context of Cervantes's Catholic faith, these passages may also be read as the author's belief in the afterlife and his endorsement of the Catholic doctrine on faith and works.[13]

The relationship that Don Quixote and Sancho share is quite unique, as Casalduero observes: "De la misma manera que el

Barbero ni se opone al Cura ni le complementa, ocurriendo lo mismo con la Sobrina respecto al Ama, Don Quijote y Sancho ni se oponen el uno al otro ni se complementan. Son dos elementos de un mismo origen, con una diferencia de grado de cuya union surge una unidad" (*Sentido y forma* 99). The one constant in their relationship from beginning to end, I posit, is Catholicism. While it is certainly not surprising to read allusions to God in the discourse of two characters who live in early modern Spain, Cervantes subtly establishes Catholicism as the baseline of their developing relationship soon after Sancho agrees to accompany Don Quixote in Part I, Chapter VII.[14]

Don Quixote's desire to die in the way prescribed by the Catholic Church and his preoccupation with his legacy as "the Good," exemplify his moral values. Sancho Panza, too, both in his words and in his actions, illustrates his belief in God and obedience to Catholic doctrine throughout the novel. In order to elucidate Cervantes's understanding of Catholic moral theology, and, specifically, the moral act, I consider the words and deeds of the knight and his squire according to 1) subjective and objective morality; 2) the condition of the moral act; 3) the physical and moral orders; and 4) the principle of double effect.[15]

The Protestant Reformation and the Counter Reformation intensified early modern Europe's understanding of the moral conscience. Protestant and Catholic churches propagated measures that promoted, for example, the moral reform of pagan beliefs and practices in popular culture (Konnert 87). Christian morality is a major theme in the literature of Cervantes and Erasmus. Cervantes's treatment of morality is veiled within the "exemplary" behavior of the characters in the *Novelas ejemplares*, the idealistic vision of a madman from La Mancha, and other literary manifestations of his authorial presence. Erasmus believed that morality is the essence of Christianity, and, therefore, a person should live his or her life in accord with the tenets of the faith, namely the New Testament and the Ten Commandments. In *Enchiridion militis Christiani* and *Encomium Moriae*, Erasmus exhorts the reader to cultivate a spiritual discipline that nurtures a moral lifestyle. Not all Christians, however, considered morality a necessary component of salvation. Martin Luther repudiated it because he did not believe a person could live a moral life without God's grace and forgiveness. Unlike Cervantes and Erasmus, who believed that free will is the first step toward a deeper relationship with God, Luther negated its existence completely (Mansch and Peters 280).[16]

Due to Don Quixote's madness, there are examples of subjective and objective Christian morality in *Don Quixote*. The question of subjective morality, however, is a complex one, especially when the subject is Don Quixote. Subjective morality may be defined based on three criteria: doing what one thinks is right and in the way one thinks is right; forming a strictly personal norm of moral action to cope with a particular and personal need; and a norm of action based on what the person thinks it should be before he or she can accept it. Subjective morality has the potential to influence a decision that leads to immoral acts when the person does not consider the well-being of the people affected by the decision. A person's decision to commit violent acts against another person because of religious differences is an example of subjective morality. Don Quixote's many adventures, especially the more physical encounters that take place in Part I, embody the criteria of subjective morality. The knight's madness, however, affects his ability to distinguish between subjective and objective morality, and he is not able to discern the difference entirely until he renounces the books of chivalry.[17]

Objective morality refers to a human act that is independent of a person's subjective disposition. In other words, it is the relationship between what a person does and the moral order: "To say that something is objective is to say that it is independent of what people think or perceive. ... To say that there are objective moral values is to say that something is good or evil independently of whether any human being believes it to be so. Similarly, to say that we have objective moral duties is to say that certain actions are right or wrong for us independently of whether any human being believes them to be so" (Craig 173). Don Quixote's actions can be viewed, objectively, as intrinsically good, which is a constitutive element of Immanuel Kant's deontological ethics:

> A good will is good because of what it effects, or accomplishes, not because of its fitness to attain some intended end, but good just by its willing, i.e. in itself, and considered by itself, it is to be esteemed beyond compare much higher than anything that could ever be brought about by it in favour of some inclination, and indeed, if you will, the sum of all inclinations. Even if by some particular disfavour of fate, or by the scanty endowment

> of a stepmotherly nature, this will should entirely lack the capacity to carry through its purpose; if despite its greatest striving it should still accomplish nothing, and only the good were to remain (not, of course, as a mere wish, but as the summoning of all means that are within our control); then, like a jewel, it would still shine by itself, as something that has its full worth in itself. (Kant 18)

In spite of Don Quixote's desire to emulate the knights about whom he has read in his books of chivalry and to achieve fame and glory while doing so, he expresses his belief that heavenly glory is greater because it is not fleeting, most notably in Part II, Chapter VIII. Don Quixote's desire for glory in heaven is what motivates him, and Cervantes reminds the reader of the knight's desire at the end of the novel when Alonso Quijano prepares himself for death by requesting that a priest hear his confession and give him the Body of Christ. Don Quixote's actions are based on what he believes is right in order fulfill a personal need, i.e., subjective morality, but at the same time, these actions are in accord with right conduct according to the Law of God. Perhaps it can be argued that Cervantes's life followed a similar trajectory.[18]

The three criteria by which an act is judged morally good are object, end, and circumstances. The object of an act is what a person chooses to do; it is the act itself. The end is the motive of the act, or, in other words, why a person does the act. The circumstances, which include the consequences and whether the physical action is proportionate to the person's intention, refer to the external conditions of the act; for example, when, where or how a person acts. Traditional Catholic morality holds that a true evaluation of morality is not possible if all of the aspects—object, end, and circumstances—are not met. Post-Tridentine Catholic morality was primarily individualistic, act-centered, law-oriented, and sin-conscious until the Second Vatican Council (1962–65) (Gula 27). Philosopher René Descartes (1596–1650) asserts that the soul of each person consists of actions and passions, both of which form the foundation of free will:

> But the will is by its nature free in such a way that it can never be constrained; and of the two sorts of thoughts I have distinguished in the soul, of which the first are its actions—namely its volitions—and the others its passions—taking this word in its most general sense, which comprises all sorts

Chapter Three

> of perceptions—the former are absolutely in its power and can only indirectly be altered by the body, whereas the latter depend absolutely on the actions that produce them and can only indirectly be altered by the soul, except when [the soul] is itself their cause. And the whole action of the soul consists in this: merely by willing something, it makes the little gland to which it is closely joined move in the way required to produce the effect corresponding to this volition. (41)

Free will, however, is much more than, in the words of philosopher David Hume (1711–76), "a power of acting or of not acting, according to the determination of the will" (72). St. Thomas Aquinas, in addition to other medieval Aristotelians, bases his concept of free will on the relationship between human nature and God. St. Thomas believes that all humans are created in the image of God, and, therefore, each person is born with a will that is inherently directed toward a goal of goodness. Since this impulse is predetermined, free will, according to St. Thomas, is determined by how a person chooses to achieve goodness. Furthermore, he believes that free will is a cognitive and an appetitive power:

> The proper act of free-will is choice: for we say that we have a free-will because we can take one thing while refusing another; and this is to choose. Therefore we must consider the nature of free-will, by considering the nature of choice. Now two things concur in choice: one on the part of the cognitive power, the other on the part of the appetitive power. On the part of the cognitive power, counsel is required, by which we judge one thing to be preferred to another: and on the part of the appetitive power, it is required that the appetite should accept the judgment of counsel. Therefore Aristotle (Ethic. vi, 2) leaves it in doubt whether choice belongs principally to the appetitive or the cognitive power: since he says that choice is either "an appetitive intellect or an intellectual appetite." But (Ethic. iii, 3) he inclines to its being an intellectual appetite when he describes choice as "a desire proceeding from counsel." And the reason of this is because the proper object of choice is the means to the end: and this, as such, is in the nature of that good which is called useful: wherefore since good, as such, is the object of the appetite, it follows that choice is principally an act of the appetitive power. And thus free-will is an appetitive power. (*Summa Theologica* Q.83, A.3)

The ability to utilize cognitive and appetitive powers to make choices, however, may be affected by outside circumstances or agents. A person who is addicted to drugs or to alcohol, for example, no longer possesses the ability to judge for himself or herself if the desire of the appetitive power is good or not. In this case, the appetitive power overtakes the cognitive power, and the person finds himself or herself controlled by the need for drugs or alcohol, regardless of the consequences. The object and end of Don Quixote's behavior, i.e., the knight's ability to utilize his cognitive and appetitive powers, is mitigated at times by his fanciful belief that he is one of the heroes from his books of chivalry. Consequently, Don Quixote's adventures do not always represent morally good acts.

Three episodes in Part I of *Don Quixote* illustrate the condition of the moral act. In Chapter IV, the knight encounters Andrés and his master Juan Haldudo. After speaking with Andrés and Juan, Don Quixote determines that Andrés, whom the knight describes as defenseless, is a victim and should be set free. Once Don Quixote convinces Juan Haldudo to release Andrés and to pay the young boy what he owes him, Don Quixote leaves, convinced that he has had a successful first adventure.

A second episode that illustrates the condition of the moral act is from Part I, Chapter XXII, when Don Quixote encounters Ginés de Pasamonte and the other galley slaves. Once again, Don Quixote must decide how to act when faced with a situation in which there appears to be injustice at hand. After listening to the galley slaves explain the reason for their punishment, Don Quixote launches into a lengthy speech in which he defends Divine and Natural Law. Then, Don Quixote attacks the guards, and the galley slaves escape.

The third episode that illustrates the condition of the moral act is Don Quixote's encounter with the priests who escort the body of a knight to Segovia for burial in Part I, Chapter XIX. After the priests inform Don Quixote that they cannot stop to explain what they are doing, the knight, offended by what he perceives is a lack of respect, becomes angry and grabs the bridle of a mule on which one of the priest travels. The mule, startled by the knight's actions, throws the priest to the ground and falls on him, breaking the priest's leg. When Don Quixote learns the nature of the priests' procession, he asks the priest to forgive him and to inform the other priests of his repentance for his actions.

Based on the criteria of the condition of the moral act, Don Quixote's actions with Andrés can be considered a moral act because it is expected of anyone to help someone who cannot help himself or herself, and, in addition, Don Quixote's intentions are certainly good. Before the adventure begins, Don Quixote gives thanks to God for the opportunity to prove that the adventures he read about in the books of chivalry are real: "Gracias doy al cielo por la merced que me hace, pues tan presto me pone ocasiones delante donde yo pueda cumplir con lo que debo a mi profesión, y donde pueda coger el fruto de mis buenos deseos" (135).[19] Don Quixote naively believes that Juan Haldudo will cease his punishment of Andrés because Don Quixote told him: "basta que yo se lo mande para que me tenga respeto; y con que él me lo jure por la ley de caballería que ha recibido, le dejaré ir libre y aseguraré la paga" (138). Of course, Juan Haldudo is not a knight, and, therefore, not beholden to the Medieval code of chivalry, but it matters little, ironically, to Don Quixote, who then reminds Juan Haldudo of the Catholic Church's soteriology, whose foundation is Apostolic Tradition and Scripture: "Importa eso poco —respondió don Quijote—, que Haldudos puede haber caballeros; cuanto más que cada uno es hijo de sus obras" (138).[20] Cervantes intimates his disdain for society's vertical concept of honor, according to which members of the nobility have more honor than anyone else because of their privileged position in society, and affirms his belief that each person, regardless of social status, has inherent dignity, which is the foundation of a moral vision of society. In two examples of incidental irony, Cervantes revisits the concept of honor in Spain's Golden Age. In Part I, Chapter VII, the narrator describes Sancho as a "hombre de bien (si es que este título se puede dar al que es pobre. ..." (163); and in Part II, Chapter XXII, Don Quixote advises Basilio how to marry well: "El pobre honrado (si es que puede ser honrado el pobre)" (211). The narrator's feigned doubt ironizes Cervantes's ideology of Christian honor.[21] In addition, the Church's salvation theology, as delineated during Session VI of the Council of Trent (1547), is predicated on a person's desire for God's grace, which alone sanctifies and saves, and his or her willingness to work toward it:

> If anyone says that man can be justified before God by his own works, whether done by his own natural powers or by the teaching of the Law, without divine grace through Jesus Christ, let him be anathema. (*The Canons and Decrees of the Council of Trent* 69–70)

Don Quixote and Moral Theology

> If anyone says that the sinner is justified by faith alone, meaning that nothing else is required to cooperate in order to obtain the grace of justification, and that it is not in any way necessary that he be prepared and disposed by the action of his own will, let him be anathema. (*The Canons and Decrees of the Council of Trent* 71)

Of course, in spite of the moral goodness of the act, including Don Quixote's attempt to convince Juan Haldudo with a theological argument, the outcome is not what Don Quixote intended it to be because the anachronistic knight is unable to reconcile the practices of medieval knighthood with early modern mores. Andrés reappears in Part I, Chapter XXXI, and Don Quixote, after telling his version to the barber, the priest, Cardenio, and Dorotea, implores Andrés to relate the episode: "Responde; no te turbes ni dudes en nada; di lo que pasó a estos señores, porque se vea y considere ser del provecho que digo haber caballeros andantes por los caminos" (437). Juan Haldudo, after Don Quixote left Andrés alone with his master, tied him to the tree again and gave him more lashes than he had before Don Quixote's arrival. Then, Andrés condemns Don Quixote and knighthood in general, contradicting the knight's version of what happened:

> Por amor de Dios, señor caballero andante, que si otra vez me encontrare, aunque vea que me hacen pedazos, no me socorra ni ayude, sino déjeme con mi desgracia, que no será tanta, que no sea mayor la que me vendrá de su ayuda de vuestra merced, a quien Dios maldiga, y a todos cuantos caballeros andantes han nacido en el mundo. (439)

Andrés's words anger Don Quixote but entertain the others, who react with muted laughter. The other characters are not alone in their derision of Don Quixote. The knight's earlier description of himself as "el valeroso don Quijote de la Mancha, el desfacedor de agravios y sinrazones" (139) becomes folly for the narrator, who satirizes Don Quixote's vanity: "Y desta manera deshizo el agravio el valeroso don Quijote" (140). Although Don Quixote is unable to "read" his world as if it were a literary rendering, this negative consequence does not necessarily violate the criteria of the condition of the moral act, although I am sure Andrés would disagree.

The episode with the galley slaves, however, is different. While it is true that Don Quixote intends for his act to be one of goodness, his desire and subsequent actions to set the galley slaves free are not in accord with the standards of good and right conduct. Until this point in Part I, Don Quixote predicates his actions more on what he sees than what he hears. In this episode, even though Don Quixote sees twelve men who are chained together, it is only after Sancho informs him that the men are *forced* to row in the galleys as punishment for their crimes does the knight consider it his duty as a knight-errant to free them, explaining, "como quiera que ello sea, esta gente, aunque los llevan, van de por fuerza, y no de su voluntad" (305). The knight believes that he is acting accordingly, however, because his interpretation of justice is superior to the law's definition of justice:

> Todo lo cual se me representa a mí ahora en la memoria, de manera que me está diciendo, persuadiendo y aun forzando, que muestre con vosotros el efecto para que el cielo me arrojó al mundo, y me hizo profesar en él la orden de caballería que profeso, y el voto que en ella hice de favorecer a los menesterosos y opresos de los mayores. (314)

Then, he reiterates his faith in divine justice: "Dios hay en el cielo, que no se descuida de castigar al malo ni de premiar al bueno, y no es bien que los hombres honrados sean verdugos de los otros hombres, no yéndoles nada en ello" (314). Don Quixote defends his actions further by appealing to Divine and Natural Law: "porque me parece duro caso hacer esclavos a los que Dios y naturaleza hizo libres" (314). Don Quixote's theological objections evoke the rationale with which Vitoria, Montesinos, Bartolomé de Las Casas (ca. 1480–1566), and other theologians defended the Indians' natural and divine rights. Cervantes's forceful defense of individual liberty in Don Quixote is foundational to the novel's Catholicity: "La teoría de Don Quijote es la del catolicismo, y si nos atenemos a ella, comprenderemos siempre la humanidad del teatro y la novela durante el siglo XVII en España. La vida tiene un sentido moral solo porque el hombre es un ser libre, libertad de la voluntad para el bien o para el mal, en perfecta armonía con el querer de la Providencia" (Casalduero, *Sentido y forma* 373). Don Quixote's misguided defense of the galley slaves' natural and divine rights mocks his failure to uphold the high moral standards that a knight is expected to personify.[22] The irony of the situation makes it possible for Cervantes, however, to express his philosophy of liberty. Once Don Quixote frees the criminals, who repay his "noble" act by reigning blows on him, he regrets not heeding Sancho's warnings: "Si yo hubiera creído lo que me dijiste, yo hubiera excusado esta pesadumbre; pero ya está hecho; paciencia, y escarmentar para desde aquí adelante" (318).

Ironically, Cervantes, despite his objections to the enslavement of the Indians, also viewed the New World as an opportunity to exercise his freedom. In 1582, he submitted an application for a colonial post to the Council of the Indies. When Cervantes learned that there were no vacant posts, he wrote a letter to Lord Antonio de Eraso, who was a member of the Council of the Indies, and informed him that he hoped to be considered for a post in the future. In the meantime, Cervantes informed Eraso that he would continue to write his first book, *La Galatea* (1585):

> En este interín me entretengo en criar a Galatea, que es el libro que dije a vuestra merced estaba componiendo. En estando algo crecida, irá a besar a vuestra merced las manos y a recibir la corrección y enmienda que yo no le habré sabido dar. (Lucía Megías 54)

Cervantes petitioned the Council of the Indies again in 1590, but this time, he emphasizes his many years of service to the King, hoping that he would reward him with one of the posts he solicited: the auditor's office in the kingdom of New Granada, the governorship of the province of Soconusco in Guatemala, accountant of galleys at Cartagena, and magistrate of La Paz (Canavaggio 155).[23] Once again, however, his petition is denied. The disappointment of two unsuccessful petitions did not diminish his enthusiasm for the New World, as evidenced by the numerous references, albeit isolated, in his writings. Diana de Armas Wilson notes the wide range of references to the New World that appear in *Don Quixote*, including the knight's praise of Hernán Cortés (Part II, Chapter VIII), Sancho's statement that he would rather be a "cacique" (Indian chief) than be responsible for disenchanting Dulcinea by whipping himself, and the similarities between Don Quixote and Christopher Columbus (210–11).

Cervantes, perhaps recalling the events of his own life, is unequivocal in his belief that God is the author of absolute justice

Chapter Three

and liberty. The knight's words suggest that Cervantes was familiar with Molinism, the religious doctrine named after Jesuit priest and theologian Luis de Molina (1535–1600) that reconciles Divine Providence with Free Will.[24] Molinists believe that God's omniscience consists of three moments of knowledge: natural, middle, and actual. God's foreknowledge permits Him to exercise Divine Providence in a universe that He orders without any consequence to Free Will. Ignatius considered Free Will a gift from God, but he also warned against minimizing Divine Grace.[25] While Don Quixote justifies his behavior, his failure to recognize that the galley slaves are criminals does not, however, excuse his actions.[26]

Don Quixote's encounter with the priests is more complicated.[27] Unlike previous adventures, this one takes place at night. The episode begins when Don Quixote and Sancho see only the light of burning torches, whose flames the narrator describes as "estrellas que se movían" (270). As the procession of mourners who accompany the body, which Don Quixote believes belongs to a knight whose death he will avenge, approaches the knight-errant and his squire, the narrator heightens the dramatic tension by describing the torches once again, but this time in terms of spatial perception, a characteristic of the Spanish Baroque: "vieron que las lumbres se iban acercando a ellos, y mientras más se llegaban, mayores parecían" (270). Don Quixote, who sees in the dangerous adventure that awaits him an opportunity to demonstrate his courage and strength, vows to stand his ground and to do battle against the unknown adversary. Sancho, who until this episode can be counted on to rationalize previous situations his master misinterpreted, is too scared, however, to be pragmatic. After the mourners flee from Don Quixote, Sancho recognizes his master's valor: "Todo lo miraba Sancho, admirado del ardimiento de su señor, y decía entre sí: 'Sin duda este mi amo es tan valiente y esforzado como él dice'" (272). Since the battle takes place in the dark of night, the mourners, like Don Quixote, misidentify their attacker: "porque todos pensaron que aquél no era hombre, sino diablo del infierno que les salía a quitar el cuerpo muerto que en la litera llevaban" (272). When Don Quixote learns that the man died of a pestilential fever, he realizes that he will not be able to take vengeance for the knight's death: "quitado me ha Nuestro Señor del trabajo que había de tomar en vengar su muerte, si otro alguno le hubiera muerto; pero habiéndole muerto quien le mató, no hay sino callar y encoger los hombros" (273).[28] Don Quixote's explanation suggests Cervantes's belief in the active presence of God in a human being's life, a philosophy that is a cornerstone of Ignatian spirituality.

While the object and end of Don Quixote's attack are morally good, the circumstances, particularly how Don Quixote acts, are certainly not. Don Quixote's anger supersedes his ability to reason, and, therefore, the consequence is an unjust and immoral act:

> For spiritedness seems to hear reason in some way, but to mishear it ... So spiritedness, because of its heated and swift nature, hears something, and though it does not hear an order, it sets off after revenge. For speech or imagination has made clear that there is a hubristic insult or slight; and spiritedness, as if it inferred from a syllogism that one ought to wage war against such a thing, immediately becomes harsh. But as for desire, if reason or sense perception merely says that something is pleasant, it sets off after enjoyment. As a result, spiritedness follows reason in a way, but desire does not. Desire, then, is more shameful. For someone who lacks self-restraint when it comes to spiritedness is in a way conquered by reason, whereas the other person is conquered by desire and not by reason. (Aristotle 147)

Don Quixote appears to regain his ability to reason when he asks for forgiveness, but the violence he displays against the priests, especially the one who suffers a broken leg, denotes an evil act. Alonso López, the priest whom Don Quixote attacks, informs the knight that he is excommunicated as a result of his actions, but, as a priest, López does not have this authority.[29] Even so, Don Quixote does not receive any Sacrament until he requests the Sacrament of Penance on his deathbed. In spite of the "penalty," the knight maintains his faith throughout the novel.[30]

In the knight's sudden burst of anger, Cervantes parodies the *mesura*, or calm temperament, that characterizes the knight: "In his concern for his subjects and for the persons he encountered in his travels, in his interest in seeing that justice was done and that right triumphed over wrong, in his humility, chastity, and calm temperament (*mesura*), the hero of the romances of chivalry offered to the readers the supposedly beneficial picture of the ideal medieval ruler" (Eisenberg, *Romances of Chivalry* 45). Don Quixote's anger is the result of a physiological imperative, based on the humoral theory of medicine that was the dominant theory of medicine in Europe for many centuries.[31] Consequently, moral reform depends on an introspective approach where the change manifests itself inside out. In Part II, Chapter XVI, for example, Don Quixote reacts differently to a similar affront. He displays his ability to control his anger, albeit righteous in his mind, when he describes his battle with the Knight of the Mirrors:

> —Todo es artificio y traza —respondió don Quijote— de los malignos magos que me persiguen, los cuales, anteviendo que yo había de quedar vencedor en la contienda, se previnieron de que el caballero vencido mostrase el rostro de mi amigo el bachiller, porque la amistad que le tengo se pusiese entre los filos de mi espada y el rigor de mi brazo, y templase la justa ira de mi corazón, y desta manera quedase con vida el que con embelecos y falsías procuraba quitarme la mía. (153)

In this episode, Cervantes illustrates Seneca's belief that reason is the strongest faculty that a person possesses:

> We have no need for other weapons; it is enough that nature has equipped us with reason. What she has given us is firm, enduring, accommodating, with no double edge to be turned on its owner. Reason by itself is enough not merely for foresight but for action. Indeed, what could be stupider than for reason to seek protection in bad temper, for something that is stable, trustworthy and sound to seek protection in something that is unsteady, untrustworthy and sick?[32] (Seneca 35)

In Part II, Chapter XXXII, the knight once again demonstrates humoral control when the Duke and Duchess's chaplain insults him and Sancho:

> Por el hábito que tengo, que estoy por decir que es tan sandio Vuestra Excelencia como estos pecadores. ¡Mirad si no han de ser ellos locos, pues los cuerdos canonizan sus locuras! Quédese Vuestra Excelencia con ellos; que en tanto que estuvieren en casa, me estaré yo en la mía, y me escusaré de reprehender lo que no puedo remediar. (298)

Don Quixote's response is certainly not, however, what the reader expects:

Don Quixote and Moral Theology

> Yo puedo estar agraviado, mas no afrentado, porque los niños no sienten, ni las mujeres, ni pueden huir, ni tienen para qué esperar, y lo mesmo los constituidos en la sacra religión, porque estos tres géneros de gente carecen de armas ofensivas y defensivas; y así, aunque naturalmente estén obligados a defenderse, no lo están para ofender a nadie. (299)

Guillermo Serés points out that wrath, which Don Quixote displays in the episode with the priests, and reason, which the knight illustrates when he does not attack the Knight of the Mirrors, are two constitutive elements a person needs to control his or her free will:

> Este camino nos llevaría a uno de los lugares comunes más importantes del Humanismo: la ira, aliada con la razón o con la prudencia, para enfrentarse a la fortuna. En otras palabras: la defensa de la capacidad individual, poniendo en juego todas las facultades, virtudes y *virtutes* "humanas" (teologales, cardinales y *naturales* u "orgánicas," entre ellas, la "irascible"), para hacer frente a lo indeterminado; o aun en otras: la defensa del libre albedrío, que, arropado con una actuación virtuosa y provisto de los medios necesarios, no debe temer ningún embate de la fortuna; incluso debe negar su existencia. (Serés 47–48)

In other words, Don Quixote is able to utilize his cognitive power to control his appetitive power, because the knight-errant does not kill the Knight of the Mirrors, reasoning, in his unique way, that his enemies gave the Knight of the Mirrors the physical features of Don Quixote's friend: "yo confieso y creo que vos, aunque parecéis el bachiller Sansón Carrasco, no lo sois, sino otro que le parece, y que en su figura aquí me le han puesto mis enemigos, para que detenga y temple el ímpetu de mi cólera, y para que use blandamente de la gloria del vencimiento" (147). Similarly, Don Quixote's humoral balance produces a reaction to the chaplain's insults that illustrates moral reform.

Cervantine morality may also be considered according to the physical and moral orders, which, like the condition of the moral act, are valid if they are in accord with right conduct (physical order) and directed toward goodness (moral order). An act cannot be judged to be moral solely on the result of a physical action; it must follow the moral order, too, which specifically addresses the will of the person who commits the act.[33] The conformity of

Chapter Three

the physical and moral orders can be measured by how well they cultivate the dimensions of a moral life. The sacred dimension is based upon the dignity of the human person and includes the following beliefs: 1) an obligation to uphold the dignity of a human person; 2) human dignity does not depend on human achievement, but it is a gift of divine love; and 3) people must attribute this same dignity, esteem, and value to each other. The social dimension of a moral life refers to the relational nature of human beings, and it is based on the belief that people depend on other people; consequently, no one is completely in control of his or her life.

Don Quixote's actions, especially in Part I, illustrate, for the most part, the sacred and social dimensions of the Catholic life. In many of these episodes, Cervantes subtly expresses his belief that a person's actions toward the good of the individual and the collective are not independent of God's presence in his or her life. In Part II, Chapter VIII, for example, Don Quixote, during his discourse on the attainment of fame, not only views these actions and sacrifices as a means to becoming a famous knight, but they also cultivate the sacred and social dimensions of the moral life. Sancho demonstrates the same two dimensions of the Catholic moral life when he adjudicates three cases brought before him as Governor of Barataria in Part II, Chapter XLV. The guiding principles with which Sancho resolves the disagreements between the peasant and the tailor, the two old men, and the woman and the rich cattleman are based on the squire's belief in God and respect for the dignity of others: "De donde se podía colegir que los que gobiernan, aunque sean unos tontos, tal vez los encamina Dios en sus juicios" (401). In each of the cases, Sancho resolves the conflict in the most fair and equitable manner.[34] When the narrator announces the end of Sancho's governorship in Part II, Chapter LIII, he does so within the context of a core Catholic belief:

> Sola la vida humana corre a su fin ligera más que el [viento], sin esperar renovarse si no es en la otra, que no tiene términos que la limiten. Esto dice Cide Hamete, filósofo mahomético; porque esto de entender la ligereza e instabilidad de la vida presente, y de la duración de la eterna que se espera, muchos sin lumbre de fe, sino con la luz natural, lo han entendido; pero aquí nuestro autor lo dice por la presteza con que se acabó, se consumió, se deshizo, se fue como en sombra y humo el gobierno de Sancho. (469)

The appearance of the word *God* nine times during the course of the three cases may remind the reader of the moral principles on which Sancho bases his decisions. Roberto González Echevarría notes that Sancho's promotion of social equality not only prefigures the Enlightenment but also has a Christian background:

> The poor and humble can learn and advance, and novelistic characters can move up and down the social ladder. This element of the *Quixote*, which is a political element, too, anticipates the Enlightenment and ideas that lead to concepts about social equality that will eventually become modern conceptions of democracy, but it also has a profoundly Christian background. We can recall Matthew's Gospel, chapter 5, the opening words of the Sermon on the Mount: Blessed [these are the Beatitudes] are the poor in spirit for theirs is the Kingdom of Heaven; blessed are they that mourn for they shall be comforted; blessed are the meek for they shall inherit the earth. (188)

These same Christian principles that guide Sancho's decisions, however, also illustrate Erasmus's influence on Cervantes. Sancho's adjudication of the cases is the personification of the Humanist doctrine of the dignity, innate wisdom, and potential of the common man.

The sacred and social dimensions of the physical and moral orders have a direct effect on social justice, which the Catholic Church identifies as one of the three dimensions of basic justice.[35] Cervantes affirms his advocacy of distributive justice and commutative throughout the novel. In Part I, Chapter XXXVII, for example, Don Quixote, during his discourse on Arms and Letters, remarks that the goal of humane letters is to "poner en su punto la justicia distributiva y dar a cada uno lo que es suyo" (516). In Part II, Chapter XVIII, Don Quixote informs Don Lorenzo about one of the requirements for a person to be a knight-errant: "el que la profesa ha de ser jurisperito, y saber las leyes de la justicia distributiva y comutativa, para dar a cada uno lo que es suyo y lo que le conviene" (177). In Part II, Chapter LX, Roque Guinart bases the payment he makes to his squires on distributive justice: "lo repartió por toda su compañía, con tanta legalidad y prudencia, que no pasó un punto ni defraudó nada de la justicia distributiva" (534).

Chapter Three

Earlier in this chapter, I defined a moral act as satisfying three criteria: object, end, and circumstances. A legitimate question to ask is, however, can the knight's actions really be considered morally right if we consider the harm he inflicts on other characters? The principle of "double effect" may be helpful in answering this question.

According to the principle of "double effect," which St. Thomas Aquinas introduced in his *Summa Theologica*, an act may be considered good even though there may be an evil or bad consequence.[36] In order for this principle to apply to an act, however, the act must meet four conditions: the act must be good, or at least morally neutral; the evil consequence must not be the motivating factor of the act; the good consequence must not be the result of the evil consequence; and the intended good consequence must equal or outweigh the evil consequence (Cavanaugh 26). A caveat to keep in mind with respect to the principle of "double effect" is the argument of proportionate reason, which St. Thomas Aquinas cites in his explanation of self-defense: "And yet, though proceeding from a good intention, an act may be rendered unlawful, if it be out of proportion to the end … Wherefore if a man, in self-defense, uses more than necessary violence, it will be unlawful" (*Summa Theologica* Q.64, A.7).

Don Quixote's aim is not to inflict pain unless in the service of a moral act. His actions are predicated on his belief that, as a knight, he has a duty to help those who cannot help themselves. Whether Don Quixote's actions result in harm to himself, such as the adventure with the flocks of sheep the knight believes are charging armies in Part I, Chapter XVIII, or to others, such as the adventure of the galley slaves in Part I, Chapter XXII, the intention of his acts, for the most part, are in proportion to their end.[37] Since Don Quixote's moral compass is not independent of God's Natural Law, which St. Thomas Aquinas defines as "nothing else than the rational creature's participation in the eternal law," his actions, when in proportion to the end, are moral in nature (*Summa Theologica* Q.91, A.2).

The knight-errant who embarks on the third sally after a period of time at home, where he is able to convalesce and to reflect on his earlier adventures, exhibits a better balance between *ira* and *razón*, albeit not perfect by any means, culminating in his deathbed condemnation of books of chivalry in Part II, Chapter LXXIV. In Don Quixote's treatment of the priest, Cervantes reminds the reader that while the knight's actions may be considered moral and his motives admirable, he is not beyond moral reproach, a fact he alludes to on his deathbed. Cervantes, at the end of a tumultuous life, must have reflected on his own moral shortcomings, but, as a Catholic, he believed in redemption, as evidenced by his request that he be given the Sacrament of the Anointing of the Sick.

Chapter Four

Tilting at the Truth
Don Quixote's Spiritual Journey as a Contemplative in Action

> The contemplative in action, according to St. Ignatius Loyola, not only contemplates the active world and sees wonderful things, but also sees in those wonderful things signs of God's presence and activity. The contemplative in action is deeply aware of God's presence even in the midst of a busy life. It is a stance of awareness. Awareness of God.
>
> Martin 391

When Don Quixote embarks upon his quest in Part I, Chapter I, his motivation for doing so is to recreate the adventures from his books of chivalry and to retrace the footsteps of their heroes. Yet, as each adventure unfolds, Don Quixote undergoes a transformation that culminates in Part II, Chapter LXXIX in an epiphany about the same books of chivalry that inspired him to leave behind his life in search of fame:

> —Las misericordias —respondió don Quijote—, sobrina, son las que en este instante ha usado Dios conmigo, a quien, como dije, no las impiden mis pecados. Yo tengo juicio ya, libre y claro, sin las sombras caliginosas de la ignorancia, que sobre él me pusieron mi amarga y continua leyenda de los detestables libros de las caballerías. Ya conozco sus disparates y sus embelecos, y no me pesa sino que este desengaño ha llegado tan tarde, que no me deja tiempo para hacer alguna recompensa, leyendo otros que sean luz del alma.[1] (633)

Since Alonso Quijano's religious beliefs are not known before he becomes Don Quixote, the reader's only knowledge about the country gentleman's faith must be deduced from his words and actions. He first speaks of his Catholic faith in Part I, Chapter IV when he hears Andrés's cry for help as Juan Haldudo whips him:

Chapter Four

> —Gracias doy al cielo por la merced que me hace, pues tan presto me pone ocasiones delante donde yo pueda cumplir con lo que debo a mi profesión, y donde pueda coger el fruto de mis buenos deseos. Estas voces, sin duda, son de algún menesteroso, o menesterosa, que ha menester mi favor y ayuda. (135)

Then, after Don Quixote confronts Juan Haldudo, the knight continues to refer to his faith after the peasant accuses Andrés of lying:

> —¿"Miente" delante de mí, ruin villano? ... Por el sol que nos alumbra que estoy por pasaros de parte a parte con esta lanza. Pagadle luego sin más réplica; si no, por el Dios que nos rige que os concluya y aniquile en este punto. Desatadlo luego. (136)

Don Quixote's reference to God is the first of many that he will make throughout the novel. The evidence I present for Don Quixote's and Sancho's spirituality includes dialogue that may be interpreted as typical literary formulae. In Francisco de Quevedo's *El Buscón* (1626), for example, the word *Dios* appears more than eighty times. In Cervantes's dedication of the *Persiles* to the Count of Lemos (Don Pedro Fernández de Castro y Osorio; 1576–1622), who was Cervantes's most important literary patron, he expresses his trust in God when he writes to the Count of Lemos about his impending death: "Pero si está decretado que la haya de perder, cúmplase la voluntad de los Cielos, y por lo menos sepa Vuestra Excelencia este mi deseo" (32–33).

If considered within the larger context of the spirituality that knight and squire practice, however, I believe that their dialogue represents more than formulae. Of course, Cervantes may be leading the reader in a different direction. I suggest that the excessive references to God may be Cervantes's satire of Catholics who, perhaps out of fear of the Inquisition, publicly affirmed their faith but did not practice it as they should.[2] Michael McGaha suggests that Don Quixote's oaths in Part I are in accord with his identity as a knight-errant ("Oaths in Don Quixote"). In Part II, however, Don Quixote is less confident of his chivalresque identity and, consequently, the noble oaths in Part I become illicit in Part II as the knight negotiates situations that may otherwise not affect as much the Don Quixote about whom we read in Part I (564).

The knight's transformation from a heroic knight-errant who seeks to imitate the heroes in his books of chivalry to a disillusioned country gentleman who renounces the same books of chivalry altogether is not only a psychological journey but a spiritual one as well. Don Quixote's words and actions represent a spiritual awareness that exteriorizes a desire to "praise, reverence, and serve God," and, throughout the knight-errant's journey toward self-discovery, he personifies numerous times the tenets of Ignatian spirituality, and perhaps none more so than the contemplative in action, who aspires to imitate the life of Jesus when He assumed a human nature.[3] Early Christian theologians, including Origen of Alexandria (185–254), St. Gregory of Nyssa (335–94), and St. Augustine of Hippo (354–430), extolled the virtues of the contemplative life, often citing Jesus' visit to Martha and Mary's house (Luke 10:38–42) as one example of it:

> In these two women, both pleasing to the Lord, two lives were figured: the present and the future; the laborious and the quiet; the troublous and the happy; the temporal and the eternal. Both are praiseworthy; but the one is laborious, the other leisured. What Martha was doing, there we are; what Mary, that what we hope for. (Aquinas, *Summa Theologiae* 98)

Pope St. Gregory the Great (540–604) deemed the contemplative life as better than the active life:

> Everyone that is perfect is first joined to an active life in productiveness, and afterwards united to a contemplative life in rest. ... The contemplative life is less indeed in time, but greater in value than the active. ... Martha's concern is not reproved, but that of Mary is even commended. For the merits of the active life are great, but of the contemplative, far better. (Aquinas, *Summa Theologiae* 100)

The Jesuits described their theological beliefs as "mystical," as opposed to the "purely speculative," or academic, theology of scholasticism. Jerónimo Nadal (1507–80), who was one of Ignatius's earliest companions, described this mystical experience as "an inner understanding and relish of the truth translated into the way one lived" (qtd. in O'Malley, *The First Jesuits 426*). His phrase, *simul in actione contemplativus* (contemplative likewise in the midst of action) would later define a core belief of the Jesuits that faith should be a lived experience:

> La actividad sería el disponerse del sujeto para recibir la gracia, lo que tradicionalmente se ha llamado vida ascética. La pasividad sería el recibir, acoger esa gracia que, a pesar de nuestras disposiciones, siempre es un acontecimiento gratuito y que sólo depende de la benevolencia divina. Es lo que vendría identificado con la mística. Pero tanto la ascética como la mística encaminan al sujeto y se encuentran en la caridad, en la ayuda al prójimo, que es el lugar de encuentro por excelencia con la persona de Jesucristo. Ésa es la vida superior a la que está llamada la Compañía; la cual, abrazando el momento ascético y el momento místico, los actualiza en una mística de servicio. (Violero 38)

Nadal describes succinctly how the contemplative in action's incarnational view of the world fosters a greater awareness of God: "El mundo es nuestra casa" (O'Malley, *The First Jesuits* 46). An incarnational view of the world inspires the contemplative in action to act with love, imitating how Jesus lived, and the more he or she seeks to find God in those everyday moments and events, the more evident God's presence becomes.

The ways in which God is alive and active in mundane daily activities, however, are difficult to appreciate without an ascetic lifestyle.[4] It cultivates a vision informed by self-negation, not as a punishment, but, rather, as a means to see the world as it truly is, as opposed to what it appears to be. In other words, asceticism is "learning not to look in the mirror long enough that one might begin to look out the window" (Himes 233). The prototypical knight of chivalry is of royal lineage, but yet, as an ascetic, he eschews earthly possessions, especially money, which is an afterthought. Don Quixote's asceticism manifests itself in different ways throughout the novel.

In Part I, Chapter III, for example, the innkeeper, who was an avid reader of books of chivalry as a child, asks Don Quixote if he has any money. The knight informs him that he does not, explaining that he never read about any knight of chivalry who did. Nevertheless, Don Quixote, motivated by his conversation with the innkeeper, returns to his village, where he raises money and packs other provisions he will need. Yet, he still does not view money as a commodity. When the innkeeper Juan Palomeque requests payment from the knight for food and lodging in Part I, Chapter XVII, Don Quixote refuses to pay:

> Pero, pues es ansí que no es castillo, sino venta, lo que se podrá hacer por agora es que perdonéis por la paga; que yo no puedo contravenir a la orden de los caballeros andantes, de los cuales sé cierto (sin que hasta ahora haya leído cosa en contrario) que jamás pagaron posada ni otra cosa en venta donde estuviesen, porque se les debe de fuero y de derecho cualquier buen acogimiento que se les hiciere, en pago del insufrible trabajo que padecen buscando las aventuras de noche y de día, en invierno y en verano, a pie y a caballo, con sed y con hambre, con calor y con frío, sujetos a todas las inclemencias del cielo y a todos los incómodos de la tierra. (253)

Don Quixote relegates money to his chivalrous ideals, once again, in Part I, Chapter XXX. Princess Micomicona promises to marry the knight and to make him the lord of her kingdom if he is able to slay the giant Pandafilando, who threatens to destroy the kingdom. Don Quixote accepts the challenge to do battle with Pandafilando, but he refuses to marry Princess Micomicona because of his unwavering love for Dulcinea, about whom he muses: "Ella pelea en mí, y vence en mí, y yo vivo y respiro en ella, y tengo vida y ser" (424).[5] David Quint notes that Don Quixote's decision not to marry Princess Micomicona is "emblematic of his refusal of the modern world itself" (90). Quint does not portray the knight's detachment in a favorable way, however, characterizing it instead as self-serving:

> But Don Quixote's response to the real, modern present is to retreat into a fantasy past and into a premodern love—his idolatrous cult of Dulcinea—that, as we have seen in Chapter Two, Cervantes's novel shows to be anything but selfless: it is rather fueled by pride. The aggrandizement—"ensalzamiento"—of his lady that Don Quixote describes is in fact the self-aggrandizement of the man who has imagined her, who worships himself in the idol he has made. (Quint 90)

Quint is not the only critic who sees Dulcinea as a negative influence in Don Quixote's life: "Dulcinea is spiritual, a sort of religious icon, and Don Quixote's misguided attempts to worship her result in many hilarious, pathetic, and physically destructive encounters with members of society who are unable (or unwilling) to join the knight errant in his quest for the restoration of the mythical 'Age of Gold'" (*The Feminist Encyclopedia* 200).

Don Quixote is unaware that his relationship with Dulcinea is an object of irony. Consequently, his futile attempts to address Dulcinea, and other women as well, in the same elegant, articulate, and gallant way that Amadís addresses Oriana, for example, are a source of ridicule for Cervantes and the other characters. In Part I, Chapter III, Don Quixote invokes his lady Dulcinea before he attacks the muleteers who want to water their mules at the inn: "Acorredme, señora mía, en esta primera afrenta que a vuestro avasallado pecho se le ofrece; no me desfallezca en este primero trance vuestro favor y amparo" (131); "¡Oh señora de la fermosura, esfuerzo y vigor del debilitado corazón mío! Ahora es tiempo que vuelvas los ojos de tu grandeza a este tu cautivo caballero, que tamaña aventura está atendiendo" (132). The only woman in the novel whom Don Quixote addresses as if she were a deity is Dulcinea. When Don Quixote and Sancho arrive to the inn, for example, two prostitutes whom the knight believes are princesses are standing at the entrance. Don Quixote speaks to them in a chivalrous manner, but he does not invoke their protection and guidance: "No fuyan las vuestras mercedes ni teman desaguisado alguno; ca a la orden de caballería que profeso non toca ni atañe facerle a ninguno, cuanto más a tan altas doncellas como vuestras presencias demuestran" (124); "Bien parece la mesura en las fermosas, y es mucha sandez, además, la risa que de leve causa procede; pero non vos lo digo porque os acuitedes ni mostredes mal talante; que el mío non es de ál que de serviros" (124).

Unlike Quint, who interprets Don Quixote's relationship with Dulcinea as pagan narcissism because the knight "worships himself in the idol he has made," I believe that Don Quixote's "idolatrous cult of Dulcinea" is perhaps one of the most important components of the knight's spiritual journey. Dulcinea represents a mystical reality, and Don Quixote's desire to honor her when he invokes her name or sends his vanquished enemies to kneel before her, inspires him to view material reality through the lens of his relationship with her. In other words, the other worldly conditions his response to material reality. This dynamic between the knight and his lady suggests that Cervantes, either consciously or not, may have modeled their relationship after a Christian worldview, and, specifically, the Ignatian philosophy of "finding God in all things."[6] Don Quixote, as a contemplative in action, is aware of God's presence in his life, but he is not able to embrace His presence completely until he rejects Dulcinea. As a hidalgo, Alonso Quijano enjoyed a comfortable lifestyle, but the chain of events that will lead him into full reconciliation with God does not begin until he abandons it. His devotion to Dulcinea makes it possible for him to continue on his journey, untethered to the world around him.[7]

In Part I, Chapter III, Don Quixote insists on keeping vigil over his armor as a prelude to being dubbed a knight the next morning. This "act of devotion," evocative of Ignatius's vigil in Montserrat at the altar dedicated to Our Lady of Montserrat, ends soon after it begins, however, when the knight enters into battle with a muleteer who removes Don Quixote's armor from the trough in order to water his mules. Ignatius describes his vigil in his autobiography, which he wrote in the third person:

> He continued his way to Montserrat thinking, as he usually did, of the achievements he was going to perform for the love of God. Because his thoughts were fully occupied with exploits, such as he had read in *Amadís de Gaula* and other like books, similar thoughts also came to mind. He therefore determined to keep a night's vigil over his arms; he would neither sit nor lie down, but would stand and kneel before the altar of Our Lady of Montserrat, where he had decided to set aside the garment she was wearing and clothe himself in the livery of Christ.[8]
> (*A Pilgrim's Journey* 25)

The influence of the books of chivalry on Ignatius is clearly evident in this passage, but unlike Don Quixote, he is able to dedicate his entire being and existence to God. The knight, nevertheless, displays the same contemplative tendencies when he does penance in the Sierra Morena in Part I, Chapters XXV and XXVI. Unamuno notes how the knight's penance is reminiscent of Ignatius's in Manresa:

> Esta penitencia de Don Quijote en Sierra Morena nos trae a la memoria aquella otra de Íñigo de Loyola en la cueva de Manresa, y sobre todo cuando en el mismo Manresa y en el

Chapter Four

monasterio de Santo Domingo, "vínole al pensamiento—como nos dice el P. Rivadeneira, libro I, capítulo IV—un ejemplo de un santo que para alcanzar de Dios una cosa que le pedía, determinó de no desayunarse hasta alcanzarla. A cuya imitación—añade—propuso él también de no comer ni beber hasta hallar la paz tan deseada de su alma, si ya no se viese por ello a peligro de morir. (83)

Two distinctive characteristics, however, are the object and means of the knight's penance. Don Quixote chooses to isolate himself in the Sierra Morena and to practice penance for no reason except to prove to Dulcinea the profundity of his love for her, explaining: "que volverse loco un caballero andante con causa, ni grado ni gracias: el toque está desatinar sin ocasión y dar a entender a mi dama que, si en seco hago esto, ¿qué hiciera en mojado?" (345). He believes that his unmotivated penance is superior to the penance of Amadís and Roland, both of whom lamented for sentimental reasons.[9] In a rare moment of self-reflection, Don Quixote considers whether to model his penance after Amadís or Roland. He chooses to imitate Amadís because his penance was not as physically demanding as Roland's, who, upon finding out that his lady Angélica left him for Medoro, another man who is a Moor, "arrancó los árboles, enturbió las aguas de las claras fuentes, mató pastores, destruyó ganados, abrasó chozas, derribó casas, arrastró yeguas e hizo otras mil insolencias" (344). In Part I, Chapter XXVI, Don Quixote, perhaps guiado por el punishment his body endured from recent misadventures, exhibits self-knowledge in explaining to Sancho why he chose to imitate Amadís:

> Por otra parte, veo que Amadís de Gaula, sin perder el juicio y sin hacer locuras, alcanzó tanta fama de enamorado como el que más; porque lo que hizo, según su historia, no fue más de que, por verse desdeñado de su señora Oriana, que le había mandado que no pareciese ante su presencia hasta que fuese su voluntad, de que se retiró a la Peña Pobre en compañía de un ermitaño, y allí se hartó de llorar y de encomendarse a Dios, hasta que el cielo le acorrió, en medio de su mayor cuita y necesidad. Y si esto es verdad, como lo es, ¿para qué quiero yo tomar trabajo agora de desnudarme del todo, ni dar pesadumbre a estos árboles, que no me han hecho mal alguno? Ni tengo para que enturbiar el agua clara destos arroyos, los cuales me han de dar de beber cuando tenga gana. (362)

Don Quixote pledges not to end his penance until Sancho, whom he sends to Dulcinea with a letter, returns with her response. The squire happens upon the priest and the barber on the road to El Toboso in Part I, Chapter XXVI. When Sancho realizes that he no longer has the letter, which Don Quixote told him to copy on to good paper, the priest and the barber suggest that he recite it so that they could write it. Sancho recites the letter several times, unaware that its content is different each time. He is a victim of the irony of self-betrayal because he believes that he can recite the letter word for word. Cervantes seems to subvert the discipline of penance, but I suggest that Sancho's encounter with the priest and the barber is authorial strategy because it allows Cervantes to address the squire's state of mind at the midpoint of Part I. Sancho informs the priest and the barber that a favorable reply from Dulcinea would mean a future in which Don Quixote is an emperor and Sancho, following his wife's death, is the husband of a lady-in-waiting to an empress. Javier Herrero comments on the spiritual importance of Don Quixote's penance in his summary of Ramón Menéndez Pidal's literary interpretation of Dulcinea: "Rejection of the flesh and of worldly ideals, austerity and single-minded concentration in devotion and service, a spiritual loneliness from which the old love of chivalry is reborn in a transformed, more authentic form: these are the effects of Don Quijote's passion, and nowhere are they better represented than in the penance in Sierra Morena" (Herrero 26). Menéndez Pidal also addresses the moral import of the knight's penance: "Este es el momento en que su locura entrevé toda la grandeza moral de que era capaz" (252).

Ignatius considers penance one of the cornerstones of Jesuit spirituality, in addition to word and works, and he writes frequently about his life as a penitent in his autobiography. Furthermore, he teaches the importance of penance during the first week of the *Spiritual Exercises*. Both saint and knight experience significant events that have a profound impact on their lives as contemplatives in action a short time after their penance. Ignatius's abstinence from food and drink lasted one week, at which time a confessor insisted that he break it for health reasons. Subsequently, he fasted, and it was during this time, in Manresa, he had several visions in which he encountered God, and, from that moment forward, Ignatius saw creation in a new and more

Chapter Four

meaningful way.[10] Don Quixote's first encounter with the world around him after his penance is the Princess Micomicona episode. As a result of their respective penances, Ignatius and Don Quixote are properly disposed to cooperating with God's grace.

Don Quixote reveals his faith in more detail in his response to the bachelor, who informs the knight-errant of his excommunication from the Church after the attack on the priests, during which one of the priests breaks his leg after his mule falls on him, in Part I, Chapter XIX:

> Mas yo sé bien que no puse las manos, sino este lanzón; cuanto más, que yo no pensé que ofendía a sacerdotes ni a cosas de la Iglesia, a quien respeto y adoro como católico y fiel cristiano que soy, sino a fantasmas y a vestiglos del otro mundo. Y cuando eso así fuese, en la memoria tengo lo que le pasó al Cid Ruy Díaz, cuando quebró la silla del embajador de aquel rey delante de Su Santidad del Papa, por lo cual lo descomulgó, y anduvo aquel día el buen Rodrigo de Vivar como muy honrado y valiente caballero. (276)

Edward Friedman observes that Don Quixote acknowledges that his behavior is subject to a higher power: "The episode commands special attention because it could be called the most 'natural' adventure, because it brings the Church into the frame, and because Don Quixote concedes that there is a higher agency, or agent, at work in the forging of his history" (n. pag.). Don Quixote, startled by the realization that he harmed a priest, attempts to ameliorate his actions by pointing out that his hands never touched the priest. Immediately thereafter, however, he pleads ignorance, but, then, he not only acknowledges his respect for priests but also for "things of the Church." Cervantes challenges his knight's assertion, as well as the reader's interpretation of these words and their significance with respect to the author's religious beliefs, in the numerous instances that scholars believe exemplify Cervantes's subversion of Catholicism.

In one of the more intriguing episodes in which Don Quixote manifests his sacramental view of the world, the knight-errant confects a pseudo-sacramental in Part I, Chapter XVII. As a contemplative in action, Don Quixote believes that he receives Christ through material reality. In Chapter XVII, the knight prepares the Balsam of Fierabrás, which he thinks will cure him of the injuries he receives after the officer of the Holy Brotherhood smashes an oil lamp on his head:

> En resolución, él tomó sus simples, de los cuales hizo un compuesto, mezclándolos todos y cociéndolos un buen espacio, hasta que le pareció que estaban en su punto. Pidió luego alguna redoma para echallo, y, como no la hubo en la venta, se resolvió de ponello en una alcuza o aceitera de hoja de lata, de quien el ventero le hizo grata donación. Y luego dijo sobre la alcuza más de ochenta paternostres y otras tantas avemarías, salves y credos, y a cada palabra acompañaba una cruz, a modo de bendición. (250)

Fierabrás, a giant Saracen from the chivalric romance *Historia del Emperador Carlomagno*, stole two containers of the embalming fluid that Joseph of Arimathea and Nicodemus used for the burial of Jesus Christ.[11] Don Quixote's confection of the ingredients may be interpreted as reminiscent of the Eucharistic Prayer, which the priest prays during the process of transubstantiation that converts the bread and wine into the Body and Blood of Christ during the Mass. After calling the Holy Spirit down upon the bread and the wine, the priest makes the sign of a cross over each species. The scandalous nature of this episode, however, also suggests that Cervantes intended it to be a criticism of the Catholic Church.[12] If we take a step back from the episode itself, however, and consider Cervantes's Catholicism and his literary proclivities, I propose a third hermeneutic that is more subtle. Cervantes neither assigns an overtly Catholic meaning nor subverts Catholic liturgy, but, instead, invokes the incarnational and sacramental tradition of Roman Catholicism. The Eucharistic implications of the episode mediate its irreverent tone because Don Quixote, who is not far removed from the influence of books of chivalry at this point in the novel, seeks a cure for his injuries that he believes will cure him as if it were the Body of Christ. Unfortunately for Don Quixote, and soon after Sancho, the balsam has the opposite effect, as both knight and squire become violently ill. The knight's physical constitution is no match for the balsam's sickening potency, but he demonstrates in this episode a desire to experience Christ's presence in everyday life. Don Quixote's ritualistic preparation of the balsam, while humorous, underscores the unitive process that takes place when the contemplative in action exteriorizes his or her spirituality.

Sixteenth-century Catholics sought Divine Favor for the Spanish soldiers who participated in the Battle of Lepanto by praying the rosary.[13] On the morning of October 7, 1571, the Holy League, which consisted of the naval fleets of European Catholic territories, including Spain, Naples, Sicily, Venice, and Genoa, entered into battle with the Ottoman Empire.[14] Each galley was not able to set sail, however, until the priest who served as its chaplain finished celebrating a pre-dawn Mass.[15] During this engagement, Pope Pius V (1566–72) and many faithful prayed the rosary, invoking the intercession of the Virgin Mary. That day, the wind inexplicably changed direction and provided the Holy League with the advantage it needed to defeat the Turkish Muslims. In commemoration of this important victory, Pope Pius V incorporated a devotion to the rosary into the celebration of the Mass on October 7. In 1573, Pope Gregory XIII (1572–85) designated October 7 as the Feast of the Most Holy Rosary. In 1645, King Philip IV (1621–1665) ordered that the rosary be prayed at nightfall in all of the military barracks; Kings Charles III (1759–88) and Fernando VII (1808; 1813–33) issued the same mandate (Labarga 164).

The rosary was also a prevalent symbol of devotion for many Catholics who did not participate in military campaigns. St. Teresa writes about praying the rosary as a child in her autobiography *Vida de Santa Teresa de Jesús*: "procuraba soledad para rezar mis devociones, que eran hartas, en especial el Rosario, de que mi madre era muy devota y ansí nos hacía serlo" (Teresa de Jesús 24). The Protestant Reformation was the impetus for increased devotion to the Virgin Mary during Cervantes's lifetime.

There are seven episodes in *Don Quixote* in which the rosary is mentioned, although the knight is not directly involved with all of them: Part I, XXII; Part I, XXVI; Part I, XXVII; Part I, XXX; Part II, XXIII; Part II, XLVI; and Part II, LXXI. One of the most well-known and controversial episodes involving a rosary takes place in Part I, XXVI after Don Quixote isolates himself in the Sierra Morena to perform acts of devotion to Dulcinea. The knight proposes to imitate Amadís of Gaul, who, upon being sent away by the Lady Oriana, retreats to the company of a hermit where Amadís commends his soul to God. Don Quixote, knowing that Amadís prayed, asks himself what he can use as a rosary:

> En esto, le vino al pensamiento cómo le haría, y fue que rasgó una gran tira de las faldas de la camisa, que andaban colgando, y diole once ñudos, el uno más gordo que los demás, y esto le sirvió de rosario el tiempo que allí estuvo, donde rezó un millón de avemarías. Y lo que le fatigaba mucho era no hallar por allí otro ermitaño que le confesase y con quien consolarse.[16] (362–63)

I do not believe that the absence of a hermit can be attributed entirely to Cervantine satire. In Part II, Chapter XXIV, Cervantes insinuates his disdain for hermits when Don Quixote compares the hermits who lived in the deserts to the hermits of his day:

> Y no se entienda que por decir bien de aquéllos no lo digo de aquéstos, sino que quiero decir que al rigor y estrecheza de entonces no llegan las penitencias de los de agora; pero no por esto dejan de ser todos buenos: a lo menos, yo por buenos los juzgo; y cuando todo corra turbio, menos mal hace el hipócrita que se finge bueno que el público pecador. (234)

The absence of the hermit reflects, I propose, the degree of Cervantes's animus toward the practice of unorthodox Catholicism. Hermits in seventeenth-century Spain often served as the custodians of chapels and shrines, which were a staple of towns and villages, whose faithful did not practice orthodox Catholicism (Taylor 377). The role of religion in Cervantes's lifetime was inextricably linked to social order. While the Inquisition established, for the most part, religious homogeneity in Spain, unlike the public conflicts between Catholic and Protestants in other parts of Europe, the existence of two forms of Catholicism betrayed a subtle division. The aristocracy adhered to the doctrinal reforms that began with the Catholic Monarchs and continued through the Council of Trent.[17] The populace of Spain, however, practiced an unorthodox form of Catholicism that emphasized the material reality of images and incorporated local beliefs that often bordered on superstition. While the absence of the hermit may be attributed to other factors, the knight's harsh words in Part II, Chapter XXIV suggest there is more at play.

Don Quixote's desire to pray the rosary certainly reflects the mindset of a contemplative in action, but the conditions surrounding it are problematic for two reasons. First, one can argue that Don Quixote's act of prayer is founded more on his desire to imitate the knights from his books than on religious devotion: "Ea, pues, manos a la obra: venid a mi memoria cosas de Amadís, y enseñadme por dónde tengo de comenzar a imitaros. Mas ya sé que lo más que él hizo fue rezar y encomendarse a Dios; pero, ¿qué haré de rosario, que no le tengo?" (Part I, Chapter XXVI, 362).[18] The knight chooses this exercise, I believe, because of a predisposition to devotion. In addition, while Don Quixote is motivated in part by his desire to imitate Amadís, the frequency with which he invokes God throughout the novel admits room to consider that a part of him wants to pray the rosary for other reasons.[19] Furthermore, Don Quixote does not state that Amadís prayed the rosary during his penitence, only that "él hizo fue rezar y encomendarse a Dios" (362).

The second reason this episode is a source of debate consists of two aspects that Carroll Johnson, among others, notes deserve special attention:

> The censors were alert to the offhand reference to a million prayers, recognized in it Erasmus's aversion to the repetition of formulas, and eliminated it. They seem to have missed the more scandalous proposition, that the use of the rosary itself is either irrelevant or downright un-Christian, implied in the fact that Don Quixote fashions his rosary from what people used before the invention of toilet paper. (Don Quixote 13–14)

Perhaps the censors, as Johnson notes, "missed the more scandalous proposition" of the episodes, or maybe they did not view it as such. In the second edition from 1605, however, changes were made, most notably to the number of Hail Marys and the material Don Quixote uses to fashion the rosary: "Y sirviéronle de Rosario unas agallas grandes de un alcornoque, que ensartó, de que hizo un diez" (Rico 292n12). Martín de Riquer does not believe that Cervantes was the author of this change: "Nada justifica la opinión de que fuera el propio Cervantes quien enmendara aquellas palabras por poder parecerle irreverentes" (Riquer 274n2). Bataillon, however, attributes the change to Cervantes, whom he believes "lamenta haberse dejado llevar por su vena satírica. Espontáneamente, o guiándose por la opinión de algún censor, discurre una manera más decente de improvisar un Rosario"

(788). Bataillon's explanation is certainly plausible if we consider Cervantes's literary style and the satiric nature of the novel. While Don Quixote's actions here may not be held up as a paragon of saintly devotion, the spirit with which he undertakes the fashioning of the rosary cannot be summarily dismissed as heretical or irrelevant. After all, why would Cervantes treat so irreverently the symbol under which he served Spain as a soldier in the Battle of Lepanto?[20]

In Part I, Chapter XXX, Don Quixote, in defense of his liberation of the galley slaves in Part I, Chapter XXII, describes the chained men as a metaphorical rosary:

> A los caballeros andantes no les toca ni atañe averiguar si los afligidos, encadenados y opresos que encuentran por los caminos van de aquella manera, o están en aquella angustia, por sus culpas, o por sus gracias; sólo le toca ayudailes como a menesterosos, poniendo los ojos en sus penas, y no en sus bellaquerías. Yo topé un rosario y sarta de gente mohína y desdichada, e hice con ellos lo que mi religión me pide. (418)

The mention of the rosary in this context may be interpreted in a number of ways. The critics who consider Cervantes's treatment of it as purely a source of derision will attach a negative connotation to the knight's metaphoric description: "El rosario se vuelve ahora una cadena de significantes que sirve para recordar delitos comunes; cada una de sus cuentas son equiparadas a delincuentes cuyos antecedentes penales fueron descritos detalladamente en el capítulo 22" (Véguez 97). If we extend this negative interpretation, however, one can argue that the metaphor reminds the reader that the comparison is not necessarily an irreverent one because it establishes a connection between the purpose of the rosary, i.e., petitioning the intercession of the Virgin Mary, and the lives of the galley slaves, who are in need of divine providence. Furthermore, Don Quixote's metaphor, when examined within the context of his journey as a contemplative in action, serves as a reminder to the reader of the knight's spiritual quest.

In Part II, Chapter XLVI, as Don Quixote dresses to attend his "audience" with the Duke and Duchess, Cervantes writes that the knight "asió un gran rosario que consigo contino traía" (405). In this episode, the reader becomes more aware of Don Quixote's life as a contemplative in action, and, specifically, his Catholicity. First, it appears that the knight carries a rosary with him.[21] Second, Don Quixote makes sure to include a rosary as a symbolic appendage of who he is in his quest to present himself in the best and most complete way possible to the Duke and Duchess: "se vistió su acamuzado vestido y se calzó sus botas de camino, por encubrir la desgracia de sus medias; arrojóse encima su mantón de escarlata y púsose en la cabeza una montera de terciopelo verde, guarnecida de pasamanos de plata, colgó el tahelí de sus hombros con su buena y tajadora espada" (405). The ridiculous, and perhaps even duplicitous, nature of the situation, is open to debate, yet the inclusion of the rosary, which one can argue Don Quixote holds in his hand, may symbolize the knight's faith.[22]

While Cervantes's engagement with the rosary in *Don Quixote* may be attributed to Erasmus's influence, it would be erroneous to discount two other considerations. First, Don Quixote's seeming indifference to the rosary may represent Cervantes's satire of those Catholics whose beliefs are superstitious in nature. How the knight fashions the rosary in the Sierra Morena and the exaggerated number of Hail Marys, for example, symbolize a religious practice void of sincere devotion. The object of Cervantes's satire would have been the religious practices of the lower class. Second, Cervantes's portrayal of Don Quixote as an anti-hero consists of a systematic deconstruction of the knight-errant's accoutrements, including the rosary. As the quintessential symbol of a knight's ascetic lifestyle, the rosary is an extension of the knight's identity and symbolizes the renunciation of earthly possessions. It would seem to make sense that Cervantes would satirize, therefore, even a religious artifact so as not to compromise his literary objectives. Furthermore, it is for this reason that Cervantes's supposed subversion of the Catholic Church merits reconsideration within the context of his life as a Catholic and an author.

Don Quixote, as a contemplative in action, is acutely aware of the presence and role of God in his life, and, consequently, he commends himself to God and encourages other characters to do the same often throughout the novel. In Part I, Chapter XX, Don Quixote attempts to console a frightened Sancho, for example, by reminding him to place his trust in God:

> Y así, te ruego, Sancho, que calles; que Dios, que me ha puesto en corazón de acometer ahora esta tan no vista y tan temerosa

aventura, tendrá cuidado de mirar por mi salud y de consolar tu tristeza. (281)

When a forlorn Sancho expresses his frustration about not becoming governor of an island yet in Part II, Chapter III, Don Quixote reminds Sancho that God has a plan for him: "Encomendadlo a Dios, Sancho —dijo don Quijote—, que todo se hará bien, y quizá mejor de lo que vos pensáis; que no se mueve la hoja en el árbol sin la voluntad de Dios" (56). In Part II, Chapter XXV, Cervantes exemplifies his knowledge of St. Thomas Aquinas's philosophy on God's relationship to time when Don Quixote explains to Sancho that he would expect *maese* Pedro's divining ape not to be able to reveal future events: "que a solo Dios está reservado conocer los tiempos y los momentos, y para Él no hay pasado ni porvenir; que todo es presente" (247).[23] After Don Quixote's Thomistic observation, which also reflects the Ignatian belief that God is present in the here and now, the knight accuses the ape of being demonic and expresses his surprise that the Inquisition does not know about the ape yet. Don Quixote's journey as a contemplative in action leads him to this awareness, a movement that French Jesuit Jean-Pierre de Caussade describes as a powerful source of spiritual growth:

> The present moment holds infinite riches beyond your wildest dreams but you will only enjoy them to the extent of your faith and love. The more a soul loves, the more it longs, the more it hopes, the more it finds. (62)

Erasmus's doctrine of incarnational humanism also places Jesus at the center of daily spirituality:

> You love the arts and sciences. That is good if you do so because of Christ. If you love them, however, for knowledge's sake, then you stop where one should proceed. But if you desire the arts and sciences, because they help you to see Christ more clearly, who is hidden in the mysteries of the holy scriptures, and if you want to enjoy your love and knowledge of Christ and share it with others, so prepare for studying them. But only pursue these studies to the extent that they further, in good conscience and to your knowledge, a good attitude (*bonum mentem*). ... [I]t is better to know less and to love more than to know much and not love. (Zimmerman 100–01)

Chapter Four

The knight's incarnational view of the world to this point provides him with the spiritual sensitivity to recognize God's presence and omnipotence. Cervantes and Erasmus concur that daily spirituality is foundational to a person's relationship with God, although the means to this end is different.

Even though Don Quixote sees himself as superior to nearly all of the characters who participate in his adventures, he exhibits his blind faith in God often throughout the novel, and especially in his conversation with one of the millers in Part II, Chapter XXIX. When the miller questions Don Quixote about the castle from which he hopes to free a prisoner, the knight attributes the miller's ignorance to the actions of an enchanter, who made the castle disappear. Don Quixote, frustrated with his conversation with the miller, seeks God's intervention, realizing his own human limitations:

> Y en esta aventura se deben de haber encontrado dos valientes encantadores, y el uno estorba lo que el otro intenta: el uno me deparó el barco, y el otro dio conmigo al través. Dios lo remedie; que todo este mundo es máquinas y trazas, contrarias unas de otras. Yo no puedo más. (279)

When Don Quixote experiences Baroque disillusionment, "Yo no puedo más," he surrenders himself completely to God's will, making it possible for him to grow in holiness and to become more aware of God's presence in his life.

The contemplative in action seeks a greater awareness of God in everyday life "para mayor gloria de Dios" (Loyola, *Ejercicios* 162). Ignatius believed that the gift of free will that every person possesses should be directed toward this end. Ignatius utilizes the comparative *greater*, acknowledging that a person can always do more to give glory to God. One example of *ad majorem Dei gloriam* about which Ignatius writes in the *Spiritual Exercises* can be found in the rules for alms giving:

> La Segunda: quiero mirar á un hombre que nunca he visto ni conoscido, y deseando yo toda su perfeccion en el ministerio y estado que tiene, como yo querria que él tuviese medio en su manera de distribuir, para mayor gloria de Dios Nuestro Señor, y mayor perfeccion de su ánima; yo haciendo asi ni mas ni menos, guardaré la regla y medida que para el otro querria y juzgo ser tal. (*Ejercicios* 162)

Consequently, the contemplative in action seeks choices that he or she perceives to be opportunities to praise God and to perfect the soul:

> Segundo, es menester tener por objeto el fin para que soy criado, que es para alabar á Dios Nuestro Señor, y salvar mi ánima: y con esto hallarme indiferente, sin afeccion alguna desordenada; de manera que no esté más inclinado ni afectado á tomar la cosa propuesta, que á dexarla; ni mas á dexarla, que á tomarla, mas que me halle como en medio de un peso para seguir aquello que sintiere ser mas en gloria y alabanza de Dios Nuestro Señor, y salvacion de mi ánima. (Loyola, *Ejercicios* 81)

In a conversation with one of the galley slaves in Part I, Chapter XXII, Don Quixote not only professes his belief in absolute free will, but he also exalts its strength:

> Sólo digo ahora que la pena que me ha causado ver estas blancas canas y este rostro venerable en tanta fatiga por alcahuete, me la ha quitado el adjunto de [ser] hechicero. Aunque bien sé que no hay hechizos en el mundo que puedan mover y forzar la voluntad, como algunos simples piensan; que es libre nuestro albedrío, y no hay yerba ni encanto que le fuerce. Lo que suelen hacer algunas mujercillas simples y algunos embusteros bellacos es algunas misturas y venenos, con que vuelven locos a los hombres, dando a entender que tienen fuerza para hacer querer bien, siendo, como digo, cosa imposible forzar la voluntad. (310)

Free will, however, according to Don Quixote, is so precious that the exercise of it supersedes its consequences. In the case of the galley slaves, Don Quixote wants them to go free, arguing that God will decide their fate:

> Pero, porque sé que una de las partes de la prudencia es que lo que se puede hacer por bien no se haga por mal, quiero rogar a estos señores guardianes y comisario sean servidos de desataros y dejaros ir en paz; que no faltarán otros que sirvan al rey en mejores ocasiones; porque me parece duro caso hacer esclavos a los que Dios y naturaleza hizo libres. Cuanto más, señores guardas —añadió don Quijote—, que estos pobres no han cometido nada contra vosotros. Allá se lo haya cada uno con su pecado; Dios hay en el cielo, que no se descuida de castigar

Chapter Four

al malo, ni de premiar al bueno, y no es bien que los hombres
honrados sean verdugos de los otros hombres, no yéndoles nada
en ello. (314)

In this same discourse with the galley slaves, Don Quixote
not only affirms his belief in free will, but he also espouses the
Catholic doctrine of Final Judgment:

> The first takes place when each one of us departs this life; for
> then he is instantly placed before the judgment seat of God,
> where all that he has ever done or spoken or thought during life
> shall be subjected to the most rigid scrutiny. This is called the
> particular judgment.
> The second occurs when on the same day and in the same
> place all men shall stand together before the tribunal of their
> Judge, that in the presence and hearing of all human beings
> of all times each may know his final doom and sentence. The
> announcement of this judgment will constitute no small part of
> the pain and punishment of the wicked; whereas the good and
> just will derive great reward and consolation from the fact that
> it will then appear what each one was in life. This is called the
> general judgment. (*The Catechism of the Council of Trent* 141)

Don Quixote's application of this doctrine appears to be misplaced in this particular episode, but he, nevertheless, reveals an understanding of this important theological concept. The knight chooses to exercise his free will for the greater glory of God.

Don Quixote, as a contemplative in action, is not able to experience his death-bed epiphany without the presence of evil in his life: "We are said to be led into temptation by Him who, although He Himself does not tempt us nor cooperate in tempting us, yet is said to tempt because He does not prevent us from being tempted or from being overcome by temptations when He is able to prevent these things. In this manner God, indeed, suffers the good and the pious to be tempted, but does not leave them unsupported by His grace" (*Catechism of the Council of Trent* 639). The word *devil*, as the personification of evil, appears 120 times (Part I: 45 times; Part II: 75 times) in *Don Quixote*, and, in addition to the frequent appearance of the word, Cervantes portrays the devil in ways that especially resonate with Catholics.

Cervantes presents several elements of the novel, including Clavileño, Antonio Moreno's enchanted head, the Cave of

Montesinos, and the cats who "attack" Don Quixote at the castle of the Duke and Duchess, in a context that suggests the presence of the devil.[24] Unlike Erasmus, who believed that a person's flawed human nature was responsible for the evil in his or her life, Cervantes's concept of it was not as easily defined. He recognized that the devil was an allegory for the existence of evil in the world, but he also understood that the source of that evil was an entity beyond human nature. Literature provided Cervantes with the vehicle by which he could express this ambiguity.

The elements I cited above, for example, are the machinations of another character's deception, but they represent for Cervantes the existence of a diabolical force. In Part II, Chapter XLVI, the narrator describes the cats who enter Don Quixote's room as a "legión de diablos" (408). In the Gospel of St. Mark, Chapter 5, a man who is possessed by a demon, who calls himself Legion because he is one of many unclean spirits inside of the man, begs Jesus to drive the demons out of him. Jesus performs this miracle in front of a large number of people, and subsequently instructs the man to go home and to proclaim to his family what Jesus did for him, to convert the non-believers into believers. Cervantes satirically depicts the "legion of cats," another joke the Duke and Duchess play on Don Quixote, as an instrument of conversion that Altisidora hopes will convince Don Quixote to forget about Dulcinea:

> Todas estas malandanzas te suceden, empedernido caballero, por el pecado de tu dureza y pertinacia; y plega a Dios que se le olvide a Sancho tu escudero el azotarse, porque nunca salga de su encanto esta tan amada tuya Dulcinea, ni tú la goces, ni llegues a tálamo con ella, a lo menos viviendo yo, que te adoro. (409)

Whether the devil manifests itself allegorically or in a more concrete way, Cervantes does not deny the existence of evil in the world. Furthermore, it functions as a constitutive element of God's Plan of Salvation. Each episode in which Don Quixote fails to slay a giant or to rescue a character in distress, for example, tests his resolve as a Christian knight who commends his actions to God.[25] In this episode, Altisidora tempts Don Quixote to renounce his love for Dulcinea, but he remains faithful to her:

Chapter Four

> No—dijo creyendo a su imaginación, y esto, con voz que pudiera ser oída—; no ha de ser parte la mayor hermosura de la tierra para que yo deje de adorar la que tengo grabada y estampada en la mitad de mi corazón y en lo más escondido de mis entrañas, ora estés, señora mía, transformada en cebolluda labradora, ora en ninfa del dorado Tajo, tejiendo telas de oro y sirgo compuestas, ora te tenga Merlín, o Montesinos, donde ellos quisieren; que adondequiera eres mía, y a doquiera he sido yo, y he de ser, tuyo. (420)

In spite of each setback, the knight continues forward, pursuing the Truth that he finds at the end of the novel.

The decrees of the Council of Trent define three aspects of the devil that Cervantes reflects in Don Quixote. In its declaration of the Nicene-Constantinopolitan Creed in Session III (1546), the council acknowledged the existence of evil in the world, specifying that the enemy consists of "spirits of wickedness" and that only the word of God can act as a shield against the "fiery darts of the most wicked one" (*The Canons and Decrees of the Council of Trent* 39). In Cervantes's day, the corruptive influence of the devil was a primary concern of society, as evidenced by the Inquisition. Any person who renounced the teachings of the Church, for example, faced Inquisitorial prosecution, such as Jeronimite monk Juan Bautista de Cubas, who questioned the dogmas of the Assumption and the Immaculate Conception of the Virgin Mary (*The Spanish Inquisition, 1478–1614* 249).[26] The numerous references to the devil, as well as many more to the existence of evil in the world, establish the background against which Don Quixote travels the spiritual journey of a contemplative in action. He is consciously aware of the presence of evil in the world, and this recognition allows him to confront and overcome it. In doing so, he exercises his freedom of will and cooperates with God, whose role in the knight's life makes this choice possible: "But *why did God not prevent the first man from sinning?* St. Leo the Great responds, 'Christ's inexpressible grace gave us blessings better than those the demon's envy had taken away.'" And St. Thomas Aquinas wrote, "There is nothing to prevent human nature's being raised up to something greater, even after sin; God permits evil in order to draw forth some greater good. Thus St. Paul says, 'Where sin increased, grace abounded all the more'; and the Exsultet sings, 'O happy fault, ...

which gained for us so great a Redeemer!'" (*Catechism of the Catholic Church,* paragraph 412).

Cardinal Marcello Cervini, one of Pope Paul III's legates, presided over Session V (1546) of the Council of Trent. The council agreed to discuss two questions: justification (doctrine) and residence (reform). The Decree Concerning Original Sin recognizes the existence of sin in the world, and, specifically, the power of the devil over humanity: "captivity under the power of him who thenceforth had the empire of death, that is to say, the devil" (*The Canons and Decrees of the Council of Trent* 22). The characters in *Don Quixote* manifest their fear of the devil. In Part I, Chapter VI, for example, the priest reminds the reader of the omnipresence of the devil when he declares that Alonso de Salazar's *El Caballero de la Cruz* (1521) should be burned during the inquisition of Don Quixote's library of books: "Por nombre tan santo como este libro tiene se podía perdonar su ignorancia; mas también se suele decir, 'tras la cruz está el diablo': vaya al fuego" (153).[27] The title of the book, as the priest notes, is misleading. Its original title was *Libro del invencible caballero Lepolemo,* and it lacks many of the elements that characterize the books of chivalry, such as magic spells and jousting tournaments. Lepolemo's adventures, however, which include slaying a giant, would no doubt fuel Don Quixote's irrational behavior.[28]

The oath that Don Quixote takes to seek revenge on the Basque in Part I, Chapter X consists of two parts: to punish the Basque and to deprive himself of certain luxuries in emulation of the Marqués de Mantua, who did the same when he swore to punish whoever killed his nephew.[29] Don Quixote's oath is representative of the degree to which his madness affects his relationship with God at this point in the novel:

> Yet an oath becomes a source of evil to him that makes evil use of it, that is who employs it without necessity and due caution. For if a man calls God as witness, for some trifling reason, it would seemingly prove him to have but little reference for God, since he would not treat even a good man in this manner. Moreover, he is in danger of committing perjury, because man easily offends in words. ... (Aquinas, *Summa Theologica* Q.89, A.2)

Chapter Four

With respect to the first part, Sancho convinces Don Quixote not to pursue the Basque, reasoning that he will have restored the knight's honor by paying homage to Dulcinea del Toboso. Don Quixote decides to fulfill, however, the second part of the oath, much to the chagrin of Sancho, who points out to his master that oaths are inherently evil: "Que dé al diablo vuestra merced tales juramentos, señor mío —replicó Sancho—; que son muy en daño de la salud y muy en perjuicio de la conciencia" (188–89). The reader may be reminded of this stage of Don Quixote's madness when he finds the barber's basin in Part I, Chapter XXI: "Digo esto, porque, si no me engaño, hacia nosotros viene uno que trae en su cabeza puesto el yelmo de Mambrino, sobre que yo hice el juramento que sabes" (293).[30]

The dichotomy of Good versus Evil is a theme of the conversation between Don Quixote and Sancho in Part I, Chapter XLVII. The knight asks his squire to explain why he is locked up in an oxcart when the knights from the books of chivalry are carried away in a more suitable and dramatic way: a dark cloud, a chariot of fire, or a hippogriff. Sancho, even though he has not read the books of chivalry, admits that much of what they experience is not "católico."[31] The word "catholic," however, is not a reference to the religion, but rather an adjective to describe a situation that is dubious. The knight-errant, however, thinking that the word "catholic" refers to the religion, exclaims that the apparitions they encounter are not Catholic because they are devils who, in this case, placed Don Quixote in the oxcart. Furthermore, Don Quixote warns Sancho about the craftiness of the devils who rely on deception as a weapon against Good.[32] Instead of returning to his village and resuming his life as Alonso Quijano, Don Quixote seeks more adventures, and each one, especially the ones orchestrated by the "enchanters," because they represent evil in his mind, contribute to his spiritual edification.

When Alonso Quijano becomes Don Quixote, he discovers a new passion for life. The simple, mundane, and repetitive lifestyle he lived for years is replaced by the exciting and blood-pumping adventures he reads about in his books of chivalry. For the first time in his life, Alonso Quijano experiences life at its fullest. As a knight-errant, Don Quixote "seeks God and seeks to find God in action," and a definitive aspect of that quest is the knight's relationship with Dulcinea (Martin 391). Herrero notes that

Unamuno and Menéndez Pidal offer the most cogent explanation of the religious, as well as national, significance of Don Quixote's devotion to Dulcinea:

> Don Quijote had loved Aldonza with unrevealed passion for twelve years; but suddenly he is born to a new faith, to the search for *eterno nombre y fama*. The symbol of eternal glory is Dulcinea, the creation of Don Quijote's faith. Such faith, as the root of Man's search for eternity, is a religious one. Don Quijote's *yo vivo y respiro en ella* is the equivalent of St. Paul's "Christ lives in me." This effort to seek (which is, also, an effort to create) a reality which goes beyond mortality, beyond earthly aims, toward the immense expanse of eternity (so the naked landscape of Castile gazes at the blue expanse of unclouded sky) is, of course, the symbolic expression of the Spanish spirit. (Herrero 26)

The knight's spiritual evolution becomes more evident when he admits to the Duchess that he does not know if Dulcinea exists or not in Part II, Chapter XXXII:

> —En eso hay mucho que decir —respondió don Quijote—. Dios sabe si hay Dulcinea o no [en] el mundo, o si es fantástica, o no es fantástica; y éstas no son de las cosas cuya averiguación se ha de llevar hasta el cabo. Ni yo engendré ni parí a mi señora, puesto que la contemplo como conviene que sea una dama que contenga en sí las partes que puedan hacerla famosa en todas las del mundo, como son: hermosa sin tacha, grave sin soberbia, amorosa con honestidad, agradecida por cortés, cortés por bien criada y, finalmente, alta por linaje, a causa que sobre la buena sangre resplandece y campea la hermosura con más grados de perfección que en las hermosas humildemente nacidas. (303–04)

When Don Quixote is in the company of the Duke and Duchess, he does not, Casalduero notes, see his appearance as a knight-errant through the images and adventures he reads about in the books of chivalry, and when that self-perception is removed the knight who will renounce the same books of chivalry and embrace his relationship with God emerges: "Don Quijote, hombre espiritual, ve su imagen de Caballero andante, que él siempre habían contemplado en la pureza de su acción: imagen de su ser externo. Los honores, la posición, la fama que la sociedad puede otorgar al hombre espiritual no son otra cosa que una imagen burlesca, deformación de la vida interior" (*Sentido y forma* 303). The consequences of Don Quixote's recognition are apparent in Part II, Chapter LVIII, when he and Sancho encounter the twelve peasants who transport the statues of St. George, St. Martin of Tours, St. James, and St. Paul for an altarpiece in their village.[33] After noting St. Paul's *metanoia*, Don Quixote reflects on his life as a knight-errant and expresses hope that he will experience a similar transformation: "pero si mi Dulcinea del Toboso saliese de los que padece, mejorándose mi ventura y adobándoseme el juicio, podría ser que encaminase mis pasos por mejor camino del que llevo" (508). As if to complete Don Quixote's prayerful wish, Sancho responds, "—Dios lo oiga y el pecado sea sordo—" (508). Even though Don Quixote acknowledges that each saint was a knight like him, he chooses to address their heavenly accomplishments, explaining: "Por buen agüero he tenido, hermanos, haber visto lo que he visto, porque estos santos y caballeros profesaron lo que yo profeso, que es el ejercicio de las armas; sino que la diferencia que hay entre mí y ellos es que ellos fueron santos y pelearon a lo divino, y yo soy pecador y peleo a lo humano" (508). Cervantes reveals in this episode an acute understanding of the Catholic Church's doctrine that saints are venerated, not worshiped, and serve as role models for the faithful on earth. Furthermore, Don Quixote's nuanced explanation of the differences between these fours saints and him is particularly telling of Cervantes's knowledge about the role of saints in the Catholic Church. Based on Don Quixote's spiritual maturation to this point in the novel, I do not believe that he would have been capable of extolling the saints' heavenly virtues over their earthly accomplishments as knights in Part I.

In the end, Don Quixote continues to seek God. Near death, he speaks in a way that reinforces my assertion that this contemplative in action, in spite of his numerous eccentricities, possesses a real awareness of God in his life. Furthermore, Don Quixote's commitment to the Catholic tradition of service of faith sustains him as he perceives the many ways in which God is active in his life: "Don Quixote is a hero of the indomitable power of Christian optimism, Christian imagination, and the glorious Christian folly that perceives the highest realities in the lowliest realities."[34] The knight asks that his friends tend to the salvation of his soul, and when he wakes up after sleeping for more than six hours, he cries out, "¡Bendito sea el poderoso Dios, que tanto bien me ha hecho! En fin, sus misericordias no tienen límite, ni las abrevian ni impiden los pecados de los hombres" (633). Then, Don Quixote, who recognizes now that his judgment is "libre y claro" (633), explains how the books of chivalry he read distanced him from God, wishing now that he could compensate by reading books "que sean luz del alma" (633). The priest hears Don Quixote's confession. Finally, the notary who is present when Don Quixote dies, comments that he had never read in any of the books of chivalry about a knight who dies in such a Christian way as Don Quixote.[35]

Michel Foucault observes that Don Quixote's journey is "a quest for similitudes: the slightest analogies are pressed into service as dormant signs that must be reawakened and made to speak once more" (52). Don Quixote's pursuit to imitate the great knights from the books he reads takes him from tilting at windmills to a magical journey on a wooden horse, but this same quest, however, also has more profound consequences: it provides him with the opportunities to grow closer to God in ways that were not possible before he became Don Quixote.

Chapter Five

The Anthropological Vision of *Don Quixote*

Among the many important changes enacted by the Council of Trent was its illumination of a Catholic Christian anthropological view of the human person. This vision does not consist of empirical studies but rather a Christocentric understanding of humanity in relation to God, as the Creator, and what He reveals Man and Woman to be. The Book of Genesis, for example, reveals that God created humanity in His image and likeness. In its treatment of Original Sin, the Council of Trent understood Adam to be a prototype of humanity whose disobedience in the Garden of Eden supersedes his individualism and illustrates concupiscence.[1] Church tradition has upheld the belief that rationality and volition are two traits of humanity that make it most like God, as these characteristics endow humanity with a sense of morality. As such, humanity also possesses inherent dignity, the core and catalyst of which is conscience. Observable behavior can inform an anthropological study of humanity, but only by focusing on its relationship with God can a deeper and more meaningful vision be developed. In this chapter, I examine Cervantes's vision of humanity vis-à-vis an anthropological reading of *Don Quixote* based on how the knight's adventures may be interpreted according to three principles of Catholic social teaching: 1) the inviolable dignity of every human person; 2) the essential centrality of community; and 3) the significance of human action (Sachs 9).[2]

The foundation of the Renaissance Church's belief in the inviolable dignity of every person is the *imago Dei*, the theological doctrine that God created human beings in His likeness and image.[3] The degree to which the *imago Dei* can be a catalyst of the soul's transformation is proportionate to the disposition of the intellect, i.e., knowledge of the self and of God. Devotional practices such as Ignatian contemplation and Erasmus's "philosophy of Christ" cultivated a deeper and more personal relationship with God. The layered nuances of Christianity during Cervantes's lifetime, as illustrated by the doctrine of the *imago Dei*, make it problematic to label a person definitively as Erasmian or anti-Erasmian, especially an author like Cervantes, whose engagement with Catholicism's multivalent tradition is deep-rooted in *Don Quixote*.

Lest we elevate Don Quixote as a paragon of charity and good will, the knight's desire to right the wrongs in the world is a consequence of his esthetic admiration for the books of chivalry, and not, as Allen writes, an ethical consideration (*Don Quixote* 97). Nevertheless, Don Quixote, in pursuit of fame as the heroes from his books of chivalry, seeks to uphold the ideals of social justice and the dignity of the human person like the knights from his books of chivalry, who achieve their fame by promoting the common good when, for example, they go to the aid of a king or queen whose kingdom is under attack or free someone who is imprisoned unjustly. The moral value of the knight's actions is questionable, however, because the ends are personal fame. Dominican friar Ambrosius Catharinus (1484–1553), while addressing the Council of Trent, reiterated St. Thomas Aquinas's philosophy that an act cannot be judged to be morally good if one of the aspects—object, end, and circumstances—is defective. In Part I, Chapter II, Don Quixote, on his first sally, muses about the fame he will achieve for the first time.[4] Cervantes does not resolve this doctrinal tension until Part II, which Henry Sullivan describes as a "salvation epic, in which Don Quixote and Sancho are made to pass through a Purgatory in this life" (6). In Part II, Chapter VIII, Don Quixote renounces the earthly fame he seeks in Part I in favor of heavenly glory because it is eternal. While it may be argued that the knight's spiritual transformation is an example of psychological egoism, it is more accurate, I believe, to point to this episode as the harbinger of his salvation.[5] Furthermore, it is reasonable to conclude that this episode also denotes Cervantes's spiritual maturation during the decade between the publication of Parts I and II, which Juan de la Cuesta published less than a year before Cervantes's death. This doctrinal complication illustrates the complex nature of the novel's religious ideology, and, especially, the abstract ways in which it can be interpreted.

The Catholic Church's social teaching does not admit the possibility that a person's individual desires and aspirations are independent of society because human beings are social and relational beings whose actions impact others. In *De regno* (*On Kingship*), St. Thomas Aquinas underscores this relationship: "Yet through virtuous living man is further ordained to a higher good, which consists in the enjoyment of God. ... Consequently, since society must have the same end as the individual man, it is not the ultimate end of an assembled multitude to live virtuously, but through virtuous living to attain the possession of God" (42). The dignity of the human person and the common good must be kept in balance. Once the efforts toward this goal affect the dignity of the human person, however, the common good should be subjugated. Of course, Don Quixote does not observe this balance in all instances. Yet, by endeavoring to succor those whom he perceives need assistance, the knight elevates their human dignity and reinforces the fabric of the common good.[6]

One of the episodes that is representative of Cervantes's promotion of the common good is Camacho's wedding (Part II, Chapters XX and XXI). Moments before the rich and powerful Camacho is to marry Quiteria, whose father arranges for her to marry Camacho for his wealth, Basilio, who is in love with Quiteria, arrives to stop the wedding. Basilio falls on a dagger and refuses to make a last confession if Quiteria does not marry him. Quiteria, fearing that Basilio will spend eternity in hell because he takes his own life, agrees to marry him. After she does, however, Basilio reveals that he staged his suicide in order to obligate Quiteria to marry him.

This episode is replete with social and religious implications. The Council of Trent addresses suicide as a violation of the Fifth Commandment, *Thou shall not kill*: "It also forbids suicide. No man possesses such power over his own life as to be at liberty to put himself to death. Hence we find that the Commandment does not say: *Thou shalt not kill another*, but simply: *Thou shalt not kill*" (*The Catechism of the Council of Trent* 485). The Council of Trent also declared that Confession, in addition to its religious connotations, also has an impact on society:

> Another advantage of Confession, which should not be overlooked, is that it contributes powerfully to the preservation

Chapter Five

of social order. Abolish sacramental Confession, and that moment you deluge society with all sorts of secret and heinous crimes—crimes too, and others of still greater enormity, which men, once that they have been depraved by vicious habits, will not dread to commit in open day. The salutary shame that attends Confession restrains licentiousness, bridles desire and checks wickedness. (*The Catechism of the Council of Trent* 344)

Cervantes further subscribes to the Council of Trent's ideology when Quiteria and Basilio recite their wedding vows: "Marriage is not a mere donation, but a mutual agreement; and therefore the consent of one of the parties is insufficient for marriage, the consent of both being essential" (403). Quiteria's vows emphasize the necessity of free will for a marriage to be valid: "Ninguna fuerza fuera bastante a torcer mi voluntad; y así, con la más libre que tengo te doy la mano de legítima esposa, y recibo la tuya, si es que me la das de tu libre albedrío, sin que la turbe ni contraste la calamidad en que tu discurso acelerado te ha puesto" (207). The themes of freedom, civic responsibility, and self-fulfillment that Cervantes explores within the context of marriage in his literature denote an author who is concerned about the disorder of the world that surrounds him, a contributing cause of which was Philip III's expulsion of the *moriscos* during the same period that Cervantes must have been writing Part II (1609–14). The episode of Camacho's wedding suggests that Cervantes leaned on his faith for the cure that ailed society. González Echevarría asserts the sacramental nature of marriage and its impact on society: "The story of Camacho's wedding is about the issue of marriage as a sacrament, a transformation of matter for transcendental purposes, that of creating a new human life and how it is institutionalized through civil and canon law, that is, by society and religion" (231). In the end, both Quiteria and Basilio illustrate agape love.[7]

The second tenet of Catholic social teaching that I would like to discuss as it applies to Cervantes's masterpiece is the essential centrality of community.[8] Don Quixote fights for a social order founded on the principle of solidarity, the Catholic teaching that the members of a community promote the common good by safeguarding the human dignity of every person in that community.[9] In his study of the romances of chivalry in the Golden Age, Eisenberg lists several reasons that motivate a knight to travel, which include serving a king or queen in need of military assistance to combat invaders or to claim what is rightfully theirs, obtaining a healing remedy for someone who is ill, and freeing someone who is held captive (*Romances of Chivalry* 62). Knight-errants like Amadís of Gaul, Palmerín of Olive, and even Don Quixote, personify the Catholic doctrine of solidarity when they help those in need. Don Quixote is not the prototypical knight-errant, of course, yet he aspires to sow the seeds of peace by strengthening the bonds of community. In the knight's discourse on Arms and Letters, Part I, Chapter XXXVII, once again Cervantes echoes St. Thomas Aquinas: "Peace is the work of justice indirectly, in so far as much peace removes the obstacles to justice" (*Summa Theologica* Q.9, A.3):

> Y así, las primeras buenas nuevas que tuvo el mundo y tuvieron los hombres fueron las que dieron los ángeles la noche que fue nuestro día, cuando cantaron en los aires: "Gloria sea en las alturas, y paz en la tierra, a los hombres de buena voluntad"; y a la salutación que el mejor maestro de la tierra y del cielo enseñó a sus allegados y favoridos fue decirles que cuando entrasen en alguna casa, dijesen: "—Paz sea en esta casa;" y otras muchas veces les dijo: "—Mi paz os doy; mi paz os dejo; paz sea con vosotros," bien como joya y prenda dada y dejada de tal mano; joya, que sin ella, en la tierra ni en el cielo puede haber bien alguno.[10] (516)

In the same way that Don Quixote made a Thomistic observation about time in the episode with the divining ape, here the knight speaks authoritatively about peace and justice in the context of a speech that Allen notes is the first time Don Quixote is the object of pity (*Don Quixote* 145).[11] The manner in which Cervantes inserts Thomism in the midst of the madman's dialogue serves a literary and a biographical purpose. Serious interjections about religion reinforce the portrayal of Don Quixote as a "cuerdo loco," but his madness and sanity manifest themselves alternately, not simultaneously, which adds complexity to the knight's characterization because he cannot conceal one or the other. Cervantes's ability to contextualize Thomistic theology within the novel suggests that he was well-versed in the Roman Catholic tradition.[12]

The third tenet of an anthropological vision of Don Quixote is the significance of human action. It is similar to the Renaissance Humanists's ideology of civic humanism, which incorporates

Chapter Five

intellectual life into the political or social environment in which they serve. Civic humanism began in earnest in Florence, where "a humanist's way of life, and the objects of his studies, had to be in harmony with his duties as a citizen. The experience of living in the 'citizen's world of action' dissolved the humanists' earlier loyalty to contemplation" (Seigel 5). The Humanist's political goal of "moral humanity" depended primarily on the education of a society's ruler. In Catholicism, however, questions of morality and faith are uniformly universal. Catholic Humanists like Thomas More shared Erasmus's passion for Christian reform, but, in addition to *imitatio Christi*, they believed that reform was not possible without the Catholic Church, and, specifically, the participation of clergy who exemplified Christ's teachings: "The combination of Scripture, the Church Fathers' writings, and the decrees and practices of the Catholic Church are, in More's eyes, the finest and most effectual manner in which both to reform and to maintain individuals and societies" (J. Nelson, "Sir Thomas More" 65). The expansion of the Protestant Reformation, however, suppressed the Catholic Humanists' reform movement.

When Alonso Quijano becomes Don Quixote, he embarks on a multi-faceted adventure that will take him to the depths of the Cave of Montesinos and to new "heights" on Clavileño. The knight also travels on a pilgrimage of self-awareness, along which he endeavors to become a famous knight-errant whose legend will be passed down from generation to generation. Yet, in the end, Don Quixote does not attain fame for the reasons that he wanted to be famous. Instead, when the knight's madness gives way to rational thought, he understands for the first time in the novel that true glory awaits him as he prepares for death by confessing his sins and consuming the Body of Christ. While it may be more expeditious to explain Don Quixote's desire for a Catholic Christian death as Cervantes's way of placating the inquisitorial censors, I prefer to elaborate on three anthropological components that define the significance of human actions and make Don Quixote's last wishes a logical conclusion.

The first anthropological component is transcendence. God created humanity in His image, and, therefore, people have a desire to discover who they are as a being created in God's image and to discern the meaning of their existence. A person attempts to answer these existential questions by transcending himself or herself in order to confront and to understand new experiences that are foreign to the world where the person feels most comfortable. The narrator describes Alonso Quijano as a fifty-something-year-old hidalgo who is "de complexión recia, seco de carnes, enjuto de rostro, gran madrugador y amigo de la caza" (114). The reader knows nothing about Alonso Quijano's early life or his spiritual proclivities. A voracious reader of books of chivalry, Alonso Quijano transcends his mundane existence and decides to imitate the heroes he reads about in his books. This illogical decision thrusts the humble country gentleman into a series of adventures and encounters that challenge his view of the world and the people who live in it. Furthermore, the truth of the real world he perceives as present in the books of chivalry also demystifies his fabricated world, leaving him to go beyond what he knows in order to understand himself and the world that surrounds him.

As Don Quijote progresses from one unsuccessful adventure to the next, he begins to realize this world is nothing like the stories from the books of chivalry. In Part II, especially, the defeats, which exact more physical consequences than in Part I, challenge Don Quixote's perception of truth, culminating with Don Quixote and Sancho's visit with the Duke and Duchess. The knight's faith in God does not wane, however, in spite of his misfortunes. In Part II, Chapter LXXIV, after Don Quixote awakens from his sleep as Alonso Quijano, he proclaims loudly that God's mercies are limitless. His niece, confused by her uncle's declaration, asks: "¿Qué misericordias son éstas, o qué pecados de los hombres?" (633). In response, he manifests his personal relationship with God when he tells his niece: "Las misericordias son las que en este instante ha usado Dios *conmigo*, a quien, como dije, no las impiden *mis* pecados" (633; my emphasis). Argentine author Jorge Luis Borges (1899–1986) suggests that this moment is transformative: "Aquí se declara la recuperada cordura de don Quijote y, para que ello sea más verosímil, se insinúa la posibilidad de un milagro. A esta altura de la novela, ya podemos creer en ese milagro, porque don Quijote es para nosotros no sólo un amigo querido sino también un *santo*" (Borges 32; my emphasis). Unamuno also acknowledges the significance of Alonso Quijano's last moments, invoking the spiritual transformation of St. Ignatius of Loyola: "¿Será cosa de recordar aquí, una vez más, a Íñigo de Loyola en cama, herido, en Pamplona, pidiendo le llevasen libros de caballerías para matar con ellos el tiempo y dándole la vida de Cristo Nuestro Señor y el *Flos Sanctorum*, los que le empujaron a meterse a ser caballero andante a lo divino?" (Unamuno 216).[13] As a result of their respective transcendence, both Alonso Quijano and Ignatius discover the many ways in which God is active in their lives.

The second anthropological component is freedom. As rational beings that possess free will, each person is able to make choices that he or she feels are most fulfilling. This choice is influenced to some extent by a person's past experiences, but it also affects the person's future due to the unintended consequences, either good or bad, that may arise. Don Quixote exercises freedom throughout the novel, although to what extent because of his madness is debatable. While his irrational behavior is due to his mental state, the moments of lucidity he experiences from time to time indicate that he is aware of his surroundings. When he realizes that the world in which he lives is not idyllic like the literary world from his books of chivalry, however, he chooses to surrender to rationality, a decision that would inspire the Russian writer Dostoyevsky to write: "This book, the saddest of all books, man will not forget to take with him to the Last Judgement. There he will show the most profound and fateful secret of man and humanity revealed … The sight of so many great and noble forces which are lost in vain is enough to drive more than one friend of humanity to despair, to arouse him not to laughter but to bitter tears, and to embitter for always by doubt a heart until then pure and believing" (qtd. in Catteau 47). While I understand Dostoyevsky's sentiments, I do not share his pessimism. Rationality, the only foe capable of conquering the knight's idealism, becomes the catalyst for Alonso Quijano to discover the mystical and to accomplish what truly was an "impossible dream" before he became Don Quixote. This realization, however, would not have been possible without the books of chivalry:

> His imitation of the heroes of chivalresque novels aims at such completeness that it becomes an attempt to live literature. He is not inspired to a vague sort of emulation, nor does he merely ape the habits, manners, and dress of knights errant; he does not simply adapt chivalresque ideals to some other causes, like St. Ignatius Loyola; he is not even acting a part, in the usual sense. He is content with nothing less than that the whole of the fabulous world—knights, princesses, magicians, giants

and all—should be part of his experience. Once he believes he really is a knight errant, and believes in his world of fiction, he steps off the pinnacle of inspired idealistic emulation into madness. He cannot play his part as he would like except in this fabulous world. In this sense he is trying to live literature.
(Riley, *Cervantes's Theory of the Novel* 36–37)

In other words, in his quest to create an idyllic world, he discovers one of the foundational principles of Ignatian spirituality—a life that is most conducive to a more intimate relationship with God: "Our only desire and one choice should be this: I want and I choose what better leads to God's deepening life in me" (O'Brien 69). To what extent did Cervantes's own itinerant and adventurous lifestyle affect his religious beliefs is limited to suppositions, but we do know that Cervantes had direct contact with Catholicism during the formative and last years of his life. His beliefs in the intermittent period will continue to be a source of debate for many years to come, but like Don Quixote, Cervantes's life ends in accord with the Catholic Church's rites of death and burial. In Part II, Chapter LXXIV, Sancho tries to convince Alonso Quijano to return to the world of adventures dressed as shepherds, telling him, "cuánto más que vuestra merced habrá visto en sus libros de caballerías ser cosa ordinaria derribarse unos caballeros a otros, y el que es vencido hoy ser vencedor mañana" (636). Truer words have never been spoken. Don Quixote no longer exists, but Alonso Quijano does, and he makes a choice to commend himself to God.

The third anthropological component is levels, and they include natural, social, human, and divine interests. In the search for truth, a person integrates each interest into a world vision and discerns that which is more important in order to satisfy his or her values. In other words, the individual transcends the different levels in order to discover the truth he or she longs to find. The process by which the person transcends the different levels is a cognitive, practical, and affective one.

In the books of chivalry, Alonso Quijano finds a doorway to a world in which he is able to transcend the mental, physical, and spiritual parameters of his life as a hidalgo. The finiteness of his life now enters the realm of infinite possibilities, where he is able to learn more about who he is and the meaning of his life. When Don Quixote utters the words, "—Yo sé quién soy...y sé que puedo ser no sólo los que he dicho, sino todos los doce Pares de

Chapter Five

Francia, y aun todos los Nueve de la Fama, pues a todas las hazañas que ellos todos juntos y cada uno por sí hicieron, se aventajarán las mías" (146), he commences that journey of self-discovery that will lead him to an anthropological understanding of his identity.

The first step occurs when he appropriates who he is by saying, "I know who I am," instead of, "I am who I am." The anthropological vision of Don Quixote necessarily begins with a study of who he is and not what: "In a world reconfigured as an enterprise, the self is no longer necessarily defined through bloodline but may indeed be realized as a process" (Castillo and Spadacchini 187). Mary Louise Pratt points out that language, and not just behavior, is an unpredictable, yet necessary, component of the human condition:

> People always speak from and in a socially constituted position, a position that is, moreover, constantly shifting, and defined in a speech situation by the intersection of many forces. On this view, speaking "for oneself," "from the heart" names only one position among the many from which a person might speak in the course of her everyday life. At other points, that person will be speaking, for instance, as a member of some collective, or as a rank in a hierarchy, and so forth ... the context and the subject continually mutually determine each other. (9)

Don Quixote's language, as much as his behavior, defines his identity as it gradually transitions from chivalric exaggerations and nonsense, interspersed with lucid rhetoric from time to time, such as the speech about the Golden Age, to a language that reflects his reality on his deathbed. For Cervantes, language is a reflection of the reality the character perceives to inhabit, and, the language that Don Quixote and Alonso Quijano speak define who they are.

An anthropological vision of humanity concerns itself with the relationship between the material and immaterial aspects of a person's life. It is based on the philosophy that human beings are made in the image and likeness of God. This vision of ourselves, however, is tested and challenged throughout our entire lives. Cervantes's anthropological vision of humanity, for example, anticipates the moral and social problems that would define Spain during the nineteenth century. The emergence of Liberalism in Spain after Emperor Napoleon installed his brother Joseph

Bonaparte as King of Spain in 1808 challenged the spiritual and intellectual revival that the Catholic Church experienced after the Battle of Waterloo (1815).[14]

Alonso Quijano's journey to self-awareness in God begins when he assumes the identity of Don Quixote. His life as a knight-errant teaches him that truth is not independent of God:

> There is, however, a need to recognize that the quest for truth does not make sense, if we do not see that the quest for truth and the quest for God are inseparable. There can be no question that, in Chesterton's view, to seek truth is to seek God, even though the seeker may not be aware of this, and that to find truth is to find God, even though, as in his own case, the implications of that finding may be long in coming through, even if, indeed, they never quite succeed in getting through. (Lauer 43–44)

As much as Don Quixote attempts to emulate the success of the heroes from the books of chivalry, his failures make him realize that literary fiction, such as the books of chivalry, and reality, i.e., seventeenth-century Spain, cannot be reconciled as easily as he once thought: "The written word and things no longer resemble one another. And between them, Don Quixote wanders off on his own" (Foucault 48). The first book of chivalry that Alonso Quijano reads sets in motion a journey that promises much and delivers little. In the end, however, he recovers his anthropological identity, denounces books of chivalry, laments that he did not read hagiographical literature, and embraces fully his relationship with God. The words, "I know who I am," take on a vastly different meaning now.

Chapter Six

From La Mancha to Manresa
Sancho Panza's Incarnational Spirituality

Before Ignatius and the other founders of the Society of Jesus (Francis Xavier, Peter Faber, Diego Laínez, Alfonso Salmerón, Nicolás de Bobadilla, and Simão Rodrigues) were Jesuits, they were humanists whose classes at the University of Paris centered on Renaissance humanism, especially Classical Latin, Theology, and Philosophy. Renaissance humanists lived a life of action and contemplation, one that Ronald Modras describes as a "balance born of complementarity" (11):

> The fifteenth-century *umanisti* were not only engaged in but devoted to the *studia humanisti*, in which *humanitas* entailed the development of human virtue in all its forms and to its fullest extent, not only insight and understanding but eloquence and action. For the humanists, the study of the classics led to an active, not sedentary or reclusive, life. Insight without action was barren, and action without insight was barbaric. Holding up *humanitas* as an ideal meant striving to strike a balance between action and contemplation. (Lauer 43–44)

The Renaissance complementarity of action and contemplation inspired the Jesuits' doctrine of "contemplation in action," a constitutive element of which was a world view grounded in incarnational spirituality:

> Christian theology holds that God became human, or "incarnate," in the person of Jesus of Nazareth. (The word *incarnation* comes from the Latin root *carn*, for "flesh.") More broadly, an incarnational spirituality means believing that God can be found in the everyday events of our lives. God is not just *out there*. God is right here, too. If you're looking for God, look around. To this end, one of the best definitions of prayer is

Chapter Six

> from Walter Burghardt, a twentieth-century Jesuit theologian, who called it a "long, loving look at the real." Incarnational spirituality is about the real. (Martin 8)

By integrating the secular and the sacred, incarnational spirituality emphasizes the immanence of God in the lives of the faithful. Everyday words, actions, and experiences become the means by which God communicates his love, grace, and divinity. The essence of Ignatius's spiritual philosophy is the presence of a God who labors in the outer, public world. Furthermore, incarnational spirituality is predicated on the belief that an awareness of God's presence cultivates a greater love for Him and a deeper appreciation for His creation. In this chapter, I discuss the numerous ways in which Sancho personifies Cervantes's understanding of an incarnational spirituality, focusing, particularly, on how the squire's religiosity is a significant component of his characterization.

Don Quixote enlists the services of Sancho Panza as his squire in Part I, Chapter VII, during the two weeks the knight recovers at home from the beating inflicted on him by the merchants of Toledo in Part I, Chapter IV. Noted scholar James Fitzmaurice-Kelly cites Cervantes's ambiguous characterization of Sancho early in Part I as evidence that Cervantes developed the character of Sancho as he developed the plot of *Don Quixote*:

> Cervantes does not venture to introduce Sancho Panza in person till near the end of the seventh chapter, and he is visibly ill at ease over his creation. It is quite plain that at this stage Cervantes knew very little about Sancho Panza, and his first remark is that the squire was an honest man (if any poor man can be called honest), "but with very little sense in his pate." This is not the Sancho who has survived; honesty is not the most preeminent quality of the squire, and if anybody thinks Sancho Panza a born fool, he must have a high standard of ability. In the ninth chapter Cervantes goes out of his way to describe Sancho Panza as a long-legged man; obviously up to this point he had never seen the squire at close quarters and was as yet not nearly so well acquainted with him as you and I are. He was soon to know him more intimately. Perceiving his mistake, he hustled the long-legged scarecrow out of sight, observed the real Sancho with minute fidelity and created the most richly humorous character in modern literature. The only possible

> rival to Sancho Panza is Sir John Falstaff; but Falstaff is emphatically English, whereas Sancho Panza is a citizen of the world, stamped with the seal of universality. (Walsh 425)

As the novel progresses, it becomes evident, especially in Part II, that the narrator's description of Sancho's mental acuity, i.e., "muy poca sal en la mollera" (163) in Part I, Chapter VII is a false and misleading description. Bakhtin presents another characterization of Sancho: "Sancho's role in relation to Don Quixote can be compared to the role of medieval parodies versus high ideology and cult, to the role of the clown versus serious ceremonial, to *charnage* versus *carême*" (22). Sancho begins his sojourn with Don Quixote as a realist whose primary motivation is power and riches, but episode after episode reveals a squire who is much more than "not very smart." In the end, as Don Quixote lay dying, it is Sancho, the "realist," who recognizes that life is about much more than power and riches:

> —¡Ay! —respondió Sancho, llorando—. No se muera vuestra merced, señor mío, sino tome mi consejo, y viva muchos años; porque la mayor locura que puede hacer un hombre en esta vida es dejarse morir, sin más ni más, sin que nadie le mate, ni otras manos le acaben que las de la melancolía. Mire no sea perezoso, sino levántese desa cama, y vámonos al campo vestidos de pastores, como tenemos concertado: quizá tras de alguna mata hallaremos a la señora doña Dulcinea desencantada, que no haya más que ver. Si es que se muere de pesar de verse vencido, écheme a mí la culpa, diciendo que por haber yo cinchado mal a Rocinante le derribaron; cuanto más que vuestra merced habrá visto en sus libros de caballerías ser cosa ordinaria derribarse unos caballeros a otros, y el que es vencido hoy ser vencedor mañana. (635–36)

Antonio Barbagallo also addresses the fluidity of Sancho's intellectual and moral development:

> Mientras la crítica trata de definir a Sancho de forma categórica y absoluta, dividiéndose así entre los que lo ven con buenos ojos, los que lo miran casi con desprecio y los que encuentran una "quijotización" del personaje, yo opino que Sancho, si bien de carácter formado, no termina de ser completo, ya que está enfrentándose de continuo a experiencias nuevas, y amoldándose a las circunstancias que van surgiendo. (Barbagallo 48)

Chapter Six

While Sancho's wit and ingenuity are on display in Part I, the most substantive evidence of the squire's evolution takes place in several episodes in Part II. In Part II, Chapter VIII, Sancho offers the reader a self-portrait: "bien es verdad que soy algo malicioso, y que tengo mis ciertos asomos de bellaco; pero todo lo cubre y tapa la gran capa de la simpleza mía, siempre natural y nunca artificiosa" (91). The internal contradiction of the statement, however, negates the self-portrait. The irony behind Sancho's affirmation of his simplicity becomes evident in Part II as the reader discovers that the squire's façade does indeed conceal more than meets the reader's eye. In Part II, Chapter LXXI, for example, Sancho negotiates payment with Don Quixote for the more than three thousand lashes he must give himself in order to disenchant Dulcinea:

> —Ellos —respondió Sancho— son tres mil y trecientos y tantos; dellos me he dado hasta cinco: quedan los demás; entren entre los tantos estos cinco, y vengamos a los tres mil y trecientos, que a cuartillo cada uno (que no llevaré menos si todo el mundo me lo mandase), montan tres mil y trecientos cuartillos, que son los tres mil, mil y quinientos medios reales, que hacen setecientos y cincuenta reales; y los trecientos hacen ciento y cincuenta medios reales, que vienen a hacer setenta y cinco reales, que juntándose a los setecientos y cincuenta, son por todos ochocientos y veinte y cinco reales. Estos desfalcaré yo de los que tengo de vuestra merced, y entraré en mi casa rico y contento, aunque bien azotado; porque no se toman truchas … y no digo más. (613)

Sancho's ability to apply one of his proverbs in a way that suits the situation is also indicative of the character's development.[1] In the same scene, Sancho deceives Don Quixote into thinking that he whips himself. Instead, the squire lashes a tree, and with each lash the squire cries out in pain, eliciting the sympathy of his master. The true depth of Sancho's character, however, is perhaps most evident during his governorship of the island. Victor Oelschläger notes how Sancho's governorship and subsequent abandonment of it can be viewed as defining moments in the squire's evolution:

> Then, finally, the most pathetic and profoundly human touch of all: after Sancho has met and bested his mockers at their own

> game, after he has practiced his master's advice to perfection, after he has delivered himself of the most masterfully brilliant and honest administration imaginable, after he has achieved the most admirable and meritorious success of his entire career (within the confines of the novel), when we are truly proud of Sancho and he has every reason to be proud of himself, he solemnly abdicates in self-dissatisfaction, in frustrated disillusionment, and in paradoxical humility born of experiential wisdom. (22)

The judicious and intelligent manner in which Sancho judges the three cases before him dispels any doubts the reader might have about the validity of the narrator's description of Sancho's seeming ignorance in Part I, Chapter VIII. The evolution of Sancho's character is noted by many critics, including Mancing, who writes: "That SP grows in self-confidence, worldly wisdom, and moral stature throughout the course of the novel (a process sometimes called quixotization) seems clear" (*The Cervantes Encyclopedia, Vol. II* 651).

Sancho reiterates throughout the novel that he is an "Old Christian." It is not surprising that an Old Christian like Sancho, therefore, would not hesitate to proclaim the purity of his blood whenever possible. In Part I, Chapter XXI, while Sancho and Don Quixote discuss what their future might hold, Sancho commends himself to God's will: "—Sea par Dios —dijo Sancho—, que yo cristiano viejo soy, y para ser conde esto me basta" (303).[2] Don Quixote's response reasserts Cervantes's belief that all human life possesses dignity and that it cannot be bought or inherited: "—Y aun te sobra —dijo don Quijote— y cuando no lo fueras, no hacía nada al caso; porque, siendo yo el rey, bien te puedo dar nobleza, sin que la compres ni me sirvas con nada" (303). In Part I, Chapter XLVII, after the barber accuses Sancho of being "impregnated" with Don Quixote's nonsensical beliefs and ideas, Sancho reminds him of his social status:

> —Yo no estoy preñado de nadie —respondió Sancho—, ni soy hombre que me dejaría empreñar, del rey que fuese; y aunque pobre, soy cristiano viejo, y no debo nada a nadie; y si ínsulas deseo, otros desean otras cosas peores; y cada uno es hijo de sus obras; y debajo de ser hombre puedo venir a ser papa, cuanto más gobernador de una ínsula, y más pudiendo ganar tantas mi señor, que le falte a quien dallas. (617)

Chapter Six

Sancho informs Sansón Carrasco in Part II, Chapter III that he is an Old Christian during a conversation that the two characters have about the publication of Sancho's and Don Quixote's adventures from Part I: "que infinitamente me ha dado gusto que el autor de la historia haya hablado de mí de manera que no enfadan las cosas que de mí se cuentan; que a fe de buen escudero que si hubiera dicho de mí cosas que no fueran muy de cristiano viejo, como soy, que nos habían de oír los sordos" (56–57). If there were any doubts about Sancho's faith, he dispels them in Part II, Chapter VIII: "Y cuando otra cosa no tuviese sino el creer, como siempre creo, firme y verdaderamente en Dios y en todo aquello que tiene y cree la santa Iglesia Católica Romana, y el ser enemigo mortal, como lo soy, de los judíos" (91). The ambiguous message of Sancho's profession of faith, however, is yet another example of Cervantine irony, which, according to Allen changes throughout the novel: "The successive strategies of Cervantes's irony in the course of the novel involve a change in the field of observation (from the esthetic to the ethical or moral). ..." (*Don Quixote: Hero or Fool* 188). While the irony that a Moor (Cide Hamete Benengeli) would praise the behavior of someone who exhibits religious intolerance against the members of another persecuted religion does not undermine Cervantes's affirmation of Catholicism, it does reflect Cervantes's social consciousness in Part II, which González Echevarría describes as the first political novel (184).[3]

In one of the more humorous scenes in the novel, Sancho's words denote his goodness but also his naiveté. In Part II, Chapter XXXIV, the "devil," who is a young man in costume, arrives to inform Don Quixote how to disenchant Dulcinea. When the "devil" does not recognize Don Quixote, who is standing in front of him, the "devil" swears "En Dios y en mi conciencia" (323) that he did not recognize Don Quixote because it slipped his mind why he was there in the first place.[4] Sancho, after hearing the "devil" swear before God and his conscience, admits that Hell must not be as he imagined it: "Sin duda —dijo Sancho— que este demonio debe de ser hombre de bien y buen cristiano, porque, a no serlo, no jurara *en Dios y en mi conciencia*. Ahora yo tengo para mí que aun en el mesmo infierno debe de haber Buena gente" (323; author's italics). John Moore asserts that Sancho's faith in God is one reason he accepts Don Quixote's invitation to be his squire without inquiring about specific details.[5] Sancho's religious faith, especially his status as an Old Christian, is a source of pride for him, and he is not timid about the ways in which he expresses his spirituality.

While Sancho's words identify him as a Catholic, his numerous acts of charity provide more concrete evidence of his spirituality. The reader first learns about Sancho's compassionate nature in Part I, Chapter VIII, after Don Quixote loses his battle with the windmills. When Don Quixote explains to Sancho that the evil enchanter Frestón changed the giants into windmills, Sancho, who sees windmills, consolingly says, "yo lo creo todo así como vuestra merced lo dice" (169). Although it may be argued that Sancho's words are self-serving, the squire's numerous acts of kindness throughout the novel illuminate the sincerity of his sentiments.

In Part I, Chapter XXII, when Sancho hears the sad plight of the fourth galley slave, the squire takes pity on him: "Y aquí tornó a su llanto, como de primero; y túvole Sancho tanta compasión, que sacó un real de a cuatro del seno y se le dio de limosna" (310). Andrés, the boy from Part I, Chapter IV whom Don Quixote defends against the beating his master Juan Haldudo inflicts upon him, reappears in Chapter XXXI to inform Don Quixote that the result of the knight's intervention was more lashes with the belt. When Andrés asks for something to eat, it is Sancho who does not hesitate to help him: "Sacó de su repuesto Sancho un pedazo de pan y otro de queso, y dándoselo al mozo, le dijo: 'Tomá, hermano Andrés; que a todos nos alcanza parte de vuestra desgracia'" (439). Sancho's words, "que a todos nos alcanza parte de vuestra desgracia," exemplify the Catholic Church's dogmatic teaching that all of humanity is one body in Christ: "For as in one body we have many members, but all the members have not the same office; so we being many, are one body in Christ and everyone members of one of another" (Romans 24:4–5; *The Catechism of the Council of Trent* 45). After Andrés inquires to what it is that affects Sancho, the squire responds with words that embody the Church's social doctrine of solidarity:

> Esta parte de queso y pan que os doy —respondió Sancho—, que Dios sabe si me ha de hacer falta o no, porque os hago saber, amigo, que los escuderos de los caballeros andantes estamos sujetos a mucha hambre y a mala ventura, y aun a otras cosas que se sienten mejor que se dicen. (439)

In Part II, Chapter XXIII, after Don Quixote emerges from the Cave of Montesinos, the knight relates that he gave the companion of Dulcinea, who asks for six *reales*, the four *reales* Sancho had given him as alms to poor people they encounter on their adventures. Another example of Sancho's concern for others occurs after he leaves Barataria and travels in search of Don Quixote. The squire crosses paths with six foreign pilgrims who ask him for alms: "y como él, según dice Cide Hamete, era caritativo además, sacó de sus alforjas medio pan y medio queso, de que venía proveído, y dióselo, diciéndoles por señas que no tenía otra cosa que darles" (478). Sancho, more so than any other character in the novel, personifies Ignatius's words, "Love ought to manifest itself more in deeds than in words" (Ganss 94).

Sancho often exhibits a willingness to surrender his will to God, and he does so with a frequency that suggests an awareness of God's presence in his life. He appeals to God's protection and Providence in Part I, Chapter XXI, for example, after listening to Don Quixote explain how the knight's plan to marry a princess and provide for Sancho may include obstacles. Both the knight and his squire express an awareness of a conscious relationship with God in this episode:

> —Pues como eso sea —respondió Sancho—, no hay sino encomendarnos a Dios, y dejar correr la suerte por donde mejor lo encaminare.
> —Hágalo Dios —respondió don Quijote— como yo deseo y tú, Sancho, has menester, y ruin sea quien por ruin se tiene. (21)

In Part I, Chapter VIII, after Don Quixote is thrown off of Rocinante while battling the windmills, Sancho exclaims, "¡Válame Dios!" (168).[6] Shortly thereafter, after Don Quixote informs Sancho that Frestón's powers will be no match for Don Quixote's sword, Sancho responds with deference: "Dios lo haga como puede" (168). Sancho's response to Don Quixote's plan to use a tree branch for a lance like the Spanish knight Diego Pérez de Vargas exemplifies, once again, the squire's commitment to God's protection: "A la mano de Dios" (170). In Part I, Chapter XIX, Sancho places his trust in God again when Don Quixote tells him to have courage as they witness the torches of the priests who accompany the knight's body: "Sí tendré, si a Dios place" (271). McGaha notes that oaths appear twenty-seven times in Part I and sixty-five times in Part II: Don Quixote speaks them nine times in Part I and thirteen times in Part II; Sancho uses them eighteen times in Part I and fifty times in Part II (565).[7] The number of oaths that Sancho uses may be understood to be in proportion to the degree of confidence he has in himself. In Part I, for the most part, Sancho still self-identifies as the simple villager who knows that windmills are not giants. In Part II, however, the relational nature of the knight and his squire becomes evident as early as Chapter II, when Sancho explains to Don Quixote's niece that an ínsula is not a food: "No es de comer, —replicó Sancho—, sino de gobernar y regir mejor que cuatro ciudades y que cuatro alcaldes de corte" (44).

Sancho's complete trust in God reflects his awareness that God is active in his life, which is a foundational belief of incarnational spirituality. In Part I, he says that he will return to his village with the basin that Don Quixote claims to be Mambrino's helmet, for example, "si Dios me diere tanta gracia" (346). In Part II, Chapter III, Sancho manifests his conscious recognition of God's active role in his life during a conversation with Sansón Carrasco: "Pero dejando esto del gobierno en las manos de Dios, que me eche a las partes donde más de mí se sirva" (56). Sancho elaborates on his incarnational spirituality in Part II, Chapter IV, professing his belief and trust in God and acknowledging an awareness of evil in the world:

> Y ¿sé yo por ventura si en esos gobiernos me tiene aparejada el diablo alguna zancadilla donde tropiece y caiga y me haga las muelas? Sancho nací, y Sancho pienso morir; pero si, con todo esto, de buenas a buenas, sin mucha solicitud y sin mucho riesgo, me deparase el cielo alguna ínsula, o otra cosa semejante, no soy tan necio que la desechase. (65)

In a conversation with his wife Teresa (Part II, Chapter V), Sancho manifests once again his complete trust in God's plan for his life:

> Llegó Sancho a su casa tan regocijado y alegre, que su mujer conoció su alegría a tiro de ballesta; tanto, que la obligó a preguntarle:
> —¿Qué traéis, Sancho amigo, que tan alegre venís?
> A lo que él respondió:
> —Mujer mía, si Dios quisiera, bien me holgara yo de no estar tan contento como muestro. (67)

Chapter Six

Sancho's invocation of God also serves as a linguistic strategy because it emphasizes the sincerity of the guilt the squire feels that he prefers to accompany Don Quixote on another sally to staying at home with his wife. Teresa is unable to understand Sancho's nuanced explanation, but she does recognize the contradictory nature of her husband's words: "No os entiendo, marido —replicó ella—, y no sé qué queréis decir en eso de que os holgáredes, si Dios quisiera, de no estar contento; que, maguer tonta, no sé yo quién recibe gusto de no tenerle" (67). Then, Sancho defends his decision to serve Don Quixote, arguing that God would have provided what he and his family needed if He wanted the squire to stay home:

> Y si Dios quisiera darme de comer a pie enjuto y en mi casa, sin traerme por vericuetos y encrucijadas, pues lo podía hacer a poca costa y no más de quererlo, claro está que mi alegría fuera más firme y valedera, pues que la que tengo va mezclada con la tristeza de dejarte; así que, dije bien que holgara, si Dios quisiera, de no estar contento. (68)

Sancho's deference to God's will may appear to be nothing more than a peasant fatalism, but I believe that it reflects a deliberately cultivated spirituality that manifests itself early in the novel, and evidence of which includes Sancho's attendance at Mass before he became his neighbor's squire.[8] In Part I, Chapter XXXI and in Part II, Chapter XX, Sancho addresses the village priest's homilies.

In the *Spiritual Exercises*, Ignatius warns the retreatant against an unhealthy trust in God, which, when extreme, diminishes a person's ability to exercise his or her free will:

> Asimismo no debemos hablar tan largo instando tanto en la gracia, que se engendre veneno para quitar la libertad. De manera que de la fé y gracia se puede hablar quanto sea posible mediante el auxilio divino para mayor alabanza de la Su Divina Majestad: mas no por tal suerte, ni por tales modos, mayormente en nuestros tiempos tan periculosos que las obras y libero arbitrio resciban detrimento alguno, ó por *nihilo* se tengan. (*Ejercicios* 173–74; author's italics)

In Part II, Chapter LIII, Sancho exercises his free will in a productive manner, however, when he chooses to abandon his governorship and return to the life he believes God created him to live:

> —Abrid camino, señores míos, y dejadme volver a mi antigua libertad; dejadme que vaya a buscar la vida pasada, para que me resucite de esta muerte presente. Yo no nací para ser gobernador, ni para defender ínsulas ni ciudades de los enemigos que quisieren acometerlas. Mejor se me entiende a mí de arar y cavar, podar y ensarmentar las viñas, que de dar leyes ni de defender provincias ni reinos. Bien se está San Pedro en Roma: quiero decir, que bien se está cada uno usando el oficio para que fue nacido.[9] Mejor me está a mí una hoz en la mano que un cetro de gobernador; más quiero hartarme de gazpachos que estar sujeto a la miseria de un médico impertinente que me mate de hambre; y más quiero recostarme a la sombra de una encina en el verano y arroparme con un zamarro de dos pelos en el invierno, en mi libertad, que acostarme con la sujeción del gobierno entre sábanas de holanda y vestirme de martas cebollinas. (474)

Sancho's decision to eschew social standing in favor of what he perceives to be God's plan for his life implies the squire's conscious awareness of moral responsibility: "This is not only shown in his homiletic discourses but also in his acts, particularly in the readiness that he shows, before the governorship and during it, to renounce his 'island' should climbing the social ladder endanger the salvation of his soul" (Close 355). This decision, when compared to Sancho's attitude in Part I, especially in Chapters X and XXXI, seems to illustrate his spiritual maturation.[10] Before Sancho departs, the steward cites Sancho's spirituality as one of the reasons he should stay: "que su ingenio y su cristiano proceder obligan a desearle" (475). The irony of the steward's comment within the context of the charade is evident, but Sancho's disposition of the cases suggests to the reader that the squire may not be a victim of irony after all.

Castro notes that Cervantes values the virtues that Jesus shares with His disciples in the Sermon on the Mount: "Entre las virtudes cristianas, las que más destacan, las que sin duda pone Cervantes en primer plano, por entender que son la base de la armonía de amor predicada en el Evangelio, son la humildad y la caridad" (*El pensamiento* 299).[11] Sancho exemplifies Cervantine humility and charity in Part II, Chapter XI, when he informs Don Quixote that he will not attack the demon dancer who beats Sancho's donkey with the bladders inflated with air:

> —No hay para qué, señor —respondió Sancho—, tomar venganza de nadie, pues no es de buenos cristianos tomarla de los agravios; cuanto más que yo acabaré con mi asno que ponga su ofensa en las manos de mi voluntad, la cual es de vivir pacíficamente los días que los cielos me dieren de vida. (120)

Don Quixote seems to experience somewhat of a transformation after listening to Sancho's words, as the knight no longer encourages his squire to attack the demon dancer. Instead, Don Quixote notes Sancho's charity and humility, perhaps facetiously, calling his squire in Part II, Chapter XI, "Sancho bueno, Sancho discreto, Sancho cristiano y Sancho sincero" (120). The knight's choice of these words—good, discreet, Christian, sincere—is the subject of much debate. Allen is insistent in his belief that these words cannot be interpreted in any other way than as Cervantine irony:

> If they are not wholly ironic, Don Quijote's words are not acceptable as simply naïve. As expressions of ingenuous naiveté they are incoherent, the words strangely chosen. To stress that Sancho's reply is "*sincere*," to single out, underline, and praise his *sincerity* is inexplicable in any sort of naïve response. If Cervantes has chosen to have Don Quijote characterize Sancho here with four emphasized adjectives, adjectives that he, Cervantes, or we, were we in his place, might well have chosen to use ironically with Sancho in this context, our assumption has to be that he knew what he was about. Selected to contribute to an ironic effort, each of these particular words makes a contribution to the effect. ("The Importance of Being an Ironist" 438; author's italics)

In the same article, however, Allen acknowledges that Anthony Close and Ruth El Saffar do not consider the knight's words to be ironic ("Importance" 440).[12] I submit for consideration that Don Quixote's description of Sancho does not necessarily have to be interpreted as ironic if understood within the context of the squire's intellectual and moral development.[13] In addition, as early as Part I, Chapter XV, Sancho cites his religious beliefs as the reason he will not fight:

> —Señor, yo soy hombre pacífico, manso, sosegado, y sé disimular cualquiera injuria, porque tengo mujer e hijos que sustentar y criar. Así, que séale a vuestra merced también aviso (pues no puede ser mandato) que en ninguna manera pondré mano a la

> espada, ni contra villano ni contra caballero; y que, desde aquí
> para delante de Dios, perdono cuantos agravios me han hecho
> y han de hacer, ora me los haya hecho, o haga, o haya de hacer,
> persona alta o baja, rico o pobre, hidalgo o pechero, sin exceptar
> estado ni condición alguna. (232)

Ironically, the squire's religious beliefs are the reason he volunteers to help Don Quixote slay the pagan Alifanfarón, who is in love with the daughter of Pentapolín, a Christian who refuses to accept Alifanfarón unless he renounces his faith in Muhammad and converts to Christianity. Sancho's eagerness to defend his faith and refusal to fight for a secular cause (e.g., demon dancer and Galicians, respectively) are not lost on Don Quixote, whose description of the squire as good, discreet, Christian, and sincere may denote, I propose, the knight's admiration of Sancho's incarnational faith. Furthermore, Sancho's willingness to fight only if his faith is threatened underscores Cervantes's commitment to Catholicism and evinces his defense of it at Lepanto. Sancho's humane treatment of Ricote, a Moor who was Sancho's neighbor until Felipe III's expulsion of the *moriscos*, in Part II, Chapter LIV not only ameliorates Cervantes's characterization of him as an enemy of the Moors in Part I but also exemplifies the evolution of Cervantes's attitude toward their presence in Spain.

Sancho displays concern for the plight of the poor when he assumes the governorship of his island: "Hizo y creó un alguacil de pobres, no para que los persiguiese, sino para que los examinase si lo eran, porque a la sombra de la manquedad fingida y de la llaga falsa andan los brazos ladrones y la salud borracha" (II, 460).[14] Sancho's appointment of an overseer for the poor is not whimsical in the least, as it reflects the reality of Spanish society during the sixteenth century. The economic crises created a class of poor people, as well as a faction of people who pretended to be poor. Dominican priest and theologian Domingo de Soto (1494–1560) was very much in favor of the right of the poor to beg, and he places their welfare ahead of the contemptuous behavior of the false beggars:

> [Q]ue en duda si uno es pobre o no, antes en favor de
> la pobreza se ha de aprobar por pobre que en favor de la
> justicia reprobarse por no pobre. Porque mayor daño y
> mayor crueldad será que a vuelta de veinte fingidos pobres

> se excluyesen cuatro verdaderos, que será injusticia por no hacer injuria a cuatro verdaderos sufrir que hubiese veinte fingidos.[15] (Cruz 24–25)

Cristóbal Pérez de Herrera (1558–1620), a royal physician whose military service as a doctor on Spain's galleys inspired him to dedicate his life to ministering to the poor and downtrodden, aims to rid Spain of false beggars, vagabonds, law breakers, and others of the same ilk he describes as "ladrones de la caridad y limosna Cristiana" (Pérez de Herrera xiii) in his book *Discursos del amparo de los legítimos pobres* (1598). He provides several examples of ways in which false beggars attempted to practice their craft, including parents who blind their children, beggars who pay a mother to rent her newborn for the day, and a man who beat his own children if they did not bring him the amount of alms he expected each night. Pérez de Herrera stipulates that each house he proposes be built to shelter the poor has a supervisor.[16] Sancho's appointment of an overseer of the poor, an action that removes the burden from the individual and places it on the state, denotes his concern for the well-being of society as a whole and not only the welfare of a few individuals. Don Quixote also appears to recognize Sancho's spirituality, as the following exchange between the knight and the squire in Part II, Chapter XX illustrates:

> —A buena fe, señor —respondió Sancho—, que no hay que fiar en la descarnada, digo, en la muerte, la cual también come cordero como carnero; y a nuestro cura he oído decir que con igual pie pisaba las altas torres de los reyes como las humildes chozas de los pobres.[17] Tiene esta señora más de poder que de melindre; no es nada asquerosa: de todo come y a todo hace, y de toda suerte de gentes, edades y preeminencias hinche sus alforjas. No es segador que duerme las siestas; que a todas horas siega, y corta así la seca como la verde yerba, y no parece que masca, sino que engulle y traga cuanto se le pone delante, porque tiene hambre canina, que nunca se harta; y aunque no tiene barriga, da a entender que está hidrópica y sedienta de beber solas las vidas de cuantos viven, como quien se bebe un jarro de agua fría.[18]
> —No más, Sancho —dijo a este punto don Quijote—. Tente en buenas, y no te dejes caer, que en verdad que lo que has dicho de la muerte por tus rústicos términos es lo que pudiera decir un buen predicador. Dígote, Sancho que si como tienes

> buen natural y discreción, pudieras tomar un púlpito en la mano e irte por ese mundo predicando lindezas.
> —Bien predica quien bien vive —respondió Sancho—, y yo no sé otras tologías. (201–02)

Sancho's practice of the Christian virtues of charity and humility suggest the squire's willingness to respond to Christ's call from the Sermon on the Mount to be "perfect just as His Father is perfect." Furthermore, the Church's doctrine of solidarity informs the decisions he makes. Pérez de Herrera concludes his speeches with an exhortation that King Philip II implement his recommendations because if Spain's mendicants are able to live a productive lifestyle, "todo será de aquí adelante próspero y abundante" (Pérez de Herrera 72).

Sancho Panza's pragmatic yet whimsical character is one of the many reasons *Don Quixote* continues to fascinate scholars and non-scholars alike. The reader learns early in the novel that Sancho's character is neither static nor one-dimensional. While Sancho's ingenuity, guile, and intellect become more apparent to the reader, the squire's spiritual acumen provides another dimension to his unpredictable behavior. His penchant for divine succor and guidance may be viewed within the context of an Ignatian awareness of God's presence in his daily life:

> En toda buena eleccion, y en cuanto es de nuestra parte, el ojo de nuestra intencion debe ser simple, solamente mirando para lo que soy criado; es á saber, para alabanza de Dios Nuestro Señor y salvacion de mi ánima. Y así, cualquier cosa que eligiere, debe ser á que me ayude para el fin que soy criado, no ordenando ni trayendo el fin al medio, mas el medio al fin. (Loyola, *Ejercicios* 76)

This incarnational view of the world differs from Erasmus, who rejected any spirituality based on finding Christ in physical or material forms. Furthermore, Erasmus, unlike Ignatius, does not necessarily see everything in this world as a means to an end:

> De igual modo, el vulgo de los hombres sienten la mayor admiración por las cosas puramente corporales, y casi piensan que son lo único que existe. Por el contrario, los hombres piadosos lo que más desprecian es lo que está más relacionado con el cuerpo y se entregan por entero a

> la contemplación de las cosas invisibles. Así pues, los unos conceden el primer papel a las riquezas, después a las comodidades corporales, y relegan el alma al último lugar, que la mayoría ni siquiera creen que exista, porque no llega a verse con los ojos. (Vilanova, "Erasmo, Sancho Panza y su amigo Don Quijote" 49)

I believe it is worth remembering that Sancho facilitates, however, Don Quixote's madness often throughout the novel for personal gain. Unlike Sansón Carrasco, who participates in Don Quixote's adventures in Part II for his own amusement from the moment he meets the knight in Chapter III until the end of the novel, Sancho's relationship with his friend and neighbor evolves.[19] The squire, in tears, pleads that Don Quixote, near death, does not succumb, and although at this point in the novel he is no longer a squire to a knight, he recognizes that only the essence of the knight's existence could possibly save him: "quizá tras de alguna mata hallaremos a la señora doña Dulcinea desencantada, que no haya más que ver" (636).[20] Sancho's dream to live out the rest of his days as the governor of an island does not come to fruition, but his adventures with Don Quixote are not meaningless. The physical journey Sancho undertakes unleashes a metaphorical journey of the soul along which the squire recognizes the presence of God in the people, places, and things of everyday life.

Conclusion

The Cervantine criticism I discuss in this book clearly illustrates the degree to which perspectivism influences conclusions about spirituality in *Don Quixote*. Although we, the readers, accompany the knight throughout *Don Quixote* in different ways—spiritually, emotionally, and mentally—, in the end we reach different conclusions. Lowry Nelson attributes this hermeneutic to Cervantes's universal irony:

> Universal ironists contemplate the world with a kind of gentle resignation and compassion in full knowledge of both the grandeurs and miseries of human life. ... It is he who can encompass a broader span of human types and human experiences. It is he who can best present the inviolability and unique essence of the particular and the individual. It is precisely this ability ... to create particularized essence that leads us ... to draw the general conclusion to see the individual as representative. Hence, the seeming plenitude of humanity we find in such odd and peculiar figures as Don Quixote and Sancho Panza, not to mention Sansón Carrasco, the curate, Marcela, Ginés de Pasamonte, and others. (10)

If we underestimate the novel's interpretative malleability, Cervantes's literary techniques, especially his satire of the romances of chivalry, may lead us to interpret the nuances in the novel as subversion of the faith. We are unable to depend on the narrator to guide us throughout the novel, for example, because unlike the episode with the windmills, the narrator does not explicitly name the signifiers all of the time. In addition, Sancho, whom we can count on at the beginning of the novel, is not as dependable later on, especially when he negates reality for personal gain.[1] The

Conclusion

fine line between illusion and reality that the reader negotiates throughout the novel is further blurred by the multiplicity of religious identities, especially the diversity of Catholicism, in Golden Age Spain:

> Cervantes incorpora a Don Quijote todo el sentido cristiano de los libros de caballerías. El caballero andante del Gótico es un Cristo; sus hazañas resultan grotescamente pueriles en el Barroco; pero su espíritu, su anhelo, su consumirse tras un ideal, su aspiración heroica, son semejantes a los sentimientos de la época de Cervantes. Todo el problema reside en darse cuenta de cómo esa vida espiritual encarnada en franciscanos y dominicos, en los cruzados y las órdenes militares, con su fondo de conventos, catedrales y castillos; con su horizonte lejano de Tierra Santa—concretización de la distancia infinita—, se transvasa a la Contrarreforma, el Oratorio, a los humanistas y jesuitas, llenos de la sabiduría de Grecia y Roma, viendo surgir ese imponente e inmenso edificio de la Razón—crítica, matemática, ciencias de la Naturaleza, astronomía—, queriendo desconcretizar la lejanía de Tierra Santa y revelar todo su sentido espiritual. (Casalduero, *Sentido y forma* 72)

If we take into account, however, the events of Cervantes's life, the socio-political milieu of Golden Age Spain, especially the diversity of early modern Catholicism, and Cervantes's literary proclivities, I believe that the mocking and ironic tone of Cervantine spirituality in *Don Quixote* defines Cervantes neither as an author who subverts Catholicism nor affirms it. The theological prisms through which I present my reading of *Don Quixote*—moral theology, Ignatian spirituality, particularly the contemplative in action and incarnational spirituality, the Catholic Church's anthropological vision, and Christian Humanism—suggest instead that when the totality of biographical and socio-historical events and influences that shaped Cervantes's religiosity are considered, the result is a new appreciation of *Don Quixote*'s moral didactic and spiritual orientation.

Notes

Introduction

1. Dates following a person's name refer to birth and death; the names of kings and popes are followed by the dates of reign.

2. Forcione also addresses Cervantes's literary style as it pertains to the Christian themes in his literature: "The variety and inconsistency that mark Cervantes's works dealing with Christian themes attest to an informing religious sensibility that is concerned but restless, one that is capable of experiencing the mysteries of spiritual exaltation and despair, of remorse in sinfulness and joy in righteousness, one that is vitally concerned with the great existential questions that traditionally had been answered by theological systems of thought and eager to explore fearlessly the suitability and the unsuitability of the orthodox answers. While there is very little in Cervantes's writing that can be construed in a strict sense as atheistic or heterodox, it is certainly wrong to describe his religious mentality as strictly orthodox. But it is just as wrong to classify him as a totally secular writer because a strong vein of criticism is visible in much of his writing and because his greatest work is focused almost exclusively on the 'marvelous' desires and disappointments of man living in this unmiraculous, desacralized world" (353).

3. While the focus of my study is a textual analysis of *Don Quixote*, I refer the reader to the scholarship that relates to the complex historical and theological context of the time throughout the book.

Chapter One

1. *Bachiller* is the title earned by a person who graduated from college. All translations are mine unless noted otherwise.

2. While the exact date of Cervantes's birth is unknown, most critics, including Fernández Álvarez (24) and Mancing (Don Quixote 1), cite the custom of naming a child for his or her saint's day as evidence that the date of Cervantes's birth is September 29. St. Michael, in addition to combatting Satan, escorts the faithful to heaven at the time of their death, protects all Christians and the Church itself, and calls the faithful to their heavenly judgment.

3. The Third Order of St. Francis consists of vowed and lay members, including married men and women. St. Francis established the Third Order for men and women who were not able to take the habit of the First or Second Order because of their state of life.

4. Members of the Brotherhood of the Slaves of the Most Holy Brotherhood were required to wear a scapular, practice fasting and abstinence on prescribed days, pray the Liturgy of the Hours throughout the day, visit hospitals, and live a simple life.

5. Cervantes's most well-known play is *El cerco de Numancia*. The valor of the inhabitants of this Celtiberian city against the invading Romans in 133

BC inspired Spaniards centuries later who defended Spain against foreign threats.

6. Erasmus was also a priest, ordained in 1492.

7. Cervantes's sojourn in Rome inspired him to write a beautiful sonnet about the Eternal City that appears in *Los trabajos de Persiles y Sigismunda* (1617). One of the pilgrims who visits Rome recites the poem, a part of which reads: "La tierra de tu suelo, que contemplo / Con la sangre de mártires mezclada, / Es la reliquia universal del suelo. / No hay parte en tí que no sirva de ejemplo / De santidad, así como trazada / De la ciudad de Dios al gran modelo" (*Los trabajos* 435).

8. An excellent study of the interpolated stories is Edwin Williamson's "Romance and Realism." See Works Cited.

9. Cervantes writes these words in response to Avellaneda's attack on Cervantes's character in the prologue to Avellaneda's spurious Part II (1614). Even though Avellaneda's tome is not a focus of my study, I note its treatment of Catholicism wherever appropriate to provide the reader with a different perspective (Spanish citations, Martín de Riquer). I do not believe this information can illuminate our understanding of Cervantes's Catholicism, however, because its source is an anonymous author of an apocryphal publication. Many critics have written about the numerous differences between Avellaneda's false Part II and Cervantes's Part II, including Tom Lathrop, "Cervantes's Treatment of the False *Quijote*;" Edward T. Aylward, *Toward a Revaluation of Avellaneda's False "Quijote;"* and Howard Mancing, *The Cervantes Encyclopedia, A–K*. Quotations from *Don Quixote* are taken from the edition of John Jay Allen.

10. Cervantes writes about his captivity in Part I, Chapters XXXIX–XLI. In the interpolated story of *The Captive's Tale*, Arnaut Mamí takes Ruy Pérez de Viedma prisoner and makes him his slave. Dalí Mamí, whose nickname was *El Cojo* (The Cripple) was Cervantes's first owner in Algiers and later sold him to Hassan Pasha, the king of Algiers, ca. 1577.

11. Garcés also notes that the total number of Spanish captives in Algiers at the end of the sixteenth century was nearly the equivalent of ten percent of the population of the Crown of Castile during the same time period.

12. According to one witness, the inhabitants of Algiers lived a care-free existence: "All they do is eat, drink, and make merry" (Canavaggio 78). Captives, like Cervantes, of course, did not enjoy Algiers' festive ambience. Cervantes mediates his impression of the city in *Los trabajos de Persiles y Sigismunda* through a character who is a captive: "Ésta, señores, que aquí veis pintada, es la ciudad de Argel, gomia y tarasca de todas las riberas del mar Mediterráneo, puesto universal de cosarios, y amparo y refugio de ladrones, que, deste pequeñuelo puerto que aquí va pintado, salen con sus bajeles a inquietar el mundo, pues se atreven a pasar el *plus ultra* de las colunas de Hércules, y a acometer y robar las apartadas islas, que, por estar rodeadas del inmenso mar Océano, pensaban estar seguras, a lo menos de los bajeles turquescos" (332; author's italics).

13. The following examples are representative of Cervantes's invective language. In Part I, Chapter IX of *Don Quixote*, Cervantes writes that the veracity of Cide Hamete Benengeli's manuscript could be suspect because of its Arabic author, "siendo muy propio de los de aquella nación ser mentirosos; aunque, por ser tan nuestros enemigos, antes se puede entender haber quedado falto en ella que demasiado" (182). In the play *Los baños de Argel* (1615), the sacristan Tristán rebukes young Moors who make fun of him with invective language: "¡Oh hijo de una puta, / nieto de un gran cornudo, / sobrino de un bellaco, / hermano de un gran traidor y sodomita!" (Cervantes, *Teatro completo*, 228). Armando Cotarelo believes that Cervantes wrote *Los baños de Argel* near the end of his life, perhaps a year or two before its publication in *Ocho comedias y ocho entremeses, nunca representados* (1615). Rodolfo Schevill and Adolfo Bonilla place the date of composition closer to the beginning of Cervantes's career as a playwright (1580s). If Schevill and Bonilla are correct, the acrimonious tone of Tristán's language may be indicative of Cervantes's sentiments toward Muslims in the years immediately following his captivity. (See Márquez Villanueva, *Personajes y temas del Quijote* 58–59n20)

14. According to the Council of Trent (Session VII, Canon 5, 1547), "If anyone says that baptism is optional, that is, not necessary for salvation, let him be anathema" (*The Canons and Decrees of the Council of Trent* 85).

15. In a ceremony on June 11, 2015, Elena Fernández de Velasco Hernández, the mayor of Esquivias, bestowed on Miguel de Cervantes the honorary title Adopted Son and on Catalina de Salazar y Palacios the title of Favorite Daughter.

16. Excommunication is a spiritual penalty that prohibits the excommunicant from receiving all of the Sacraments except the Sacrament of Penance. The Seven Sacraments are Baptism, Penance, First Communion (Eucharist), Confirmation, Marriage, Holy Orders, and Anointing of the Sick.

17. The Trinitarians procured the ransom and negotiated Cervantes's freedom from captivity in 1580. Cervantes's mother, Leonor de Cortinas (1520–93), who made many sacrifices to free Miguel and his brother Rodrigo from captivity, paid Fray Juan Gil (1535–1604), who was the attorney general of the Order of Trinity, two hundred fifty ducats for her sons' ransom. Cervantes's sister, Andrea de Cervantes, contributed fifty ducats. Cervantes believed that he owed his life to this order, whose nuns arranged for him to be buried on the grounds of their convent, and, in particular, to Fray Juan Gil, who Cervantes immortalizes in the fourth act of *El trato de Argel* (1582). The captives in this play, like Cervantes in real life, are liberated from captivity by a Trinitarian named Fray Juan Gil. Cervantes was buried in the habit of a Trinitarian Third Order. In 2015, archaeologists and forensic anthropologists located what are believed to be Cervantes's remains in a splintered wooden coffin with the initials M.C. A formal burial of Cervantes's remains occurred on June 11, 2015. For a more detailed account of Fray Juan Gil's role in the negotiations, see Garcés, *Cervantes in Algiers* 107–10.

18. Today, Extreme Unction is known as the Anointing of the Sick. The Sacrament of Anointing of the Sick may be administered to a person who is seriously ill or close to death. The *Catechism of the Council of Trent* refers to it as the Sacrament of Extreme Unction, "because among all the unctions prescribed by Our Lord to His Church, this is the last to be administered" (369). The Sacrament of Anointing of the Sick is different from Last Rites, which today consists of *viaticum*, the Prayer of Commendation of the Dying, and the Prayers for the Dead.

19. Swiss historian Jacob Burckhardt, on the other hand, views the humanist spirit of the Middle Ages quite differently: "In the Middle Ages both sides of human consciousness—that which was turned within as that which was turned without—lay dreaming or halfawake beneath a common veil. The veil was woven of faith, illusion, and childish prepossession, through which the world and history were seen clad in strange hues. Man was conscious of himself only as a member of a race, people, party, family, or corporation—only through some general category" (98).

20. In a letter to Fr. Luis González de Cámara (1520–75), Ignatius describes how he composed the *Exercises*: "Yo no compuse los *Ejercicios* todo de una sola vez. Cuando cualquier cosa resultante de mi propia experiencia me parecía que podía ser de utilidad a otros, tomaba nota de ello" (Roca 22). Ignatius wrote the first draft of the *Spiritual Exercises* in summary form at Manresa in 1522; the earliest extant version is the autograph copy that Ignatius left when he died in 1556. It was not until 1548, however, after Pope Paul III approved the *Spiritual Exercises*, that they appeared as we know them today.

21. Cervantes's formative years transpired during a time in which the Sacrament of Confession was a staple of Spanish society: "Spaniards participated in the sacrament of penance from their youth. They discussed it in church, on the streets, and at home. They understood, with a perspective born of experience and necessity, the ins and outs of confession" (O'Banion 11).

22. Session XIV, Canon 13 (1551).

23. The four sets of mysteries are the Joyful (prayed on Mondays and Saturdays), Sorrowful (Tuesdays and Fridays), Glorious (Wednesdays and Sundays), and Luminous (Thursdays). St. John Paul II introduced the Luminous mysteries in his Apostolic Letter *Rosarium Virginis Mariae* (2002). Each mystery centers on five events from the life of Jesus. The faithful contemplate on one of the five events as they pray the Hail Mary ten times, keeping count with each of the beads. For example, the Glorious Mysteries begin with the Resurrection of Jesus.

24. Erasmus writes in the *Adagia* (1500), an extensive annotated collection of Greek and Latin proverbs: "If you remain on the surface, a thing may sometimes appear absurd; if you pierce through to the spiritual meaning, you will adore the divine wisdom" (Phillips 82).

25. Erasmus refused Cardinal Cisneros's invitation: "Non placet Hispania" ("I do not like Spain").

26. Erasmus's anti-monastic views were not an indictment of Francis or the other founders of the mendicant orders, whose ascetic lifestyle he admired. The hypocrisy and impiousness of the friars of these orders, however, were the target of his sardonic criticisms: "He is a very good Son of St. *Francis,* who does not disdain to wear an Ash-colour'd Habit, and a Canvas Girdle; but compare their Lives, and nothing can be more disagreeable: I speak of a great many, but not of all. And this may be carried thro' all Orders and Professions. A preposterous Confidence springs from an erroneous Judgment, and from them both, preposterous Scandals. Let but a *Franciscan* go out of Doors with a Leather Girdle, if he has chanc'd to lose his Rope; or an *Augustine* with a Woollen one, or one that uses to wear a Girdle without one; what an Abomination would it be accounted? What Danger is there, that if some Women should see this, they would miscarry! And from such Trifles as these, how is brotherly Charity broke in upon! what bitter Envyings, how virulent Slanderings! The Lord exclaims against these in the Gospel, and so does *Paul* vehemently, and so ought Divines and Preachers to do" (*The Colloquies,* vol. II 97; italics are Erasmus's). In 1529, Erasmus wrote a letter to the Swiss theologian Johann Von Botzheim in which he names several monks, including the Dominican prior Laurens Laurensen. Erasmus describes Laurensen's vitriolic sermons as "Old Comedy, for it seemed as though he had smeared himself with dirt and was speaking from a cart rather than proclaiming the message of the gospel from the sacred pulpit" (*The Correspondence of Erasmus* 10). In the same letter, Erasmus writes that the Franciscans first removed his books from their libraries and then attacked his reputation in public lectures (12).

27. The Inquisition's Index of prohibited books condemned Erasmus's publications, beginning in 1551 with his *Colloquies.* Fourteen more works, including the *Enchiridion,* appeared on the Index of 1559. The Index of 1612 prohibited all of Erasmus's publications in Spanish and declared him an *auctor damnatus* (Kamen 126).

28. St. Teresa's mother, Beatriz de Ahumada y Cuevas (1495–1529), was an avid reader of chivalric tales: "Era aficionada a libros de caballería, y no tan mal tomaba este pensamiento como yo le tomé para mí, porque no perdía su labor … y por ventura lo hacía para no pensar en grandes trabajos que tenia, y ocupar sus hijos, que no anduviesen en otras cosas perdidos" (*El libro de la vida* 4).

29. "En este tiempo me dieron las Confesiones de San Agustín, que parece el Señor lo ordenó, porque yo no las procuré ni nunca las había visto. Yo soy muy aficionada a San Agustín, porque el monasterio adonde estuve seglar era de su Orden; y también por haber sido pecador, que en los santos que después de serlo el Señor tornó a Sí, hallaba yo mucho consuelo, pareciéndome en ellos había de hallar ayuda y que, como los había el Señor perdonado, podía hacer a mí; salvo que una cosa me desconsolaba, como he dicho: que a ellos sólo una vez los había el Señor llamado, y no tornaban a caer, y a mí eran ya tantas, que esto me fatigaba. Mas considerando en el amor que me tenía, tornaba a animarme,

que de su misericordia jamás desconfié; de mí muchas veces ... Como comencé a leer las Confesiones, paréceme me vía yo allí; comencé a encomendarme mucho a este glorioso Santo. Cuando llegué a su conversión y leí cómo oyó aquella voz en el Huerto, no me parece sino que el Señor me la dio a mí, según sintió mi corazón" (*El libro de la vida* 51).

30. Teresian spirituality consists of many characteristics. First, in all of St. Teresa's writings, she describes in vivid detail how God is active in her life. She writes in *El castillo interior* that God, for example, can always be found within us, especially if we cannot find Him outside of the "castillo." A second characteristic is her belief that the mystical union of the soul with God is for everyone and should be viewed as a way to teach others about God. Mutual support was also a key characteristic of St. Teresa's spirituality, for she believed that everyone needed to walk with others on their spiritual journey. Even though she encouraged her followers to master the inner world, she recognized the importance of the communal experience. A fourth characteristic of Teresian spirituality is her devotion to the humanity of Christ. She reminds us in *El castillo interior* that it is important not to avert the corporal aspects of Christ in favor of only the spiritual: "Creo queda dado a entender lo que conviene, por espirituales que sean, no huir tanto de cosas corpóreas que les parezca aún hace daño la Humanidad sacratísima" (Molins 62). The fifth characteristic of St. Teresa's spirituality is the vivid descriptions and accounts of the spiritual journey.

31. The Spanish soldiers who fought alongside Ignatius wanted to surrender to save their lives, but Ignatius convinced the commander to defend the fortress. Ignatius's courage inspired the other soldiers to remain in the battle, but they surrendered soon after Ignatius's injury.

32. *Flos Sanctorum* is a book about the life of Jesus and the saints. Alonso de Villegas (1533–1603) translated it from Latin to Spanish in 1588. This book figures prominently into the religiosity of Avellaneda's Don Quixote, who in Chapter I informs Sancho about it: "Este libro trata de las vidas de los santos, como de San Lorenço, que fue asado; de San Bartolomé, que fue dessollado; de Santa Catalina, que fue passada por la rueda de las navajas, y assímismo de todos los demás santos y mártyres de todo el año. Siéntate, y leerte he la vida del santo que oy, a veynte de agosto, celebra la Iglesia, que es san Bernardo" (24). Based on the many references to Catholicism, dogma, the saints, and the Church, it is reasonable to conclude that Avellaneda was a member of the clergy, or, at the very least, a devoted and practicing Catholic. Four authors who meet this criterion because they were priests are Lope de Vega (1562–1635), Tirso de Molina (1579–1648), Fray Luis de Aliaga (1555–1626), and Pedro Líñan de Riaza (ca. 1556–1607). If Lope had been Avellaneda, Part II of *Don Quixote* would not have been the first work of literature he appropriated; he continued Ariosto's Angelica, and he wrote his own version of Sanazzaro's *Arcadia* (1504). While Lope's sincere desire to change his life was noble, he continued his sordid behavior after ordination. In 1616, two years after his ordination, Lope fell in love with Marta de Nevares, who was Lope's lover until her death in 1632. Lope often based female characters on the women in his life. For example, Marta de Nevares appears as Amarilis in the autobiographical eclogue *Amarilis* (1633) and Marcia Leonarda in *Novelas a Marcia Leonarda* (1621, 1624).

33. The act of reading also inspires Alonso Quijano to uproot his life. Ignatius, however, never regrets the path he followed, although the life of the flesh that he lived before his conversion was anathema to him.

34. Pope Benedict XV declared Our Lady of Aránzazu the patron saint of Guipúzcoa in 1918; Ignatius is also the patron saint of Guipúzcoa.

35. In a similar episode, Don Quixote must also decide how to proceed when he arrives to a four-way crossroads in Part I, Chapter IV. The knight also drops the reins, ceding the decision to Rocinante. In this scene, however, the knight appears to emulate what other knights-errant do in the books he read.

36. Ignatius lived in a room at the Luis de Antezana Hospital in Alcalá de Henares. One night, he felt the presence of enemy spirits. Immediately, Ignatius, commending his life to God's protection, challenged the spirits to attack him. Pedro de Rivadeneira notes that not only did Ignatius conquer the spirits he encountered that night, but the courage he demonstrated provided him with the spiritual strength to defeat Satan or any enemy spirits that dared attack him again (549). In Part I, Chapter XXXV, Don Quixote illustrates his valor when he attacks a "giant," who is the enemy of Princess Micomicona. The "giant" against whom the brave knight battles is a collection of wineskins.

37. The large number of Jesuits at the time of Ignatius's death included New Christians or *conversos*, Jews who transitioned from Judaism to Christianity, and *moriscos*, Christians of Muslim ancestry in Spain. Ignatius insisted that New Christians be accepted into the Society of Jesus immediately. According to John O'Malley, Ignatius expressed a desire to be of Jewish blood so that he could belong to the same race as Jesus Christ (*The First Jesuits* 190).

38. The biographical sketch of Ignatius presented here is based on Norman O'Neal's biography of the saint, *The Life of St. Ignatius of Loyola*. The years that appear after a pope's name refer to his tenure as the Vicar of Christ.

39. Rafael Lapesa called St. Ignatius a "caballero a lo divino" (195).

40. The title of the English edition, which first appeared in London in 1755, is *The Spiritual Quixote; or, the Entertaining Story of Don Ignatius Loyola, Founder of the Order of the Jesuits*.

41. The source of Unamuno's information about Ignatius's life is Pedro de Rivadeneira's biography *Vida del bienaventurado padre Ignacio de Loyola* (1583).

42. The *Spiritual Exercises* is a thirty-day retreat, divided into four weeks. There are four Contemplations on the first day of the second week.

43. Bradley J. Nelson defines this experience as *presence*, whose effects, he asserts, are "a primary indicator of the social and political functions of literary practices in early modern Spain" (4).

44. Jon Whitman describes an emblem as a "miniature form of allegory" (388) because its singular image conveys more than what it represents. An example of an extended allegory is Plato's *The Allegory of the Cave*.

45. Álvarez notes that Bernardino Daza translates "Insani Gladius" as "La espada en la mano del loco" in his Spanish translation of Alciato's *Emblematum Liber* (151). The text of Emblem 176 reads: "Ajax was standing, sword in hand, in the midst of a bristly / herd, convinced that his sword was felling in its slaughter / the descendants of Tantalus. So such a victim as a pig paid / the penalty in the place of Laertes' son and the nobility. / Fury does not know how to confront its enemies: its blows / fall wide and, lacking any plan, it rushes to its ruin" (Alciato 203).

46. Temperance, prudence, justice, and fortitude are the four cardinal, or moral, virtues in the Catholic Church.

47. The Parisian method consisted of heavy emphasis on the humanities, an orderly system of pursuing successive knowledge, repetition of material, and active involvement of the students in their own education through argumentation, discussion, and competition. The students who studied at Jesuit schools were active learners, who, for example, composed and delivered speeches as a means to study literature. They studied drama by performing it, often with music and dance. Learning, however, was not confined to the classroom. Ignatius believed that knowledge could be shared and obtained through informal conversations as well, and perhaps even more so in this way, because knowledge enabled a person to grow in his or her relationship with God and to live a life based on the teachings of Jesus. This philosophy is perhaps best expressed by the Jesuit author and hagiologist Pedro Ribadeneira (1527–1611), who in a letter to King Philip II wrote, "y que todo el bien de la cristiandad y de todo el mundo depende de la buena institución de la juventud" (Lange Cruz 108). Alfonso de Polanco (1517–76), who was executive secretary of the Society of Jesus from 1547–72, also emphasized the mission to promote the common good: "Los que ahora son solamente estudiantes serán de mayores párrocos, funcionarios públicos, administradores de justicia y cubrirán otros puestos importantes para el provecho y ventaja de todos" (Lange Cruz 106).

48. Session XIII, Chapter 5 (1551). Pope Paul III (1534–49) convened the first session of the Council of Trent in December of 1545, and Popes Julius III (1550–55) and Pius IV (1559–65) presided over the Second (1551–52) and Third (1562–63) sessions, respectively.

49. Cervantes must have witnessed many of these celebrations at one time or another during his lifetime. While Cervantes was a resident of the town of Esquivias, a village in the province of Toledo, for example, it is likely that he attended the celebrations that took place on April 27, 1587 in Toledo in honor of the interment of the remains of St. Leocadia (d. 304). In addition to possible attendance and perhaps even participation in public celebrations of the Blessed Sacrament or the lives of saints, Cervantes was also active in the different religious activities organized by confraternities.

50. Casalduero contextualizes the rebirth of classicism in the Renaissance: "Esta imitación clásica ha sido profundamente transformada por el Cristianismo, y la Contrarreforma vuelve a incorporarse la teorías greco-latinas dándoles un sentido cristiano. La imitación cristiana es una comunión, un continuo hacer carne y sangre de la palabra. La bella externalidad clásica es sustituida por la interioridad cristiana, y para gozar del Barroco se han de sentir las dos direcciones de esta intimidad: la protestante y la católica" (*Sentido y forma* 128*).*

51. There are several non-Roman rites within the Catholic Church, including Byzantine, Alexandrian, Maronite, and Chaldean.

Chapter Two

1. In response to the Protestant Reformation's influence in Europe, King Philip II issued a decree that banned Spaniards from studying in foreign universities, even Catholic ones, in 1559. A year or so after this decree, the Inquisition prosecuted nearly 1,000 people whom it accused of practicing Protestantism (Payne 46).

2. Canisius's words "no lack of eggs for Luther to hatch" are a reference to Martin Luther's theological disagreements with Erasmus, which included, most notably, free will. In the treatise *De libero arbitrio* (*On the Freedom of the Will*; 1524), Erasmus refuted Martin Luther's doctrine of predestination, according to which humanity is void of free will because of its sinful nature. Erasmus defined free will as "the power of the human will whereby man can apply to or turn away from that which leads unto eternal salvation" (*Erasmus-Luther* 20). This belief is predicated on the doctrine of synergism whereby God, who offers His grace, and the person, who chooses whether to accept it or not, contribute equally to salvation: "But since all things have three parts, a beginning, a continuation, and an end, grace is attributed to the two extremities, and only in the continuation does the free will effect something" (*Erasmus-Luther* 85).

3. Erasmus is the author of *The Praise of Folly* (1511) and *Colloquies* (1518). The religious writers Alfonso (1490–1532) and Juan de Valdés (1500–41), who were twins, wrote the *Dialogues*, a series of literary compositions about religion and politics in sixteenth-century Spain. While the author of *Voyage to Turkey* (ca. 1557) is unknown, the possible writers of this travelogue include Cristóbal de Villalón (1510–62), Andrés Laguna (1499–1559), and Juan de Ulloa Pereira (1545–92).

4. José Antonio López Calle offers the following assessment of Castro's opinion: "Cuando Castro señala que, de acuerdo con un espíritu erasmista, en el *Quijote* se critican ciertas creencias, no quiere decir con ello que Cervantes ataque allí creencias fundamentales cristianas, cosa que, por cierto, Erasmo tampoco hizo, pues admite que en toda la obra de Cervantes, y no sólo en su gran novela, no hay ataques a creencias fundamentales, sino a ciertas formas desviadas o supersticiosas de trato con los santos y a la creencia en los milagros debidos a la superstición. Por tanto, no se atribuye a Cervantes un ataque a la creencia y culto a los santos en sí, sino sólo a las prácticas inadecuadas; igualmente, no se cuestionan los milagros en sí, sino sólo los falsos milagros o los milagros que no tienen más base que la superstición" (3).

5. In *El pensamiento de Cervantes*, Castro labeled Cervantes "un hábil hipócrita" (240). Castro later recanted, but his assessment raised the ire of Cervantine scholars, including Muñoz Iglesias, who reacted decisivamente: "Decir eso de un autor, sin más pruebas que la afirmación gratuita de que se debe entender que piensa en materia religiosa lo contrario de lo que dice, es, aparte de ofensivo e injurioso, críticamente una flagrante petición de principio. Los argumentos de Castro son absolutamente inválidos" (323).

6. If Cervantes were anticlerical, he missed an opportunity to express his sentiments in a scene from Part I, Chapter XXVII of the novel. The barber and priest's plan to convince Don Quixote to return to his village requires that one of them disguises himself as a damsel in distress. The original plan calls for the priest to do so, but he changes his mind because, according to the narrator, it would not be dignified for a priest to wear lady's clothing. It is also possible that Cervantes, however, preferred not to risk censorship.

7. Vilanova writes: "Creo poder afirmar de forma precisa que la verdadera inspiración del *Quijote* de Cervantes procede del *Elogio de la locura*" (*Erasmo y Cervantes* 22). The degree to which the Dutch humanist's treatise influenced Cervantes's masterpiece was in question, however, even before the discovery of the Spanish translation of *The Praise of Folly* (2011): "Que Cervantes leyera esta obra de Erasmo—cosa posible y aun probable—no implica que la tuviera en cuenta como modelo último y absoluto de su novela" (Erasmus, *Elogio* 53n78).

8. Session XXIV (1563).

9. The Council Fathers approved the decree on Penance in Session XIV (1551). Navarino, officially known now as Pílos, is a port town in southwestern Greece. La Goleta was an island-fortress that protected Tunis. See Lathrop, *Don Quixote* 314–15 for more information about Navarino and La Goleta.

10. The Council Fathers approved the decree on Contrition in Session XIV (1551). The Council of Trent defines attrition as "imperfect contrition, which is called attrition, since it commonly arises either from the consideration of the heinousness of sin or from the fear of hell and of punishment, the council declares that if it renounces the desire to sin and hopes for pardon, it not only does not make one a hypocrite and a greater sinner, but is even a gift of God and an impulse of the Holy Ghost, not indeed as already dwelling in the penitent, but only moving him, with which assistance the penitent prepares a way for himself unto justice." (*The Canons and Decrees of the Council of Trent* 128)

11. Carroll Johnson proffers a strict Erasmian reading of this episode: "Cervantes seems to be suggesting that there is no inherent difference between a religious procession and a vision out of hell. This is a scandalous proposition in the repressive environment of 1600, possible only to someone nurtured on Erasmus and his distaste for processions" (Don Quixote 13).

12. The word *saint* appears nearly seventy times in Avellaneda's tome. In comparison, the same word appears nearly forty-five times in Cervantes's novel, Parts I and II. These numbers include references to a specific saint,

the Holy Roman Church, holy matrimony, and any time the word *saints* (*santos* or *santas*) refer to all of the saints in non-specific terms. The numerous references to the lives of saints, as well as the frequent appearance of the words *santo, santa, santos,* and *santas,* variations of the words *saint* and *holy* in Spanish, contribute significantly to the Catholic ideology of Avellaneda's apocryphal Part II. The Catholic faithful believe that the saints, especially the example of their lives and their intercessory role with Jesus, represent another means by which a person can experience God's plan of Salvation. In addition, the word *holy* reminds the reader that the referent is dedicated to and consecrated in the service of God and His people. The saints, who represent a cross-section of the faithful (male, female, young, old), and the objects that Avellaneda describes as *holy* appeal to the reader in a relatable way because they integrate the secular aspects of life with the spiritual presence of the Holy Spirit.

13. López Calle comments on this universal call to holiness and what it means within the context of Erasmus's influence on Cervantes: "Esta declaración de que en todos los estados el hombre puede alcanzar la perfección cristiana y salvarse es complementaria de lo afirmado por don Quijote en la plática con Vivaldo: si allí admitía el hidalgo que el estado religioso es objetivamente superior al del seglar, puesto que el religioso se compromete a cumplir unos votos y un género de vida más exigente, ahora también se reconoce y se añade a ello que en todos los estados se puede uno salvar, incluso los seglares pueden ser más perfectos que los religiosos. Aceptar que el estado religioso es más perfecto que el seglar no quiere decir, no obstante, que cada monje o fraile sea por ello más perfecto que un seglar, pues naturalmente entre ellos hay pecadores y entre los seglares santos; sólo se desea decir que como forma de vida es más perfecta la del estado monacal, por el compromiso con los votos y por las mayores exigencias que entraña, pero el camino de perfección y de salvación está abierto por igual a cualquier cristiano en cualquier estado" (4).

14. Pauline theology is foundational to Erasmus's writings. In the *Enchiridion*, for example, he exhorts the soldier to whom he writes about the virtues of a Christian life to seek guidance from St. Paul: "Above all, however, make Paul your intimate friend. Him you should always cling to, 'meditating upon him day and night' until you commit to memory every word" (*The* Enchiridion *of Erasmus* 199).

15. Descouzis observes that Pauline theology is an essential aspect of *Don Quixote*'s Tridentine identity: "Los indudables paralelos del *Quijote* con la ideología paulina respiran el didacticismo destinado al cristiano enseñado por el postridentino" (*Cervantes II* 110).

16. *Fabliaux*, which is the plural form of *fabliau*, is a medieval tale in verse that contains humor and generally satirizes social institutions, such as the Church and the nobility.

17. With respect to the problems that the Catholic Church experienced in the sixteenth century, St. Teresa writes in *El libro de la vida* (ca. 1565): "Oh grandísimo mal, grandísimo mal de religiosos—no digo ahora más de

mujeres que hombres—a donde no se guarda religión, y todos casi se andan por igual. Antes mal dije, no por igual, que por nuestros pecados se camina más el más imperfecto; y como hay más de él, es más favorecido. Se usa tan poco el de la verdadera religión, que más ha de temer el fraile y la monja que ha de comenzar de veras a seguir del todo su llamamiento a los mismos de su casa, que a todos los demonios" (89–90).

18. If "face value" were the prevailing criterion, what could be deduced from the similarity between *Colloquies* (1518), the title of Erasmus's collection of dialogues about a variety of subjects, and Cervantes's *El coloquio de los perros*, one of the *Novelas ejemplares* (1613) in which two dogs converse about life and the society of their time? In Part I, Chapter IV, Don Quixote's insistence that the Toledan merchants swear allegiance to Dulcinea without having ever seen her evokes the arbitrariness of the Inquisition. When the merchants ask to see a picture of Dulcinea first, Don Quixote argues, "Si os la mostrara —replicó don Quijote—, ¿qué hiciérades vosotros en confesar una verdad tan notoria? La importancia está en que sin verla lo habéis de creer, confesar, afirmar, jurar y defender …" (141). I do not believe that Don Quixote's reply is sufficient evidence to interpret these words as exclusively subversive. The same words may also remind the reader of the foundational nature of faith: "Jesus said to him [Thomas], 'Have you come to believe because you have seen me? Blessed are those who have not seen and have believed'" (John 20:29).

19. Allen considers Don Diego de Miranda's expression of incredulity that knights-errant exist to be an example of *ingénu* irony: "¿Cómo y es posible que hay hoy caballeros andantes en el mundo, y que hay historias impresas de verdaderas caballerías? No me puedo persuadir que haya hoy en la tierra quien favorezca viudas, ampare doncellas, ni honre casadas, ni socorra huérfanos, y no lo creyera si en vuesa merced no lo hubiera visto con mis ojos" (*Don Quixote* 175).

20. The Cervantes Prize, which is the most prestigious literary award in the Spanish-speaking world, recognizes the lifetime achievements of authors from Spain and Spanish America. Past winners include Jorge Guillén, who was the first recipient of the Cervantes Prize in 1976, Juan Goytisolo, Ana María Matute, Mario Vargas Llosa, Miguel Delibes, and Elena Poniatowska.

21. Session XXII, Chapter VI (1562).

22. The characters in Avellaneda's Part II invoke the Virgin Mary twenty times. One of Avellaneda's earliest references to the Virgin Mary alludes to her apparition to St. James in 40 A.D. on top of a marble pillar in the Roman city of Casearaugusta, known today as Zaragoza. She instructed him and his disciples to build a church around the pillar. In Chapter XII, while the knight and his squire visit Zaragoza, the "giant" Bramidán de Tajayunque challenges Don Quixote to do battle. He agrees to fight the "giant" in the plaza known as "El Pilar." There are also several references to the Virgin Mary, including acts of devotion, in the hermit's story about the happy lovers in Chapter XVII. Although there are only three invocations to the Virgin Mary in Cervantes's entire novel, the paucity of references to the Mother of

God is not indicative that the Virgin Mary as a literary theme was anathema to Cervantes. In addition to "The Captive's Tale," the Virgin Mary also has a substantive role in *Los trabajos de Persiles y Sigismunda*.

23. Erasmus also expresses a derisive critique of the clergy's rigid adherence to the Church's teachings: "Now, there are some so affected that fish is poison to them, just as there are found those who in like manner shrink from wine. If one who is thus affected with regard to fishes, should be forbidden to feed on flesh and milk-food, will he not be hardly treated? Is it possible that any man can desire him to be exposed to the pains of hell, if for the necessity of his body he should live on flesh? If any constitution of Popes and Bishops involves liability to the punishment of hell, the condition of Christians is hard indeed. If some impose the liability, others not; no one will better declare his intention than the Pope himself. And it would conduce to the peace of consciences to have it declared. What if some Pope should decree that priests should go girt; would it be probable that he declared this with the intention that if one because of renal suffering should lay aside the girdle, he should be liable to hell? I think not" (*The Colloquies*, vol. I xxii).

24. In a footnote to his edition of *Don Quijote de la Mancha II* (93), Allen informs the reader that the *princeps* edition of the novel has the word *injuria* instead of *lujuria*. The only Deadly Sin not mentioned is Greed.

25. The knight's words are reminiscent of St. Paul's Second Letter to the Corinthians (5:20): "We are therefore Christ's ambassadors, as though God were making his appeal through us. We implore you on Christ's behalf: Be reconciled to God."

26. See Castro, *Cervantes y los casticismos españoles,* and Márquez Villanueva, *Cervantes en letra viva: Estudios sobre la vida y la obra.*

27. In the Foreword to Nabokov's *Lecture on Don Quixote*, Guy Davenport writes that the Russian writer's aim was "to put Cervantes's hero back into Cervantes's text" (xiv).

Chapter Three

1. The Catholic Church identifies two types of sin: mortal and venial. In order for an action to be considered a mortal sin, it must satisfy three criteria: it is grave in nature; the person who commits the sin is aware of its seriousness; and the person willingly commits the sin in spite of the recognition of its offensive nature. A venial sin is an action that is less grave in nature or if it is grave in nature, it is performed without complete consent or the will or full knowledge of the consequences.

2. Vitoria was also the author of treatises that defended the human dignity of the natives of the New World, namely *De Indis* and *De iure belli*. He expressed his sentiments about the mistreatment of the Indians in a letter to his friend Miguel de Arcos, who was also a Dominican priest: "En verdad, si los indios no son hombres, sino monas, *non sunt capaces injuriae*. Pero si son hombres y prójimos, *et quod ipsi praese ferunt,* vasallos del Emperador, *non video quomodo excusar* a estos conquistadores de última impiedad y

tiranía, ni sé que tan grand servicio hagan a Su Majestat de echarle a perder sus vasallos. Si yo desease mucho el arzobispado de Toledo, que está vaco, y me lo hoviesen de dar porque yo firmase o afirmase la inocencia destos peruleros, sin duda no lo osara hacer. Antes se me seque la lengua y la mano, que yo diga ni escriba cosa tan inhumana y fuera de toda cristiandad" (Vitoria 21; author's italics).

3. Session XXIII, Chapter XI (1563). The curriculum consisted of the following classes: grammar, singing, ecclesiastical computation, and other useful arts; shall be instructed in Sacred Scripture, ecclesiastical books, the homilies of the saints, the manner of administering the sacraments, especially those things that seem adapted to the hearing of confessions, and the rites and ceremonies (*The Canons and Decrees of the Council of Trent* 223).

4. While there are many references to the knight's faith in Part I and Part II, Cervantes presents them tacitly until the last scene when Don Quixote bares his soul and requests books about saints, like *Flos Sanctorum*. Avellaneda, on the other hand, prioritizes Don Quixote's religiosity over his knight-errantry in Chapter I. Consequently, the reader does not have to wonder about the depth or sincerity of it. While Cervantes's knight curses books of chivalry in the last chapter and laments that he did not dedicate his life to reading books about saints, Avellaneda's Don Quixote embraces books that offer spiritual edification from the beginning of the novel. Avellaneda's Don Quixote does not need to travel the same spiritual journey as Cervantes's knight because it is apparent from the outset of the novel that he is a practicing Catholic, whose knowledge about the faith and incarnational spirituality are the foundations of his identity.

5. Rachel Schmidt views Don Quixote's death as the final act of specularity in the novel in which the knight, who seeks fame and glory throughout the novel, has his final "adventure," which he hopes will immortalize his name in the annals of history: "His repentance has little to do with his salvation, but much to do with the clearing of his name and the reestablishment of the esteem in which others hold him" ("The Performance and Hermeneutics of Death" 113). While I do agree that he wants to reestablish his good name, I suggest that it represents Alonso Quijano's hope that he will be remembered as a good Catholic. Perhaps this scene provides a peek into another facet of his life before he became Don Quixote.

6. According to McKendrick, the official censors had Part II of the novel in their possession by February 15, 1615 (196). Sullivan notes that Part II appeared in print in November of 1615 (13). Cervantes died in April of 1616.

7. Quevedo satirizes the deathbed scene in his ballad "Testamento de don Quijote": "De un molimiento de güesos / a puros palos y piedras, / don Quijote de la Mancha / yace doliente y sin fuerzas, / tendido sobre un paves, / cubierto con su rodela, / sacando como tortuga / de entre conchas la cabeza" (Quevedo 43; verses 1–8). Quevedo's sonnet and Avellaneda's apocryphal Part II of the novel infer that Cervantes's contemporaries considered *Don Quixote* to be a funny book above all else. In *Cervantes and the Burlesque*

Sonnet, Adrienne Martín asserts that the poems in *Don Quixote* define the novel as a parody, but she also explains that a funny book can be much more than it seems: "That is not to say, however, that it cannot have a serious purpose. The problem is one of degree and of terminology: what does 'funny' actually mean? *Don Quixote* is above all else a *humorous* rather than a funny book. And humor most often implies a serious intent" (132; author's italics). In addition to *Don Quixote*, Quevedo also parodies the *Cantar de Mio Cid* in a ballad titled "Pavura de los condes de Carrión": "Medio día era por filo, / que rapar podía la barba, / cuando, después de mascar, / el Cid sosiega la panza: / la gorra sobre los ojos / y floja la martingala, / boquiabierto y cabizbajo, roncando como una vaca" (Rivers 296).

8. Don Quixote, however, is not always the beneficiary of Divine Providence. In Part I, Chapter XLII, for example, it is ironic that Maritornes and the innkeeper's daughter string up the same hand that Don Quixote boasts is the quintessential synecdoche for knighthood.

9. "It is also frequently called the Viaticum by sacred writers, both because it is spiritual food by which we are sustained in our pilgrimage through this life, and also because it paves our way to eternal glory and happiness" (*The Catechism of the Council of Trent* 276).

10. The Sacraments of Confession and Anointing of the Sick are directed to spiritual healing, a constitutive element of which is absolution of sins. The priest is granted this faculty at ordination, whereas the deacon is not.

11. Erasmus authored his own *ars moriendi* pamphlet titled *Preparation for Death* (1534), which he wrote in Germany after becoming ill and believing that his death was imminent. He died in 1536.

12. Disdain for the court and praise of the countryside was a popular theme in Renaissance literature. Fray Antonio de Guevara (1480–1545), who was a court preacher and royal chronicler during the reign of Charles V, the Holy Roman Emperor (Charles I, King of Spain), is the author of *Menosprecio de corte y alabanza de aldea* (1539). Don Quixote alludes to this theme when he compares courtly knights and knights-errant in Part II, Chapters I, VI, XVII, and XLVI.

13. The biblical foundation of this doctrine is the following verses from the Epistle of St. James: "faith of itself, if it does not have work, is dead" (2:17); "See how a person is justified by works and not by faith alone" (2:24); "For just as a body without a spirit is dead, so also faith without works is dead" (2:26). The Council of Trent reaffirmed the necessity of faith and works: "If anyone says that man can be justified before God by his own works, whether done by his own natural powers or by the teaching of the Law, without divine grace through Jesus Christ, let him be anathema" (Session VI; Can. 1); "If anyone says that the sinner is justified by faith alone, meaning that nothing else is required to cooperate in order to obtain the grace of justification and that it is not in any way necessary that he be prepared and disposed by the action of his own will, let him be anathema" (Session VI: Can. 9).

14. Don Quixote and Sancho Panza's first dialogic references to God take place at the end of Chapter VII. Sancho believes that "aunque lloviese Dios

reinos sobre la tierra" (165), his wife Mari Gutiérrez would be better suited to be a countess than a queen, and even then, Sancho says, may God help her. In response, Don Quixote instructs Sancho to trust God: "Encomiéndalo tú a Dios, Sancho ... que Él le dará lo que más le convenga" (165). Cervantes calls Sancho's wife Juana Gutiérrez on the same page he refers to her as Mari Gutiérrez (her name also appears throughout the novel as Juana Panza, Teresa Panza, and Teresa Cascajo). The question whether Cervantes was aware of the mistake or not is one that scholars have debated with respect to the inconsistencies in *Don Quixote*, which also include the number of years Cervantes served Philip II; Don Quixote's bad arithmetic in Part I, Chapter XXIV, when he remarks that seven times nine is seventy three; and Don Quixote's erroneous claim that Samson removed the doors of the temple (Samson removed the gates of the city of Gaza). Tom Lathrop is the most ardent defender of the position that Cervantes was well aware of the mistakes and inconsistencies, attributing them to Cervantes's satirization of the careless literary style of the books of chivalry: "Cervantes, as a rule, simply does not make mistakes and he's not careless either. Indeed he had to be particularly keen and creative in order to *make sure* everything was contradicted. Every contradiction, every mistake, every careless turn of phrase is there because Cervantes wanted it exactly that way" (*Don Quixote* xi; author's italics).

15. These categories are from Dailey 105.

16. Mansch and Peters note that Martin Luther published *The Bondage of the Will* (1525) to contest Erasmus's assertions in *On the Freedom of the Will* (1524) (280).

17. Johnson attributes Alonso Quijano's voracious reading of books of chivalry and subsequent madness to a frustrated incestuous desire for his niece: "My Don Quixote is propelled backward into life by his flight from an unbearable environmental pressure personified in his niece and the threat of incest. When this first line of defense proves inadequate, the only mental space left to retreat into is his madness" (Don Quixote 118–19).

18. There are several allusions to fame throughout Cervantes's literature. In Part II, Chapter XXXIII, for example, Sancho tells the Duchess: "más vale el buen nombre que las muchas riquezas" (315). In *Persiles*, Periandro states: "una onza de fama vale más que una libra de perlas" (225).

19. The word *profession* is a double entendre. See Chapter 2.

20. See Philippians 2:13; James 2:17, 24, and 26.

21. According to Allen, the irony is centered on the confusion of the moral and the monetary (Don Quixote 145).

22. Eisenberg notes that the standards were so high that a lie would be grounds for a duel: "This reflects the medieval use of the duel, burlesqued in the combat with Tosilos, as a means of determining which of two disputing parties is telling the truth; God was presumed to help the more deserving combatant" (*A Study of* Don Quixote 128n69). In Part II, Chapter LVI, Don Quixote prepares to duel the man who dishonored Doña Rodríguez's daughter. Tosilos, the man's servant, agrees to replace the man after he flees the country. When Tosilos sees Doña Rodríguez's daughter, he falls in love with her and refuses to duel Don Quixote. Tosilos proposes to Doña Rodríguez's daughter, who accepts the proposal and then discovers Tosilos is not the man who dishonored her.

23. In the petition, Cervantes states that he served Felipe II for twenty-two years. Fernández Álvarez notes that Cervantes exaggerated the tenure of his service because if true, Cervantes's first year would have been 1569, the year a warrant was issued for his arrest. Cervantes's initiated his service to Felipe II in 1571, the year he fought in the Battle of Lepanto (315).

24. Molina's most important contribution to this debate is the book *Liberi arbitrii cum gratiae donis, divina praescientia, providentia, praedestinatione et reprobatione concordia* (*A Reconciliation of Free Choice with the Gifts of Grace, Divine Foreknowledge, Providence, Predestination and Reprobation*; 1588).

25. Ignatius addresses Free Will and Divine Grace in three of the eighteen rules that comprise his *Rules for Thinking, Judging, and Feeling with the Church* (1522–24). The seventeenth rule summarizes his philosophy: "De manera que de la fé y gracia se puede hablar quanto sea posible mediante el auxilio Divino para mayor alabanza de la su Divina Magestad; mas no por tal suerte, ni por tales modos, mayormente en nuestros tiempos tan periculosos, que las obras y libero arbitrio resciban detriment alguno, ó por *nihilo* se tengan" (*Ejercicios* 173–74; author's italics).

26. Sancho, perhaps swayed by Don Quixote's sentiments and his own compassion, helps Ginés de Pasamonte to escape, but immediately thereafter he regains his composure and suggests that he and his master leave in order to avoid arrest by the Holy Brotherhood, the militia that the Catholic Monarchs organized to maintain law and order, especially among nobles who sought more power. Sancho's recognition of the reality of the situation, as evidenced by his attempt to convince Don Quixote that the galley slaves are criminals who deserve to be punished, does not stop him, however, from participating in it.

27. Nabokov identifies forty episodes in which Don Quixote encounters a different opposing force, either animate or inanimate; Don Quixote's attack of the priests is the fourteenth episode. In the end, the knight is victorious the same number of times he is defeated, 20–20 (Part I: 13–13; Part II: 7–7). Nabokov attributes the equilibrium in a novel as disjointed as *Don Quixote* to Cervantes's writing style: "Este equilibrio perfecto de victoria y derrota es muy asombroso en una obra que parece tan inconexa y descuidada. Nace de un sentido secreto de la escritura, la intuición armonizadora del artista" (*Curso sobre* El Quijote 207).

28. Pestilential fever, or bubonic plague, was responsible for the death of nearly half a million Spaniards between 1596 and 1602. Jehenson and Dunn propose that Cervantes passes over national crises, such as the bubonic plague and floods, in *Don Quixote* in order to evoke a utopian society (131).

29. The only clergy who can excommunicate are those who hold a high-ranking ecclesiastical office, e.g., Bishop or Cardinal. The Council of Trent addresses excommunication in Session XXV, Chapter 3 (1563): "Although the sword of excommunication is the nerve of ecclesiastical discipline and very salutary for holding the people in their duty, it is, however, to be used with moderation and great discretion, since experience teaches that if wielded rashly or for trifling reasons, it is more despised than feared and is productive of destruction rather than salvation. Wherefore, those excommunications which after previous admonitions are customarily imposed for the purpose of eliciting a so-called disclosure, or by reason of properties squandered or alienated, shall be issued by absolutely no one but the bishop, and even then not except by reason of an unusual circumstance and after a diligent and very complete examination by the bishop of the cause which his moves his mind thereto" (*The Canons and Decrees of the Council of Trent* 290).

30. Unlike Cervantes's knight, Avellaneda's is not excommunicated, and, therefore, is able to attend Mass, which he does, carrying his rosary. He also participates in vespers, evening prayer at which the faithful chant hymns and reflect on readings from the Bible. Cervantes's Don Quixote is prohibited from attending Mass until he makes his confession, which he does on his deathbed. Riquer believes that Cervantes's Don Quixote does not go to Mass because of his appearance, a decision by the author that reflects his respect for the Catholic Church (*Cervantes, Pasamonte y Avellaneda* lx).

31. The humoral theory of medicine is based on the belief that the human body consists of four fluids: black bile, yellow or red bile, blood, and phlegm. An imbalance of these fluids produces a deleterious effect, such as disease, in the individual. The fluids also refer to four psychological temperaments: melancholic (black bile), sanguine (blood), choleric (yellow bile), and phlegmatic (phlegm). According to the ancient Greek philosopher Galen (AD 129 –ca. 210), "the mind's inclination follows the body's temperature" (Paster 87). In *El diablo y Cervantes*, Padilla postulates that Don Quixote's madness is the product of interior (a melancholic disposition) and exterior influences (lack of sleep, books of chivalry) (97). German Christian mystic and theologian Jakob Böhme (1575–1624) compares the melancholic's acquisition of knowledge through sensual experience to the mysticism of St. John of the Cross, who, in "Dark Night of the Soul" describes the arduous journey of the soul as it seeks perfect union with God. Coudert notes, "The idea that true knowledge comes through suffering, even death and the illumination that follows, was a common theme in alchemy and alchemical symbolism" (654n28).

32. For more on Aristotelian and Senecan ethics in Cervantes's literature, see Serés 37–54.

33. While it was common knowledge that the human soul consists of memory, will, and intellect, Alonso López Pinciano's (*El Pinciano*) treatise *Philosophía antigua poética* (*Ancient Philosophy of Poetry*; 1596), which addresses Aristotle's assertion that the soul is composed of faculties (memory, will, and intellect), appears to have influenced Cervantes's literary *corpus* as well. Which of the three faculties is dominant, however, is open to debate. St. Thomas Aquinas believed that there exists a hierarchy: "Will or appetition is the faculty by which the soul or vital force moves toward that which the intellect conceives as good. Thomas, following Aristotle, defines the good as 'that which is desirable.' Beauty is a form of the good; it is that which pleases when seen. Why does it please? Through the proportion and harmony of parts in an organized whole. Intellect is subject to will in so far as desire can determine the direction of thought; but will is subject to the intellect in so far as our desires are determined by the way we conceive things ... ; 'the good as understood moves the will.' Freedom lies not really in the will, which is 'necessarily moved' by the understanding of the matter presented by the intellect, but in the judgment (*arbitrium*); therefore freedom varies directly with knowledge, reason, wisdom, with the capacity of the intellect to present a true picture of the situation to the will; only the wise are truly free. Intelligence is not only the best and highest, it is also the most powerful, of the faculties of the soul ... 'The proper operation of man is to understand'" (Durant 102; author's italics). St. Augustine compared the three components of the human soul to the triune God: "Since these three, the memory, the understanding, and the will are, therefore, not three lives but one life, not three minds, but one mind, it follows that they are certainly not three substances, but one substance [...] Therefore, these three are one in that they are one life, one mind, and one essence" (311). John G. Weiger believes that the "triad" of memory, will, and intellect "underlies much of Cervantes's portrayal of the human struggle for self-realization" (139).

34. In the case between the two old men, one man borrows ten *escudos* from his friend but does not pay him back. When Sancho asks the man to swear that he returned the money, the man hands his cane to the other man and swears that he did indeed return the money. Sancho realizes that the ten *escudos* in gold, however, are in the cane that belongs to the man who swears that he returned the money. Of course, when the man is in possession of his cane again, he does not make the same oath. Sancho decrees that the ten *escudos* be paid to the man who made the loan. Next, Sancho resolves the case between the woman and the rich cattleman, whom the woman accuses of inappropriate sexual advances. Sancho orders the man to give the woman twenty *ducados* and instructs the woman to leave. Then, the Governor asks the man to follow the woman and wrestle the money away from her. Moments later, the two return, and it is evident that the woman is stronger than the man. Sancho finds in favor of the man. The conflict between the peasant and the tailor, however, is unique. While Sancho decides that neither should benefit from the decision, the squire also mandates that the cloth material, which is the source of the disagreement, should not be discarded.

35. Social justice, commutative justice, and distributive justice are the three dimensions of basic justice.

36. St. Thomas Aquinas wrote *Summa Theologica*, also known as *Summa Theologiae*, between 1265 and 1274, but it was not published in its entirety until 1485.

37. An exception is the knight's attack on Alonso López, the priest in Part I, Chapter XIX.

Chapter Four

1. Allen notes in his edition of Part II that one of the books Don Quixote regrets not having the time to read is Dominican friar Felipe de Meneses's *Luz del alma christiana contra la ceguedad y ignorancia [...]*. In Part II, Chapter LXII, Don Quixote sees a typesetter who is correcting a print of this book in the print shop in Barcelona and comments: "—Estos tales libros, aunque hay muchos deste género, son los que se deben imprimir, porque son muchos los pecadores que se usan, y son menester infinitas luces para tantos desalumbrados" (555). Allen also points out that Don Quixote's observation reflects the transformation he undergoes from the beginning of the novel: "Para darse cuenta del cambio en don Quijote reflejado en este comentario, solo hace falta recordar qué libros tenía en su biblioteca" (555n17). Allen juxtaposes this quotation with one of Kierkegaard's three essential stages of life: "There is a yearning for something further that shall lead us beyond the world of natural existence. Such an attitude of despondency at not finding what we sought ... leads to transition to the third level of the *religious*, with its awareness of an eternal power permeating existence" (*Don Quixote* 199). (Allen notes that the paraphrase of this stage of life is excerpted from Marie Collins Swabey, *Comic Laughter, A Philosophical Essay* [New Haven and London, 1961] 94–95.)

2. Christian notes that "skepticism and incredulity, if we are to trust literary accounts and Inquisition documents, were to be found as much in a small village as in a large town. In novels like *Lazarillo de Tormes*, *La vida del Buscón*, and *Persiles y Segismunda* not all hermits are holy, all pilgrims devout, or all villagers credulous. The Inquisition of Cuenca arrested persons in all sizes of towns for propositions like denying the virginity of Mary (nineteen cases between 1515 and 1535), incredulity as to the Eucharist, denial of the efficacy of prayers for the dead, and denial of the divinity of Christ (these last skeptics were priests). Those investigated included the literate and the illiterate, the rich and the poor" (148).

3. The incarnation of Jesus first became accepted doctrine at the Council of Nicaea (325 A.D.), the Council of Ephesus (431), and the Council of Chalcedon (451).

4. The Jesuits' preferred scholastic theologian was St. Thomas Aquinas, whose beliefs were compatible to the Jesuits' in many ways. Jesuit priest and historian John O'Malley cites three areas in which St. Thomas Aquinas's theology appealed to the Jesuits: his unquestioned orthodoxy, his understanding of the relationship between philosophy and Christian doctrine, and his Christian adaptation of Aristotle's teaching on virtue, which inspired Ignatius's teaching on moderation in ascetical practices (*The First Jesuits* 249).

5. Sancho reacts angrily to Don Quixote's decision not to marry Princess Micomicona: "¿Es, por dicha, más hermosa mi señora Dulcinea? No, por cierto, ni aun con la mitad, y aun estoy por decir que no llega a su zapato de la que está delante. Así, noramala alcanzaré yo el condado que espero, si vuestra merced se anda a pedir cotufas en el golfo. Cásese, cásese luego,

encomiéndole yo a Satanás, y tome ese reino que se le viene a las manos de vobis, vobis, y en siendo rey, hágame marqués o adelantado, y luego, siquiera se lo lleve el diablo todo" (424). Sancho's words, which reveal the sincerity of his belief that he will be the governor of an island, are a harbinger of the squire's "quixotization." I believe the squire's reaction humanizes him in a way with which the reader can empathize. Shortly thereafter, an argument ensues between the knight and his squire. Don Quixote asks Sancho to forgive him, and Sancho, in doing so, expresses regret for his behavior: "y así, en mí la gana de hablar siempre es primero movimiento, y no puedo dejar de decir, por una vez siquiera, lo que me viene a la lengua" (425). When Sancho declares that Don Quixote is crazy because he refuses to marry Princess Micomicona, Allen notes the irony that Sancho speaks the truth without realizing that the knight's madness is not restricted to this specific episode (*Don Quixote* 144).

6. In Ignatius's letters on the apostolic spirituality of finding God in all things, he discusses how God forms an inherent bond with the activities of everyday life: "Se pueden ejercitar en buscar la presencia de nuestro Señor en todas las cosas, como en el conversar con alguno, andar, ver, gustar, oír, entender, y en todo lo que hiciéremos, pues es verdad que está su divina Majestad por presencia, potencia y esencia en todas las cosas" (Giuliani 164).

7. Don Quixote's rejection of Princess Micomicona may not be due solely to the knight's profound love for Dulcinea. Several critics, including Ruth El Saffar (*Beyond Fiction* 54), Félix Martínez-Bonati (38), and Carroll B. Johnson (*Madness and Lust* 158, 167) suggest that Don Quixote invents Dulcinea because of a psychological or physical impotence. Eisenberg posits that Cervantes projects his own concerns about intimacy onto his knight (*A Study of Don Quixote* 125). Don Quixote's asexuality is a parody of the knights-errant in the books of chivalry who often marry the lady they court and father a child: "Unlike certain lusty lancemen that grace the pages of the romances, Don Quixote finds all things carnal distasteful and even repugnant. The comic irony is evident: by rejecting sexuality so vehemently, our protagonist comes to imitate not the knights-errant that fill his fantasy, but rather the damsels in distress who chastely struggle to protect their virtue" (Cull 43).

8. Joseph N. Tylenda, S.J. notes that Esplandián, the fourth son of Amadís, kept a vigil of arms in front of a statue of the Virgin Mary the night before consecration to knighthood (25).

9. Roland is a character in Ludovico Ariosto's *Orlando Furioso* (1516).

10. Ignatius states in his autobiography that the intimate encounter he had with God in the visions he had in Manresa would have been sufficient reason for him to sacrifice his life: "If there were no scriptures to teach us these matters of faith, he would still resolve to die for them on the basis of what he had seen" (Tylenda 38). Don Quixote manifests a similar commitment to the transcendental nature of the visions he saw in the Cave of Montesinos (Part II, Chapter XXII): "—Dios os lo perdone, amigos; que me habéis quitado de la más sabrosa y agradable vida y vista que ningún humano ha visto ni pasado. En efecto: ahora acabo de conocer que todos los contentos desta vida pasan como sombra y sueño, o se marchitan como la flor del campo" (217).

11. John 19:38–42.

12. The Portuguese Inquisition censored the following sentence from the novel in 1624: "Y luego dijo sobre la alcuza más de ochenta paternostres y otras tantas avemarías, salves y credos, y a cada palabra acompañaba una cruz, a modo de bendición" (*Don Quijote de la Mancha* 250). Castro affirms Cervantes's Catholicity: "Beyond a shadow of a doubt, Cervantes was a good Catholic, for Hispanicity and faith were indissolubly united" ("Incarnation in *Don Quixote*" 156).

13. It is believed that the Virgin Mary revealed the devotion to the rosary in an apparition to St. Dominic (1170–1221), a Spanish priest who founded the Dominican order. St. Dominic prayed the rosary to aid him in his missionary work to the Albigensians, who believed that the material world, and especially the Catholic Church, was evil. Dominic of Prussia (1382–1461), a Carthusian monk, is credited with creating the fifty meditations on the mysteries of the life of Christ.

14. King Philip II named John of Austria (1547–78) supreme commander of the Holy League. King Philip II presented John with an image of the Virgin of Guadalupe, and John relied on Guadalupe's intercession for a safe and victorious expedition.

15. The priests belonged to one of the major religious orders: Capuchins, Dominicans, Jesuits, and Theatines. Since it was impossible for the priests to hear individual confessions, Pope Pius V declared a general absolution, which the priests granted, to all of the soldiers who fought that day (Chesterton 60).

16. Nieto explains the absence of a monk hermit as a Cervantine "antimimetic transforming motif" (30).

17. Ruiz notes the nature and impact of these reforms: "To the average Christian, the demands of religion and spirituality became even more challenging after the Council of Trent. In the 1560s, a series of Church councils held at Trent—the Spanish clergy played an important role in the final decisions of the Council—elaborated new theological positions, liturgical changes, and stricter forms of daily religious observances" (233).

18. Roberto Véguez notes that Amadís did not use a rosary during his act of penitence at Peña Pobre. Véguez posits that either Don Quijote forgets this detail or that Cervantes added the rosary to Don Quijote's penitence in order to satirize Catholics' devotion to it (95).

19. In comparison, Avellaneda's Don Quixote, after sitting idle for several months, embarks on another adventure to serve God and Mankind. Furthermore, the knight reveals his understanding that God created him in His own image and endowed him with gifts: "Querría, pues (para que no se diga que yo he recebido en vano el talento que Dios me dio y sea reprehendido como aquel del Evangelio, que ató el que su amo le fió en el pañizuelo y no quiso granjear con él, que bolviéssemos lo más presto que ser pudiesse a nuestro militar exercicio, porque en ello haremos dos cosas: la una, servicio

muy grande a Dios, y la otra, provecho al mundo" (60–61) The Gospel reference is to the Parable of the Talents, Matthew 25:14–30.

20. Casalduero acknowledges the formative role of Lepanto in Cervantes's ideology: "The catholic Cervantes, a catholic of his epoch, that is, of the Counter Reformation, does not express the struggle between the soul and the flesh, between virtue and vice. His religious consciousness adopts the modern form of a historical-cultural feeling. He sees the world as an opposition between the faith of the past and the will of the present, between the knight errant and the *caballero* of his epoch, and he succeeds in reducing the ample circles of his emotion to the limits of his own life, of his personal experience wherein Lepanto rises like a mile-post to separate the two epochs" ("The Composition" 59; author's italics).

21. Of course, one might wonder when he began to carry the rosary. Apparently, he did not have it in Part I, Chapter XXVI.

22. Véguez believes that the large size of the rosary negates the possibility that it can be an instrument of devotion. Instead, he considers it purely a decorative feature of the knight's attire, a symbol of the knight's vanity (102). Cervantes only states that the rosary is large, however, a description that does not relegate it, I believe, to a profane appendage of clothing.

23. "God sees all things in His eternity, which, being simple, is present to all time, and embraces all time" (*Summa Theologiae*, Q.14, A.3). "With like certitude God knows, in His eternity, all that takes place throughout the whole course of time. For His eternity is in present contact with the whole course of time, and even passes beyond time" (*Aquinas's Shorter* Summa 150).

24. Padilla (78) postulates that Don Quixote assumes the role of an exorcist when he inquires to the reason of the goatherd's madness and vows to cure him of it in Part I, Chapter XXIV: "Y juro —añadió don Quijote— por la orden de caballería que recibí, aunque indigno y pecador, y por la profesión de caballero andante, que si en esto, señor, me complacéis, de serviros con las veras a que me obliga el ser quien soy, ora remediando vuestra desgracia, si tiene remedio, ora ayudándoos a llorarla, como os lo he prometido" (332).

25. As early as Part I, Chapter VIII, Don Quixote is determined to defeat the more than thirty "giants," which, in reality, are windmills, in God's name: "que ésta es buena guerra, y es gran servicio de Dios quitar tan mala simiente de sobre la faz de la tierra" (166).

26. The Inquisition labelled Bautista de Cubas's heretical beliefs as "propositions," which were much more serious than "scandalous words." King Philip IV issued the first official proclamation of the patronage of the Virgin Mary's Immaculate Conception in Spain in 1643. It is likely that Sister Mary of Jesus of Ágreda (María de Jesús de Ágreda, 1602–65), who was King Philip IV's spiritual advisor, was influential in the King's decision to proclaim the patronage of the Immaculate Conception. Due to the debate surrounding the immaculate conception of Mary in early modern Spain, the Inquisition had to prosecute Old Christians who denied this belief. The Virgin Mary is the subject of plays by two of Spain's

most well-known playwrights: Lope de Vega (*La limpieza no manchada*; 1624) and Calderón de la Vega (1600–81; *La hidalga del Valle*; 1640). In addition, Diego Velázquez (1599–1660) painted *The Immaculate Conception* (1618) and Bartolomé Esteban Murillo (1617–82) depicted the Immaculate Conception in *La Purísima Inmaculada Concepción* (1678).

27. St. Teresa expresses this same admonition in *El castillo interior*: "Viene el demonio con unas sutilezas grandes, y debajo de color de bien vala desquiciando en poquitas cosas de ella y metiendo en algunas que él le hace entender que no son malas, y poco a poco oscureciendo el entendimiento y entibiando la voluntad y haciendo crecer en ella el amor propio, hasta que de uno en otro la va apartando de la voluntad de Dios y llegando a la suya" (Sicari 139).

28. The Italian Pietro Lauro (1510–68) is the author of a continuation of *El Caballero de la Cruz* titled *Leandro el Bel* (1560). Its Spanish title is *Libro segundo del esforzado caballero de la Cruz* (1563).

29. "Yo hago juramento al Criador de todas las cosas y a los santos cuatro Evangelios, donde más largamente están escritos, de hacer la vida que hizo el grande marqués de Mantua cuando juró de vengar la muerte de su sobrino Valdovinos, que fue de no comer pan a manteles, ni con su mujer folgar, y otras cosas que, aunque dellas no me acuerdo, las doy aquí por expresadas, hasta tomar entera venganza del que tal desaguisado me fizo" (188).

30. González Echevarría notes the literary significance of this episode: "The novel begins to acquire ... an inner density and substance by means of these links, these connections within the plot, one related to the other, the oath and the fulfillment of the oath" (85).

31. The word *católico* has more than one meaning. Its Greek origin is *katholikos*, which means "throughout the whole" or universal. The *Diccionario de Autoridades* defines *cathólico* as something that is "perfecto, sano y cabal."

32. In Part I, Chapter XXIII, upon finding a saddle cushion and a traveling bag in the Sierra Morena, a goatherd refuses to touch them, reasoning "que es el diablo sutil; y debajo de los pies se le levanta allombre cosa donde tropiece y caya, sin saber cómo ni cómo no" (326).

33. When Don Quixote sees the statue of St. Martin (315–ca. 395) on horseback, sharing part of his cloak with the poor man, the knight's somewhat irreverent tone could be interpreted as Erasmian satire: "y sin duda debía de ser entonces invierno, que si no, él se la diera toda, según era de caritativo" (507). Sancho's response is just as flippant: "—No debió de ser eso —dijo Sancho—, sino que se debió de atener al refrán que dicen: que para dar y tener, seso es menester" (507). The same night of St. Martin's charitable act, however, he experienced a vision of Jesus, wearing the cloak he had given to the poor man. St. Martin, an unbaptized catechumen at the time, received the Sacrament of Baptism soon thereafter.

34. Fitzpatrick, n.p. Service of faith is a fundamental element of the Jesuit mission of education. In a speech delivered at the International

Congress of Jesuit Alumni in Valencia, Spain (1973), Pedro Arrupe, S.J. (1907–91) spoke about this vision, describing it as "hombres y mujeres para los demás" (Lamet 28).

35. Leo Spitzer notes another Christian reading of this episode: "the final scene of his Christian death and regeneration seems rounded out by a kind of re-baptism, as this *loco* [madman] becomes a *cuerdo* [sane man] (the change of name is thrice mentioned in this final chapter, as if the author wanted to din it into our heads that the old Adam is dead)" (165).

Chapter Five

1. "If anyone asserts that the transgression of Adam injured him alone and not his posterity, and that the holiness and justice which he received from God, which he lost, he lost for himself alone and not for us also; or that he, being defiled by the sin of disobedience, has transfused only death and the pains of the body into the whole human race, but not sin also, which is the death of the soul, let him be anathema" (Session V, 1546; *The Canons and Decrees of the Council of Trent* 47).

2. The foundation of each principle is the Bible, as the following verses illustrate: Psalm 8:5–7 (the inviolable dignity of man); Romans 13:9–10 (the essential centrality of community); and 1 Corinthians 3:22–23 (the significance of human action). The Council of Trent addresses these principles at length in its decrees on Justification (Session VI, 1547).

3. "For this single reflection, that he who is true and perfect God became man, alone is sufficient proof of the exalted dignity conferred on man by the divine bounty ..." (*The Catechism of the Council of Trent* 54).

4. "¿Quién duda sino que en los venideros tiempos, cuando salga a luz la verdadera historia de mi famosos hechos ..." (121).

5. Joel Feinberg, a social and political philosopher, defines *psychological egoism* as "the doctrine that the only thing anyone is capable of desiring or pursuing ultimately (as an end in itself) is his *own* self-interest" (183; author's italics).

6. There are numerous episodes in which Don Quixote promotes, not always successfully, of course, the common good, beginning with the episode in which he encounters Juan Haldudo and Andrés (Part I, Chapter IV). In these episodes, which include the Toledan merchants (Part I, Chapter IV), the Benedictine friars who accompany the Basque woman (Part I, Chapter VIII), the armies of Alifanfarón and Pentapolín (Part I, Chapter XVIII), the adventure with the dead body (Part I, Chapter XIX), the galley slaves (Part I, Chapter XXII), Princess Micomicona (Part I, Chapter XXX), the adventure with the penitents (Part I, Chapter LII), the destruction of the puppet theater (Part II, Chapter XXVI), and the enchanted boat (Part II, Chapter XXIX), the intent of Don Quixote's actions, although mitigated considerably by his madness, exemplify the Church's belief in the common good, which the Council of Trent addresses in its Bull of the Convocation: "if they [European royalty] feel themselves bound and under obligation to the Lord for His great favors toward them, they will not abandon His cause and interests but will come personally to the celebration of the holy council, where their piety and virtue would be greatly conducive to the common good" (*The Canons and Decrees of the Council of Trent* 31).

7. Agape love is the highest form of the four types of love in the Bible. It is sacrificial, unconditional, and selfless. The other types of love are storge, philia, and eros.

8. The four pillars of social doctrine are solidarity, subsidiarity, equality, and liberty.

9. Christian Humanism had a similar objective: "'The revival of a genuine science of theology,' as Erasmus phrased it in one of his letters, was certainly his basic aim as a humanist scholar. It was not, however, his only concern, nor did scholarly pursuits blind him to the more practical questions of the Christian life and the problems of personal and social reform. Scholarship for Erasmus was never an end in itself, but was intended to conduct men to a better life. Learning was to lead to virtue, scholarship to God; and thus the restoration of theology was to be the means toward the revival of a more vital Christianity" (Erasmus, *Christian Humanism and the Reformation* 8).

10. The words in quotations are biblical verses, respectively: Luke 2:14 (it begins "Glory to God," not "Glory in the highest"); Luke 10:5; 14:27; and John 20:19.

11. At the conclusion of Don Quixote's speech, the narrator relates the reaction of his audience: "En los que escuchado le habían sobrevino nueva lástima de ver que hombre que, al parecer, tenía buen entendimiento y buen discurso en todas las cosas que trataba, le hubiese perdido tan rematadamente en tratándole de su negra y pizmienta caballería" (521).

12. There is no doubt that the theology of St. Thomas Aquinas influenced the Council of Trent's decrees (e.g., the *Catechism of the Council of Trent* may be considered a compendium of Thomistic principles), but what is not as certain is the belief that the Council placed the *Summa Theologiae* on the high altar as second only to the Bible (Kreeft 2).

13. Mario Casella presents a different perspective of the knight and the saint: "In England the rancor which was directed at Catholic Spain led to the identification of Don Quixote with St. Ignatius of Loyola so as to ridicule both one and the other at the same time" (200).

14. Signs of the Catholic Church's revival included new religious orders, more seminaries, and the re-establishment of the Society of Jesus in 1814 (the Suppression of the Jesuits occurred in 1773).

Chapter Six

1. The complete proverb is *no se toman truchas a bragas enjutas* ("you don't catch trout with dry pants").

2. The oath "Par Dios" is an unsophisticated yet more polite form of "Por Dios." Michael McGaha posits that Sancho's frequent use of "Par Dios" may be the reason Don Quixote uses only "Por Dios." McGaha also notes, however, that between Chapter XL and Chapter XLIII (Part II), Sancho uses "Pardiez," which is a variant of "Par Dios," and "Por Dios," respectively ("Oaths" 566). These chapters consist of the Clavileño episode and Don Quixote's advice to Sancho before the squire assumes the governorship of Barataria. Erasmus condemned oaths, citing Matthew 5:33–37 as the reason.

3. González Echevarría bases his assertion that Part II is the first political novel on Cervantes's treatment of the expulsion of the *moriscos* from Spain (1609–14) in the novel, which he was writing at the time.

4. The oath "en mi conciencia" is not blasphemous unless it is a reference to God or used in any way to disparage the Catholic faith (McGaha, "Oaths" 563).

5. "How does he go? What danger, toil, and suffering does he encounter? The peasant does not ask these questions, for he has faith, a faith nourished equally by the deep wells of religion and the shallow waters of wishful thinking" (Moore 74).

6. The phrase "Válame Dios" is employed to seek favor from God or to exclaim wonderment.

7. McGaha's numbers encompass the following oaths: "Por Dios," and its variants "Par Dios" and "Pardiez"; "Por quien Dios es"; "Por un solo Dios"; "en Dios y en mi ánima"; "Vive Dios" ("Vive el Señor"); "Voto a Dios" ("Voto ..." and "Voto a tal"); "A fe" ("a buena fe" and "mía fe"); "Vál(g)ame Dios"; and "Cuerpo de (Dios)" ("Oaths" 565).

8. The preponderance of religious celebrations in Spain offered peasants respite from the challenges they faced on a daily basis. To what extent the peasants' participation in these activities shaped their spirituality is difficult to ascertain, but they were active participants: "Los pobres formaban parte de la sociedad estamental y tenían una función que cumplir. Su presencia resultaba imprescindible en numerosas actividades religiosas, por ejemplo en las frecuentes procesiones, sobre todo, durante la Semana Santa; misas o entierros, donde acompañaban a los clérigos, a las órdenes religiosas y a la nobleza, formando 'un solo pueblo.' También participaban en el Lavatorio de pies de Jueves Santo, practica que hoy continúa, en honor al acto que realizó Jesucristo con sus Apóstoles. Se celebraba en edificios religiosos y cofradías, donde un personaje destacado de la sociedad les lavaba los pies; incluso un cronista señalaba que el Rey se quitaba la capa, espada y sombrero, se colocaba una toalla, se arrodillaba y les lavaba los pies a los pobres con un poco de agua" (Pizarro Alcalde 81).

9. Once again, Sancho applies a proverb in a proper manner. There are several references to the universal Catholic Church and Catholicism in Avellaneda's Part II. Sancho makes a reference to the Church and Rome several times: Chapter III, Chapter XXIV, Chapter XXVI, Chapter XXXII, and Chapter XXXV. In Chapter XXVI, Sancho tells Don Quixote that he believes in Jesus Christ and His commandments and "en las santas iglesias de Roma" (41). Sancho invokes the universal Church in Chapter XXXV as the reason it is not necessary for his wife Mari Gutiérrez to sign her name to any document, and, specifically, the letter in which Sancho informs her that they

will live in Madrid and work as servants to the nobleman Archipámpano and his wife: "cree bien firme y verdaderamente todo lo que tiene y cree la Santa Madre Iglesia de Roma" (205).

10. In Part I, Chapter X, Sancho offers to give up the governorship of an island in exchange for the recipe to the Balm of Fierabrás, explaining: "yo renuncio desde aquí el gobierno de la prometida ínsula, y no quiero otra cosa en pago de mis muchos y buenos servicios sino que vuestra merced me dé la receta de ese estremado licor; que para mí tengo que valdrá la onza adondequiera más de a dos reales, y no he menester yo más para pasar esta vida honrada y descansadamente" (187). In Part I, Chapter XXXI, after listening to Don Quixote talk about the unconditional love a knight feels for his lady, Sancho comments on the agape love about which the village priest preaches: "—Con esa manera de amor —dijo Sancho— he oído yo predicar que se ha de amar a Nuestro Señor, por sí solo, sin que nos mueva esperanza de gloria o temor de pena. Aunque yo le querría amar y servir por lo que pudiese" (436).

11. "But I say to you, love your enemies, and pray for those who persecute you, that you may be children of your heavenly Father, for he makes his sun rise on the bad and the good, and causes rain to fall on the just and the unjust. For if you love those who love you, what recompense will you have? Do not the tax collectors do the same? And if you greet your brothers only, what is unusual about that? Do not the pagans do the same? So be perfect, just as your heavenly Father is perfect" (Matthew. 5:38–48; *The Catholic Study Bible*).

12. I include Close's and El Saffar's articles in the bibliography. Allen describes Close and El Saffar as "two of the most brilliant *cervantistas* of their generation" ("The Importance" 440).

13. The narrator notes this development at the beginning of Part II, Chapter V: "Llegando a escribir el traductor desta historia este quinto capítulo, dice que le tiene por apócrifo, porque en él habla Sancho Panza con otro estilo del que se podía prometer de su corto ingenio, y dice cosas tan sutiles, que no tiene por posible que él las supiese; pero que no quiso dejar de traducirlo, por cumplir con lo que a su oficio debía" (67).

14. The overseer is reminiscent of the *syphogrant* from Thomas More's *Utopia*, whose only duty is to ensure that no person lives a life of idleness. My thanks to Ryan Schmitz for drawing my attention to this reference.

15. Cruz cites the Spanish from *Deliberación en la causa de los pobres (y replica de Fray Juan de Robles, O.S.B.)* (Madrid: Instituto de Estudios Políticos, 1965), 15–17.

16. A large house requires three supervisors, who consist of an administrator, a local politician, and a member of the Catholic clergy. The supervisors of smaller shelters are a priest and the town's mayor.

17. The words "A fe," while not an oath, affirm the speaker's enthusiasm for what is to follow.

18. In Part II, Chapter XII, Sancho expresses similar thoughts about death: "como aquella del juego del ajedrez, que mientras dura el juego, cada pieza tiene su particular oficio, y en acabándose el juego, todas se mezclan, juntan y barajan, y dan con ellas en una bolsa, que es como dar con la vida en la sepultura" (122). In the same episode, Don Quixote also states that death is the great equalizer: "—Pues lo mesmo —dijo don Quijote— acontece en la comedia y trato deste mundo, donde unos hacen los emperadores, otros los pontífices, y, finalmente, todas cuantas figuras se pueden introducir en una comedia; pero en llegando al fin, que es cuando se acaba la vida, a todos les quita la muerte las ropas que los diferenciaban, y quedan iguales en la sepultura" (122).

19. Sansón offers to write pastoral or courtly poetry to entertain Don Quixote and Sancho while the three characters travel.

20. In *Vida de Don Quijote y Sancho* (*Life of Don Quijote and Sancho*), Unamuno writes that Sancho's desire that Don Quixote live is entirely self-serving: "No, Sancho, no; tú no eres ni puedes ser señor de ti mismo, y si mataras a tu amo, en el mismo instante te matarías para siempre a ti mismo" (455).

Conclusion

1. Johnson cites the *baciyelmo* episode as an example. Don Quixote believes the basin is Mambrino's helmet, but he identifies the barber's saddle as a mule's packsaddle because it does not fit within the chivalresque narrative. Sancho wants to place the saddle on Dapper, but he can only take it if Don Quixote believes that he is in possession of Mambrino's helmet. As a compromise, Sancho calls it a *baciyelmo*, a combination of basin and *yelmo* (helmet) (95).

Bibliography

Alciati, Andrea. *A Book of Emblems: The* Emblematum Liber *in Latin and English*. Trans. John Francis Moffitt. Jefferson, NC: McFarland, 2004.

Allen, John Jay. *Don Quixote: Hero or Fool? Remixed*. Newark, DE: Juan de la Cuesta Hispanic Monographs, 2008.

———. "The Importance of Being an Ironist." *ehumanista / Cervantes* 1 (2012): 437–47.

Alonso Lasheras, S.J., Diego. *Luis de Molina's* De Iustitia et Iure: *Justice as Virtue in an Economic Context*. Leiden: Brill, 2011.

Álvarez, Marissa C. "Emblematic Aspects of Cervantes's Narrative Prose." *Cervantes* 8 (1988): 149–58.

Aquinas, St. Thomas. *Aquinas's Shorter* Summa: *St. Thomas Aquinas's Own Concise Version of His* Summa Theologica. Manchester, NH: Sophia Institute Press, 1993.

———. *On Kingship: To the King of Cyprus*. Trans. Gerald Phelan. London: Aeterna Press, 2015.

———. *Summa Theologica*. Vol. 1, Part I. Trans. Fathers of the English Dominican Province. New York: Cosimo Classics, 2007

———. *Summa Theologiae: Volume 46. Action and Contemplation*. Ed. Jordan Aumann. Cambridge: Cambridge UP, 2006.

Aristotle. *Aristotle's Nicomachean Ethics*. Trans. Robert C. Bartlett and Susan D. Collins. Chicago: U of Chicago P, 2011.

Armstrong-Roche, Michael. *Cervantes's Epic Novel: Empire, Religion, and the Dream Life of Heroes in* Persiles. Toronto: U of Toronto P, 2009.

Augustine. *The Trinity*. Trans. Stephen McKenna. Washington, D.C.: Catholic U of America P, 1963.

Aylward, Edward T. *Toward a Revaluation of Avellaneda's False "Quijote."* Newark, DE: Juan de la Cuesta Hispanic Monographs, 1998.

Bakhtin, Mikhail. *Rabelais and His World*. Trans. Hélène Iswolsky. Bloomington: Indiana UP, 1984.

Bandera, Cesáreo. *The Humble Story of* Don Quixote: *Reflections on the Birth of the Modern Novel*. Washington, D.C.: Catholic U of America P, 2006.

———. *A Refuge of Lies: Reflections on Faith and Fiction*. East Lansing: Michigan State UP, 2013.

Barbagallo, Antonio. "Sancho no es, se hace." *Cervantes* 15 (1995): 46–59.

Bataillon, Marcel. *Erasmo y España*. Trans. Antonio Alatorre. México, D. F.: Fondo de Cultura Económica, 2007.

Bibliography

Bireley, S.J., Robert. "Early-Modern Catholicism as a Response to the Changing World of the Long Sixteenth Century." *The Catholic Historical Review* 95.2 (2009): 219–39.

Boccaccio, Giovanni. *The Decameron.* Trans. Wayne A. Rebhorn. New York: W. W. Norton, 2013.

Borges, Jorge Luis. "Análisis del último capítulo del Quijote."*Revista de la Universidad de Buenos Aires* V Época 1 (1956): 29–36.

Bowle, John. "A Letter to Dr. Percy." Ed. Daniel Eisenberg. *Cervantes* 21.1 (2001): 95–146.

Bradatan, Costica. "God is Dreaming You: Narrative as *Imitatio Dei* in Miguel de Unamuno." *Janus Head* 7.2 (2004): 453–67.

Burckhardt, Jacob. *The Civilization of the Renaissance in Italy.* New York: Penguin Classics, 1990.

Canavaggio, Jean. *Cervantes.* Trans. J.R. Jones. New York: W. W. Norton, 1990.

The Canons and Decrees of the Council of Trent. Trans. Rev. H.J. Schroeder, O. P. Charlotte: TAN Books, 1978.

Casalduero, Joaquín. "The Composition of *Don Quixote*." Trans. Esther Sylvia. *Cervantes Across the Centuries: A Quadricentennial Volume.* Ed. Angel Flores and M.J. Bernardete. New York: The Dryden Press, 1948. 56–93.

———. *Sentido y forma del* Quijote. Madrid: Insula, 1966.

Casas, Bartolomé de las. *Brevísima relación de las destruyción de las Indias.* Ed. Jean-Paul Duviols. Stockcero, 2006.

Casella, Mario. "Critical Realism." *Cervantes Across the Centuries.* Eds. Angel Flores and M. J. Bernadete. New York: The Dryden Press, 1947. 195–214.

Cassirer, Ernst. *The Individual and the Cosmos in Renaissance Philosophy.* Trans. Mario Domandi. Chicago: U of Chicago P, 1963.

Castillo, David and Nicholas Spadaccini. "Models of Subjectivity in Early Modern Spain." *Subjectivity in Early Modern Spain.* Ed. Oscar Pereira Zazo. *Journal of Interdisciplinary Literary Studies* 6.2. Lincoln: University of Nebraska-Lincoln, 1994. 185–204.

Castro, Américo. *Cervantes y los casticismos españoles.* Madrid: Ediciones Alfaguara, 1966.

———. "Incarnation in *Don Quixote*." *Cervantes Across the Centuries: A Quadricentennial Volume.*Ed. Angel Flores and M. J. Bernardete. New York: The Dryden Press, 1948. 136–78.

———. *El pensamiento de Cervantes.* Barcelona: Editorial Noguer, S.A., 1972.

Bibliography

The Catechism of the Catholic Church. Vatican City: Libreria Editrice Vaticana, 1994.

The Catechism of the Council of Trent. Charlotte, TAN Books, 1982.

The Catholic Study Bible. Ed. Donald Senior. New York: Oxford UP, 1990.

Catteau, Jacques. *Dostoyevsky and the Process of Literary Creation*. Cambridge: Cambridge UP, 1989.

Caussade, Jean-Pierre. *The Sacrament of the Present Moment*. Trans. Kitty Muggeridge. New York: HarperCollins, 1989.

Cavanaugh, T.A. *Double-Effect Reasoning: Doing Good and Avoiding Evil*. Oxford: Oxford UP, 2006.

"Cervantes and His Writings." *American Monthly Magazine* 1 (1836): 342–54.

Cervantes Saavedra, Miguel de. *Don Quijote de la Mancha*. Ed. Martín de Riquer. Barcelona: Planeta, 1980.

———. *Don Quijote de la Mancha I*. Ed. John Jay Allen. Madrid: Cátedra, 1998.

———. *Don Quijote de la Mancha II*. Ed. John Jay Allen. Madrid: Cátedra, 2005.

———. *Don Quixote*. Trans. Tom Lathrop. Newark, DE: Cervantes & Co., 2005.

———. *Novelas ejemplares II*. Ed. Harry Sieber. Madrid: Cátedra, 1992.

———. *Teatro completo*. Eds. Florencio Sevilla Arroyo and Antonio Rey Hazas. Barcelona: Editorial Planeta, S.A., 1987.

———. *Los trabajos de Persiles y Sigismunda*. Ed. Stephen Hessel. Newark, DE: Cervantes & Co., 2011.

Chesterton, G.K. *Lepanto*. San Francisco: Ignatius Press, 2012.

Christian, Jr., William A. *Local Religion in Sixteenth-Century Spain*. Princeton: Princeton UP, 1981.

Close, Anthony J. "Sancho Panza: Wise Fool." *The Modern Language Review* 68.2 (1973): 344–57.

Colston, Ken. "Misreading a Masterpiece." *New Oxford Review*. Web. 27 February 2016.

Cordero Pando, Jesús, ed. *Francisco de Vitoria: Relectio de Potestate Civili. Estudios sobre su filosofía política*. Madrid: Consejo Superior de Investigaciones Científicas, 2008.

Coudert, Allison P. "Melancholy, Madness, and Demonic Possession in the Early Modern West." *Mental Health, Spirituality, and Religion in the Middle Ages and Early Modern Age*. Ed. Albrecht Classen. Berlin: De Gruyter, 2014. 647–89.

Bibliography

Craig, William Lane. *Reasonable Faith: Christian Truth and Apologetics.* Wheaton, IL: Crossway Books, 2008.

Cruz, Anne J. *Discourses of Poverty: Social Reform and the Picaresque Novel in Early Modern Spain.* Toronto: U of Toronto P, 1999.

Cull, John T. "The 'Knight of the Broken Lance' and His 'Trusty Steed': On Don Quixote and Rocinante." *Cervantes* 10.2 (1990): 37–53.

Curran, Charles E. *The Development of Moral Theology: Five Strands.* Washington, D.C.: Georgetown UP, 2013.

Dailey, S.J., Robert H. *Introduction to Moral Theology.* New York: The Bruce Publishing Company, 1970.

De Armas, Frederick A. *Cervantes, Raphael, and the Classics.* Cambridge: Cambridge UP, 1998.

———. *Quixotic Frescoes: Cervantes and Italian Renaissance Art.* Toronto: U of Toronto P, 2006.

Delgado, Mariano. "El cristianismo místico y mesiánico del *Quijote*." *Anuario de Historia de la Iglesia* 15 (2006): 221–35.

Derowitsch, Brent. "Preparing Christians to Die Faithfully By Living Well." *Obsculta* 6.1 (2013): 37–42.

Descartes, René. *The Passions of the Soul.* Trans. Stephen H. Voss. Indianapolis: Hackett Publishing, 1989.

Descouzis, Paul M. *Cervantes, a nueva luz. I. El Quijote y el Concilio de Trento.* Frankfurt am Main: Vittorio Klostermann Verlag, 1966.

———. *Cervantes, a nueva luz. II. Con la Iglesia hemos dado, Sancho.* Madrid: Ediciones Iberoamericanas, S. A., 1973.

———. "Reflejos del Concilio de Trento en el 'Quijote.'" *Hispania* 47.3 (1964): 479–84.

Diccionario de Autoridades. Madrid: Gredos, 1990.

Durant, Will. *The Age of Faith: The Story of Civilization.* New York: Simon and Schuster, 2011.

Eisenberg, Daniel. "La actitud de Cervantes ante sus antepasados judaicos." *Cervantes y las religiones: Actas del Coloquio Internacional de la Asociación de Cervantistas.* Eds. Ruth Fine and Santiago López Navia. Madrid: Iberoamericana, 2008. 55–78.

———. *Romances of Chivalry in the Spanish Golden Age.* Newark, DE: Juan de la Cuesta Hispanic Monographs, 1982.

———. *A Study of Don Quixote.* Newark, DE: Juan de la Cuesta Hispanic Monographs, 1987.

El Saffar, Ruth. *Beyond Fiction: The Recovery of the Feminine in the Novels of Cervantes.* Berkeley: U of California P, 1984.

———. "Concerning Change, Continuity, and Other Critical Matters: A Reading of John J. Allen's *Don Quijote: Hero or Fool? Part II.*" Journal of Hispanic Philology 4 (1980): 237–54.

Enno Van Gelder, H.A. *The Two Reformations in the Sixteenth Century: A Study of the Religious Aspects and Consequences of Renaissance and Humanism.* The Hague: Martinus Nijhoff, 1961.

Erasmus, Desiderius. *Christian Humanism and the Reformation: Selected Writings of Erasmus.* Ed. John C. Olin. New York: Fordham UP, 1987.

———. *The Collected Works of Erasmus:* Colloquies, vol. I. Trans. Craig R. Thompson. Toronto: U of Toronto P, 1997.

———. *The Colloquies of Erasmus.* Trans. Nathan Bailey. London: Reeves & Turner, 1878. 2 vols.

———. *The Correspondence of Erasmus: Letters 2204–2356 (August 1529–July 1530).* Trans. Alexander Dalzell. Toronto: U of Toronto P, 2015.

———. *The* Enchiridion *of Erasmus.* Ed. and trans. Raymond Himelick. Bloomington: Indiana UP, 1964.

———. *Erasmus-Luther: Discourse on Free Will.* Trans. Ernst F. Winter. New York: Frederick Unger Publishing, 1967.

———. Moria *de Erasmo Roterodamo: A Critical Edition of the Early Modern Spanish Translation of Erasmus's* Encomium Moriae. Eds. Jorge Ledo and Harm den Boer. Leiden: Brill, 2012.

———. *The Praise of Folly.* Trans. John Wilson. Rockville, MD: Arc Manor, 2008.

Fastiggi, Robert L. *The Sacrament of Reconciliation: An Anthropological and Scriptural Understanding.* Chicago: Hillenbrand Books, 2017.

Feinberg, Joel. "Psychological Egoism." *Ethical Theory: An Anthology.* Ed. Russ Shafer-Landau. Malden, MA: Blackwell Publishing, 2007.

The Feminist Encyclopedia of Spanish Literature. Eds. Janet Pérez and Maureen Ihrie. Westport, CT: Greenwood Publishing Group, 2002.

Fernández Álvarez, Manuel. *Cervantes visto por un historiador.* Barcelona: Grupo Planeta Spain, 2011.

Fernández de Avellaneda, Alonso. *Don Quijote de la Mancha.* Ed. Martín de Riquer. Madrid: Espasa-Calpe, S.A., 1972.

Fitzpatrick, Sean. "Don Quixote and the Via Dolorosa." *Crisis.* Web. 29 May 2016.

Forcione, Alban. *Cervantes and the Humanist Vision: A Study of Four Exemplary Novels* Princeton, NJ: Princeton UP, 1982.

Bibliography

Foucault, Michel. *The Order of Things: An Archaeology of the Human Sciences*. London: Routledge Classics, 2002.

Friedman, Edward. "Making Amends: An Approach to the Structure of *Don Quixote*, Part II." *Vanderbilt e-Journal of Luso-Hispanic Studies* 2 (2005): n. pag.

Fuentes, Carlos. *Myself with Others: Selected Essays*. New York: Farrar, Strauss and Giroux, 1990.

Gallagher, Raphael. "Interpreting Thomas Aquinas: Aspects of the Redemptorist and Jesuit Schools in the Twentieth Century." *The Ethics of Aquinas*. Ed. Stephen J. Pope. Washington, D.C.: Georgetown UP, 2002. 374–411.

Ganss, S.J., George. *The Spiritual Exercises of Saint Ignatius: A Translation Commentary*. Chicago: Loyola UP, 1992.

Garcés, María Antonia. *Cervantes in Algiers: A Captive's Tale*. Nashville: Vanderbilt UP, 2005.

———. *An Early Modern Dialogue with Islam: Antonio de Sosa's Topography of Algiers (1612)*. Trans. Diana de Armas Wilson. Notre Dame: U of Notre Dame P, 2011.

Gerli, E. Michael. *Refiguring Authority: Reading, Writing, and Rewriting in Cervantes*. Lexington: UP of Kentucky, 1995.

Giuliani, S.J., Maurice. *Acoger el tiempo que viene: estudios sobre San Ignacio de Loyola*. Trans. Miguel Lop Sebastià, S.J. Bilbao: Ediciones Mensajero, 2006.

González Echevarría, Roberto. *Cervantes's* Don Quixote. New Haven: Yale UP, 2015.

Graf, E. C. "The Pomegranate of *Don Quixote* 1.9." *Writing for the Eyes in the Spanish Golden Age*. Ed. Frederick de Armas. Lewisburg: Bucknell UP, 2004. 42–62.

Gula, S. S., Richard M. *Reason Informed by Faith: Foundations of Catholic Morality*. Mahwah, NJ: Paulist Press, 1989

Hannay, David. *The Later Renaissance*. New York: Charles Scribner's Sons, 1898.

Hatzfeld, Helmut. El Quijote *como obra del arte del lenguaje*. Madrid: C.S.I.C, 1972.

Herrero, Javier. "Dulcinea and Her Critics." *Cervantes* 2.1 (1982): 23–42.

Himes, Michael. "Living Conversation: Higher Education in a Catholic Context." *An Ignatian Spirituality Reader*. Ed. George W. Traub, S.J. Chicago: Loyola Press, 2008. 225–41.

Huizinga, Johan. *Erasmus and the Age of the Reformation*. New York: Harper, 1957.

———. *The Waning of the Middle Ages: A Study of the Forms of Life, Thought and Art in France and the Netherlands in the XIVth and XVth Centuries*. Eastford, CT: Martino Fine Books, 2016.

Hume, David. *An Enquiry Concerning Human Understanding: A Critical Edition*. Ed. Tom L. Beauchamp. Oxford: Oxford UP, 2000.

J. B. P. "Don Quixote." *Notes and Queries* 10.261 (1854): 343.

Jehenson, Myriam Yvonne and Peter N. Dunn. "Discursive Hybridity: Don Quixote's and Sancho Panza's Utopias." *Miguel de Cervantes's* Don Quixote. Ed. Harold Bloom. New York: Bloom's Literary Criticism, 2010.

Jesuit Writings of the Early Modern Period: 1540–1640. Ed. and trans. John Patrick Donnelly, S.J. Cambridge: Hackett Publishing, 2008.

Jesús, Santa Teresa de. *El libro de la vida*. Madrid: Penguin Random House Grupo Editorial España, 2015.

———. *Vida de Santa Teresa de Jesús*. Ed. Fray Diego de Yepes. Buenos Aires: Emecé Editores, 1946.

Johnson, Carroll. *Cervantes and the Material World*. Champaign: U of Illinois P, 2000.

———. Don Quixote: *The Quest for Modern Fiction*. Prospects Heights, IL: Waveland Press, 1990.

———. *Madness and Lust: A Psychoanalytical Approach to* Don Quijote. Berkeley: U of California P, 1983.

Kamen, Henry. *The Spanish Inquisition: A Historical Revision*. New Haven: Yale UP, 2014.

Kant, Immanuel. *Immanuel Kant: Groundwork of the Metaphysics of Morals: A German–English Edition*. Ed. and Trans. Mary Gregor and Jens Timmerman. Cambridge: Cambridge UP, 2011.

Knox, Norman. "On the Classification of Ironies." *Modern Philosophy* 70 (1972–73): 53–62.

Konnert, Mark. *Early Modern Europe: The Age of Religious War, 1599–1715*. Toronto: U of Toronto P, 2008.

Kreeft, Peter. *A Shorter Summa: The Essential Passages of St. Thomas Aquinas' Summa Theologica*. San Francisco: Ignatius Press, 1993.

Labarga, Fermín. "Historia del culto y devoción en torno al Santo Rosario." *Scripta Theologica* 35 (2002): 153–76.

Lamet, Pedro Miguel, et. al. *Arrupe y Gárate: dos modelos*. Bilbao: Universidad de Deusto, 2008.

Lange Cruz, S.J., W. Ignacio. *Carisma ignaciano y mística de la educación*. Madrid: Universidad Pontificia Comillas de Madrid, 2005.

Bibliography

Lapesa, Rafael. "La *Vida de San Ignacio* del P. Ribadeneyra." *De la Edad Media a nuestros días*. Madrid: Gredos, 1967. 193–211.

Lathrop, Tom. "Cervantes's Treatment of the False *Quijote*." *Kentucky Romance Quarterly* (32) 1985: 213–17.

Lauer, S.J., Quentin. G.K. Chesterton: Philosopher Without Portfolio. New York: Fordham UP, 2004.

Leclerc, Jean. "L'Enthousiasme de l'Eglise Romaine demontré par quelques remarques sur la vie d'Ignace Loyola." *Bibliothèque universelle et historique*, Tome XI. Amsterdam: Henri Scheltz, 1688. 93–147.

Locke, John. *Letter Concerning Toleration*. New York: Bobbs-Merrill, 1955.

López Alemany, Ignacio. "A Portrait of a Lady: Representations of Sigismunda-Auristela in Cervantes's *Persiles*." *Ekphrasis in the Age of Cervantes*. Ed. Frederick A. de Armas. Lewisburg: Bucknell UP, 2005.

López Calle, José Antonio. "Américo Castro y la exégesis erasmista del Quijote," *El catoblepas* 112 (2011): 1–10.

Loyola, St. Ignatius of. *Ejercicios espirituales de S. Ignacio de Loyola*. Madrid: Imprenta de D. M. de Burgos, 1833.

Lucía Megías, José Manuel. *La madurez de Cervantes*. Madrid: Editorial EDAF, 2016.

Ludwig-Selig, Karl. "The Battle of the Sheep: Don Quixote I, xviii." *Revista Hispánica Moderna* 38 (1974–75): 64–72.

MacCabe, W. B. "Don Quixote." *Notes and Queries* 10.264 (1854): 407–08.

Maestro, Jesús G. "Cervantes y la religión en *La Numancia*." *Cervantes* 25.2 (2005 [2006]): 5–29.

———. *Las ascuas del Imperio. Crítica de las* Novelas ejemplares *desde el materialismo filosófico*. Vigo: Editorial Academia del Hispanismo, 2007.

Mancing, Howard. *The Cervantes Encyclopedia*. Westport, CT: Greenwood Press, 2004. 2 vols.

———. *The Chivalric World of Don Quixote*. Columbia: U of Missouri P, 1982.

———. Don Quixote*: A Reference Guide*. Westport, CT: Greenwood Press, 2006.

Mandel, Oscar. "The Function of the Norm in *Don Quixote*." *Modern Philology* 55.3 (1958): 154–63.

Maravall, José Antonio. *La cultura del Barroco*. Barcelona: Editorial Ariel, S.A., 2002.

Bibliography

Mansch, Larry D. and Curtis H. Peters. *Martin Luther: The Life and Lessons.* Jefferson, NC: McFarland, 2016.

Márquez Villanueva, Francisco. *Cervantes en letra viva: Estudios sobre la vida y la obra.* Madrid: Reverso, 2005.

———. *Personajes y temas del* Quijote. Madrid: Taurus Ediciones, S. A., 1975.

Martín, Adrienne Laskier. *Cervantes and the Burlesque Sonnet.* Berkeley: U of California P, 1991.

Martin, S.J., James. *The Jesuit Guide to (Almost) Everything: A Spirituality for Real Life.* New York: HarperCollins, 2010.

Martinengo, Alessandro. "Cervantes contro il Rinascimento." *Studi Mediolatini e Volgari* IV (1956): 177–223.

Martínez-Bonati, Félix. "El Quijote*: * Juego y significación." *Dispositio* 3.9 (1978): 315–36.

McCrory, Donald P. *No Ordinary Life: The Life and Times of Miguel de Cervantes.* London: Peter Owen Publishers, 2002.

McGaha, Michael. "Is There A Hidden Jewish Meaning in *Don Quixote?*" *Cervantes* 24.1 (2004): 173–88.

———. "Oaths in *Don Quixote.*" *Romance Notes* 14.3 (1973): 561–69.

McKendrick, Melveena. *Cervantes.* Trans. Elena de Grau. Barcelona: Salvat Editores, S.A., 1989.

Menéndez Pidal, Ramón. "Un aspecto en la elaboración del 'Quijote.'" *Mis páginas preferidas. Temas literarios.* Madrid: Editorial Gredos, 1957. 222–69.

Meregalli, Franco. "De *Los tratos de Argel* a *Los baños de Argel. Homenaje a Casalduero.* Madrid: Gredos, 1972. 395–409.

Mirandola, Giovanni Pico della. *Oration on the Dignity of Man.* Trans. A. Robert Caponigri. Washington, D.C.: Regnery Publishing, 2008.

Modras, Ronald. "The Spiritual Humanism of the Jesuits." *An Ignatian Spirituality Reader: Contemporary Writings on St. Ignatius of Loyola, the* Spiritual Exercises, *Discernment and More.* Ed. George W. Traub, S.J. Chicago: Loyola Press, 2008.

Molins, María Victoria. *Teresa de Jesús: La verdad de las Escrituras.* Barcelona: Ediciones STJ, 2003.

Moore, John. "The Idealism of Sancho Panza." *Hispania* 41.1 (1958): 73–76.

Moreno Baez, Enrique. *Reflexiones sobre* El Quijote. Madrid: Editorial Prensa Española, 1968.

Morón Arroyo, Ciriaco. "La historia del Cautivo y el sentido del *Quijote.*" *Iberomania* 18 (1983): 91–105.

Bibliography

Muñoz Iglesias, Salvador. *Lo religioso en* El Quijote. Toledo: Estudio Teológico de San Ildefonso, 1989.

Nabokov, Vladimir. *Curso sobre* El Quijote. Trans. María Luisa Balseiro. Barcelona: Ediciones B, 2016.

———. *Lectures on* Don Quixote. Ed. Fredson Bowers. New York: Harvest Books, 1984.

Nelson, Bradley J. *The Persistence of Presence: Emblem and Ritual in Baroque Spain*. Toronto: U of Toronto P, 2010.

Nelson, Julia R. "Sir Thomas More, Christian Humanism, and *Utopia*." *Archive* 7 (2004): 59–91.

Nelson, Lowry. *Cervantes: A Collection of Critical Essays*. Englewood Cliffs, NJ: Prentice-Hall, 1969.

Nieto, José C. "Don Quixote's Penance in Sierra Morena: Structure and Intentionality." *Juniata Voices* VI (2006): 29–45.

O'Banion, Patrick J. *The Sacrament of Penance and Religious Life in Golden Age Spain*. State College: Pennsylvana State UP, 2012.

O'Brien, Kevin. *The Ignatian Adventure: Experiencing the Spiritual Exercises of St. Ignatius in Daily Life*. Chicago: Loyola Press, 2011.

Oelschläger, Victor. "Sancho's Zest for the Quest." *Hispania* 35.1 (1952): 18–24.

Olin, John C. "Erasmus and St. Ignatius Loyola," *Luther, Erasmus, and the Reformation*. Ed. by John C. Olin, James D. Smart, and Robert E. McNally, S.J. New York: Fordham UP, 1969.

O'Malley, John. *The First Jesuits*. Cambridge: Harvard UP, 1993.

———. *Trent: What Happened at the Council*. Cambridge, MA: Harvard UP, 2013.

O'Neal, S.J., Norman. *The Life of St. Ignatius of Loyola*. New York: Jesuit Seminary and Mission Bureau, 1995.

Pabel, Hilmar M. "Peter Canisius's Ambivalent Assessment of Erasmus." *The Reception of Erasmus in the Early Modern Period*. Ed. Karl A. E. Enenkel. Leiden: Brill, 2013.

Padilla, Ignacio. *El diablo y Cervantes*. México, D.F.: Fondo de Cultura Económica, 2005.

Paster, Gail Kern. *Humoring the Body: Emotions and the Shakespearean Stage*. Chicago: U of Chicago P, 2004.

Payne, Stanley G. *Spanish Catholicism: An Historical Overview*. Madison: U of Wisconsin P, 1984.

Pérez de Herrera, Cristóbal. *Discursos del amparo de los legítimos pobres y reducción de los fingidos; y de la fundación y principio de los albergues destos reinos, y amparo de la milicia dellos.* Madrid: Luis Sánchez, 1598.

Phillips, Margaret Mann. *Erasmus on His Times: A Shortened Version of the* Adages *of Erasmus.* Cambridge: Cambridge UP, 1967.

Pizarro Alcalde, Felipe. "Religiosidad y pobreza en la España moderna." *Tiempo y sociedad* 10 (2013): 79–91.

Pope John Paul II. "Rosarium Virginis Mariae." Vatican: the Holy See. Rome, 16 Oct. 2002. Web. 8 Jul. 2015.

Pratt, Mary Louise. "The Ideology of Speech-Act Theory." *Centrum* 1.1 (1982): 5–18.

Quesnel, Pierre. *The Spiritual Quixote; or, the Entertaining Story of Don Ignatius Loyola, Founder of the Order of the Jesuits.* Trans. Charles Gabriel Porée. London: J. Bouquet, 1755.

Quevedo, Francisco de. *Selected Poetry of Francisco de Quevedo: A Bilingual Edition.* Ed. and Trans. Christopher Johnson. Chicago: U of Chicago P, 2009.

Quint, David. *Cervantes's Novel of Modern Times: A New Reading of* Don Quijote. Princeton: Princeton UP, 2003.

Rawlings, Helen. *Church, Religion, and Society in Early Modern Spain.* London: Palgrave Macmillan, 2002.

Reardon, Bernard M. *Religious Thought in the Reformation.* 2nd ed. New York: Routledge, 2014.

Ricapito, Joseph. *Cervantes's* Novelas ejemplares: *Between History and Creativity.* West Lafayette: Purdue UP, 2000.

Rico, Francisco, ed. *Don Quijote de la Mancha.* Barcelona: Crítica, 1998.

Riley, E.C. *Cervantes's Theory of the Novel.* Newark, DE: LinguaText Limited, 1992.

———. "Symbolism in *Don Quixote*, Part II, Chapter 73." *Journal of Hispanic Philology* 3 (1979): 161–74.

Riquer, Martín de. *Cervantes, Passamonte y Avellaneda.* Barcelona: Sirmio, 1988.

Rivadeneira, Pedro de. *Vida del bienaventurado padre Ignacio de Loyola: fundador de la religión Compañía de Jesús.* Madrid: M. Tello, 1880.

Rivers, Elias L., ed. *Renaissance and Baroque Poetry of Spain.* Long Grove, IL: Waveland Press, 1988.

Roca, Juanma. *El líder que llevas dentro.* Barcelona: Grupo Planeta, 2012.

Bibliography

Rosales, Luis. *Cervantes y la libertad*. Madrid: Instituto de Cooperación Iberoamericana, 1985.

Ruiz, Teofilo F. *Spanish Society, 1400–1600*. London: Longman, 2001.

Sachs, John Randall. *The Christian Vision of Humanity: Basic Christian Anthropology*. Collegeville, MN: The Liturgical Press, 1991.

Schmidt, Rachel. "The Performance and Hermeneutics of Death in the Last Chapter of *Don Quijote*." *Cervantes* 20.2 (2000): 101–26.

Seigel, Jerrold E. "'Civic Humanism' or Ciceronian Rhetoric? The Culture of Petrarch and Bruni." *Past and Present* 34 (1966): 3–48.

Seneca. "On Anger." *Seneca: Moral and Political Essays*. Eds. John M. Cooper and J. F. Procopé. Cambridge: Cambridge UP, 1995.

Serés, Guillermo. "La ira justa y el templado amor, fundamentos de la *virtus* en *La Galatea*." *Bulletin Hispanique* 98.1 (1996): 37–54.

Sicari, Antonio María. *En el* Castillo Interior *de Santa Teresa de Ávila*. Trans. Maria Aránzazu Ruiz de Arcaute. Pergine Valsugana: Associazione Culturale Archa, 2015.

The Spanish Inquisition, 1478–1614. Ed. and Trans. Lu Ann Homza. Indianapolis, IN: Hackett Publishing, 2006.

Spitzer, Leo. "Linguistic Perspectivism in *Don Quijote*." *Cervantes's* Don Quixote*: A Casebook*. Ed. Roberto González Echevarría. Oxford: Oxford UP, 2005.

Strauss, Leo. *Persecution and the Art of Writing*. Chicago: U of Chicago P, 1988.

Sullivan, Henry. "*Don Quixote de la Mancha: Analyzabe or Unanalyzable?*" *Cervantes* 18.1 (1998): 4–23.

Taylor, William B. *Theater of a Thousand Wonders: A History of Miraculous Images and Shrines in New Spain*. Cambridge: Cambridge UP, 2016.

Tovar Foncillas, Claudia del Val. *El protestantismo de la Edad Moderna en Alcalá de Henares*. Madrid: Editorial Bubok Publishing S.L., 2015.

Tylenda, S.J., Joseph N., ed. *A Pilgrim's Journey: Autobiography of St. Ignatius of Loyola*. San Francisco: Ignatius Press, 2001.

Unamuno, Miguel de. *Vida de Don Quijote y Sancho*. Madrid: Espasa-Calpe, 1964.

Vandebosch, Dagmar. "Quixotism as a Poetic and National Project in the Early Twentieth-Century Spanish Essay." *International Don Quixote*. Eds. Theo D'haen and Reindert Dhondt. Amsterdam: Rodopi, 2009: 15–32.

Vega, Lope Félix de. *Coleccion de las obras sueltas assi en prosa como en verso, Vol. I.* Madrid: Antonio de Sancha, 1776.

Véguez, Roberto. "'Un millón de avemarías': El Rosario en *Don Quijote*." *Cervantes* 21.2 (2001): 87–110.

Vilanova, Antonio. "Erasmo, Sancho Panza y su amigo Don Quijote." *Cervantes* 8 (1988): 43–92.

———. *Erasmo y Cervantes*. Barcelona: Editorial Lumen, 1989.

Violero, Julia. "Contemplativos en la acción: Dejarse conducir hacia la integración espiritual." *Ignaziana* 7 (2009): 29–96.

Vitoria, O.P., Francisco de. *Relecciones sobre los indios y el derecho de guerra*. Madrid: Espasa-Calpe, S.A., 1975.

Voltaire. *A Philosophical Dictionary*. Vol. 6. Eds. Tobias Smollett and John Morley. Trans. William F Fleming. New York: St. Hubert Guild, 1901.

Walsh, James J. "Cervantes and Some Romances, Old and New." *The American Catholic Quarterly Review* 41 (1916): 421–52.

Weiger, John G. *The Substance of Cervantes*. Cambridge: Cambridge UP, 1985.

Weimer, Christopher B. "The Quixotic Art: Cervantes, Vasari, and Michelangelo." *Writing for the Eyes in the Spanish Golden Age*. Ed. Frederick de Armas. Lewisburg: Bucknell UP, 2004. 63–84.

Whitman, Jon. *Interpretation and Allegory: Antiquity to the Modern Period*. Leiden: Brill, 2003.

Williamson, Edwin. "Romance and Realism in the Interpolated Stories of the Quixote." *Cervantes: Bulletin of the Cervantes Society of America* 2.1 (1982): 43–67.

Wilson, Diana de Armas. "Cervantes and the New World." *The Cambridge Companion to Cervantes*. Ed. Anthony J. Cascardi. Cambridge: Cambridge UP, 2006.

Zimmerman, Jens. *Incarnational Humanism: A Philosophy of Culture for the Church in the World*. Downers Grove, IL, 2012.

Zimic, Stanislav. *Las* Novelas ejemplares *de Cervantes*. Madrid: Siglo XXI de España Editores, S.A., 1996.

Ziolkowski, Eric J. *The Sanctification of Don Quixote: From Hidalgo to Priest*. State College: Pennsylvania State UP, 1991.

Index

Acevedo, Father Pedro Pablo, 8
Acquaviva, Cardinal Giulio, 10
Alcalá de Henares, 7, 8, 24, 31, 147n36
Alciato, Andrea, 28–29
  Emblematum Liber, 28, 148n45
Algiers, 12–13, 142nn10–12, 143n17
Allen, John Jay, 51, 61, 112, 115, 128, 134, 142n9, 152n19, 153n24, 156n21, 160n1, 161n5, 168n12
alumbrado, 24
Álvarez, Marissa C., 28
Aquinas, St. Thomas, 33, 61, 68, 80, 85, 99, 104, 112–13, 115, 158n33, 159n36, 160n4, 163n23, 166n12
  Summa Theologica, 68, 80, 85, 105, 115, 159n36, 163n23, 166n12
Aristotle, 68, 75, 158n33, 160n4
Armas, Frederick A. de, 28
Armstrong-Roche, Michael, 4
Augustine, St., 22, 85, 159n33
Austria, Don Juan de, 12, 162
Avila, St. Teresa of, 22, 45, 54
  El castillo interior, 23, 146n30, 164n27

Bandera, Cesáreo, 59–60
Barbagallo, Antonio, 125
Bataillon, Marcel, 3, 5, 22, 37–40, 42, 45–47, 96–97
Battle of Lepanto, 10–11, 94, 97, 157n
Bellay, Bishop Eustace du, 29
Bireley, Robert, 16
Boer, Harm den, 40–41
Borges, Jorge Luis, 117
Bowle, Rev. John, 26
Bradatan, Costica, 3

Brotherhood of the Slaves of the Most Holy Sacrament, 7, 141n4

Cabra, 8
Canavaggio, Jean, 7, 8, 13–14, 54, 73, 142n12
Canisius, Peter, 37
Carthusian, Ludolph the, 31
Cassirer, Ernst, 15–16
Castro, Américo, 3, 5, 21, 38–39, 42–44, 53, 149n4, 150n5, 153n26, 162n12
Caulibus, Giovanni de, 31
  Meditationes vitae Christi, 31
Cervantes, Juan de, 7–8
Cervantes, Miguel de, 1–3, 5–6
  El capitán cautivo, 12–13
  and Catholicism, 16–7, 19, 20–24, 26–31
  and Catholic social teaching, 111–16 119–20, 124, 126, 128
  El coloquio de los perros, 9, 39, 152n18
  El curioso impertinente, 10
  and the devil, 102–04
  La Galatea, 14, 73
  life of, 7–12, 14–15
  and moral theology, 57–65, 67, 69, 71–77, 79–80, 84, 87–88
  Novelas ejemplares, 9, 15, 21, 65, 152n18
  Ocho comedias y ocho entremeses, nunca representados, 15, 54, 143n13
  and Penance, 91–93
  Rinconete and Cortadillo, 4–5, 15
  and the rosary, 94–98, 100
  and saints, 108

185

Index

Cervantes *(continued)*

Segunda parte del ingenioso caballero don Quijote de la Mancha, 15
spirituality of, 34, 37–38, 40–42, 44–45, 48–53, 56, 133–35
Los trabajos de Persiles y Sigismunda, 4, 15, 142n7, 142n12, 153n22
El trato de Argel, 12, 143n17
El viaje del Parnaso, 15
Cervantes, Rodrigo de, 9
Charles V (Charles I of Spain), 21, 155n12
Christian Humanism, 16, 19–22, 35, 46, 53, 140, 166n9
Christian, Jr., William A., 17
Cisneros, García de, 16
Ejercitatorio de la vida espiritual, 16
Ciudad Real, 17
Colston, Ken, 4, 54
Complutensian Polyglot Bible, 22
Confession, 16, 18, 24, 31, 57–62, 67, 109, 144, 144n21, 154n3, 155n10, 158n30, 162n15
Convent of the Discalced Trinitarians, 15
Córdoba, 8, 14, 17, 31
Council of Trent, 4, 18, 29–30, 32, 41, 44, 48, 58, 62, 70–71, 95, 102, 104–05, 111–14, 129, 143n14, 144n18, 148n48, 150n10, 154n3, 155n9, 155n13, 157n29, 162n17, 165nn1–3, 165n6, 166n12
Counter Reformation, 37, 49, 65, 163n20
Cross, St. John of the, 33, 54, 158n31
Cuenca, 17, 160n2
Cusanus, Nicholas, 16

Delgado, Mariano, 46
Descartes, René, 67
Devotio Moderna, 16
Dictionnaire philosophique, 25
Dostoyevsky, Fyodor, 118
Dulcinea del Toboso, 18, 73, 87–91, 94, 103, 106–08, 125–26, 128, 130, 138, 152n18, 160n5, 161n7

Écija, 14
Eisenberg, Daniel, 53–54, 75, 114, 156n22, 161n7
El Saffar, Ruth, 134, 161n7, 168n12
El Sol, 11
Erasmus, Desiderius, 5, 9, 19, 21–22, 27, 33, 35–42, 44–50, 52, 65, 79, 96, 98–100, 103, 112, 116, 137, 142n6, 144nn24–25, 145nn26–27, 149nn2–3, 150n7, 150n11, 151nn13–14, 152n18, 153n23, 155n11, 156n16, 166n9, 167n2
Adagia, 144n24
Colloquies, 5, 145nn26–27, 149n3, 152n18, 153n23
Enchiridion militis Christiani, 19–20, 35, 65, 151n14
The Praise of Folly, 39–41, 49, 52, 149n3, 150n7
Sileni Alcibiades, 19
Esquivias, 14–15, 143n15, 148n49
Estella, Fray Diego de, 22

Faber, Peter, 29, 31, 36, 123
Feast of Saint Michael, 7
Fernández Álvarez, Manuel, 7, 9–11, 141n2, 157n23
Fernández de Avellaneda, Alonso, 59, 142n9, 146n32, 150n12, 152n22, 154n7, 158n30, 162n19, 167n9
Fielding, Sarah, 1

Fitzpatrick, Sean, 4, 55–56, 164n34
Fitzmaurice-Kelly, James, 124
Fonseca, Alonso de, 22
Forcione, Alban, 3–4, 21, 38, 141n2
Foucault, Michel, 109, 121
Freire de Lima, Simón, 15
Friedman, Edward, 92
Fuentes, Carlos, 3, 5, 39, 42

Gandía, 30
Garcés, María Antonia, 11, 142n11, 143n17
Gerli, Michael, 1
González Echevarría, Roberto, 79, 114, 128, 164n30, 167n3
Graf, E.C., 28
Granada, Fray Luis de, 22, 33
Guipúzcoa, 23, 147n34

Hannay, David, 5
Hatzfeld, Helmut, 4, 48–49
Holy League, 10–11, 41, 94, 162n14
Horozco, Juan de, 28
Emblemas morales, 28
Hoyos, Juan López de, 9, 21, 38
Huizinga, Johan, 15, 47, 50
Hume, David, 68

Inquisition, 22, 24, 32, 84, 95, 99, 104, 145n27, 149n1, 152n18, 160n2, 162n12, 163n26
Islam, 12–13, 35
Isuzna, Pedro, 14

Jerusalem, 24
Jesuits, 25–27, 29–31, 35, 37–38, 59, 85–86, 123, 147n37, 160n4, 162n15, 166n14
Jiménez de Cisneros, Cardinal Francisco, 8, 22, 44

Johnson, Carroll, 5, 56, 96, 150n11, 156n17, 161n7, 169n1

Kagan, Richard, 8
Kant, Immanuel, 66
Kempis, Thomas à, 31
The Imitation of Christ, 31

Laínez, Diego, 29, 123
La Marquesa, 11
Las Casas, Bartolomé de, 72
Lathrop, Tom, 2, 142n9, 150n9, 156n14
Le Jay, Claude, 29
Leclerc, Jean, 25
Bibliothèque universelle et historique, 25
Ledo, Jorge, 40–41
León, Fray Luis de, 22–33
Locke, John, 20
López Calle, José Antonio, 4, 42–45, 53, 149n4, 151n13
López de Hoyos, Juan, 9, 21, 38
Loyola, St. Ignatius of, 16, 22–27, 29–33, 35–37, 39, 49, 57, 74, 83, 85, 89, 91–92, 100, 117–18, 123–24, 130, 132, 137, 148n47, 157n25, 160n4, 161n6, 161n10, 166n13
Ejercicios espirituales (Spiritual Exercises), 16, 23, 36, 49, 100–01, 132, 137, 144n20, 147n42, 157n25
Luther, Martin, 27, 37, 58, 65–66, 149n2, 156n16

MacCabe, W. B., 27
Madrid, 7, 9–10, 15, 168n9
Madrid, Fray Alonso de, 33
Maestro, Jesús G., 53
Mamí, Arnaut, 11, 142n10
Mamí, Dalí, 11–12, 142n10
Mancing, Howard, 2, 40, 127, 141n2, 142n9

187

Index

Manresa, 24, 89, 91, 144n20, 161n10
Manrique de Lara, Alonso, 22
Maravall, José Antonio, 32
Márquez Villanueva, Francisco, 13, 47, 53, 143n13, 153n26
Martin, S.J., James, 83, 106, 124,
McCrory, Donald, 9–10, 14
McGaha, Michael, 54, 84, 130, 166n2, 167n4, 167n7
Menéndez Pidal, Ramón, 91, 107
Meregalli, Franco, 13
Messina, 30
Mirandola, Pico della, 20
Oration on the Dignity of Man, 20
Molina, Luis de, 74
Montesinos, Antonio, 57, 72
Montesinos, Cave of, 116, 130, 161n10
Montserrat, 24, 89
Moor, 13–14, 24, 54–55, 128, 135, 143n13
Moreno Baez, Enrique, 45
moriscos, 12, 57, 114, 135, 147n37, 167n3
Morón Arroyo, Ciriaco, 13
Moscoso, Francisco, 14

Nabokov, Vladimir, 153n27, 157n27
Nadal, Jerónimo, 85, 86
Nelson, Lowry, 139

Oelschläger, Victor, 126
O'Malley, John, 29, 31, 37–38, 58, 85–86, 147n37, 160n4
Order of St. Francis, 7, 141n3
Order of the Passion of Christ, 50
Our Lady of Aránzazu, 24, 147n34
Our Lady of Montserrat, 24, 89

Pamplona, 23, 117
Paris, 25, 29–31, 36, 123
Percy, Reverend Thomas, 26
Pérez, Francisco, 15

Pérez de Herrera, Cristóbal, 136–37
Discursos del amparo de los legítimos pobres, 136
Philip II, 9, 12, 21, 43, 137, 148n47, 149n1, 156n14, 162n14
Philip III, 15, 43, 114
Philip IV, 94, 163n26
Pope Paul III, 25, 29, 105, 144n20, 148n48
Regimini militantis Ecclesiae, 25
Pope Paul VI, 22
Pratt, Mary Louise, 120
Protestant Reformation, 65, 94, 116, 149n1

Quesnel, Pierre, 25
Quevedo, Francisco de, 7, 84, 154n7
Quint, David, 18, 87–88

Ricapito, Joseph, 21
Rico, Francisco, 96
Riley, Edward C., 28, 119
Riquer, Martín de, 96, 142n9, 158n30,
Rivadeneira, Pedro de, 27, 90, 147n36, 147n41
Rome, 4, 10, 25, 29, 53, 57, 142n7, 167n9
Rosales, Luis, 60

Salazar, Catalina de, 7, 14, 143n15
Salmerón, Alfonso, 29, 123
Satan (devil), 7, 38, 102–06, 128, 141n2, 147n36
Saxony, Ludolph of, 23
The Life of Christ, 23
Schmidt, Rachel, 64, 154n5
Self-flagellation, 16–18
Selig, Karl-Ludwig, 28
Seneca, 76
Serés, Guillermo, 77, 158n32
Seville, 8, 10, 14–15, 17, 31, 35
Siena, Catherine of, 31

188

Index

Society of Jesus, 25, 30–31, 141,
    147n37, 148n47, 166n14
Sosa, Antonio de, 14
Soto, Domingo de, 135
Spanish Armada, 14, 41
Spinoza, Baruch, 53
Strauss, Leo, 2

Toledo, 14–15, 17, 22, 124,
    148n49, 154n2
True Cross Brotherhood, 17

Unamuno, Miguel de, 25, 27,
    89, 107, 117–18, 147n41,
    169n20
University of Alcalá de Henares, 8,
    24, 31, 35
University of Paris, 25, 30–31, 123
University of Salamanca, 24, 58

Valladolid, 15, 35
Valois, Isabel de, 9
van den Wyngaerde, Anton, 8
Vega, Lope de, 7, 146n32, 164n26
Véguez, Roberto, 97, 162n18,
    163n22
Vilanova, Antonio, 40, 138, 150n7
Virgin Mary, 5, 13–14, 24–25, 27,
    94, 97, 104, 152n22, 161n8,
    162n13, 163n26
Vitoria, Francisco de, 57–58,
    153n2
Vives, Juan Luis, 36
Voltaire, 25
Voraigne, Jacobus de, 23
    Flos Sanctorum (*Golden Legend*),
    23, 26, 146n32, 154n4

Weimer, Christopher, 28
Wilson, Diana de Armas, 73

Xavier, Francis, 31, 123

Zimic, Stanislav, 5
Ziolkowski, Eric, 39, 45

About the Book

Don Quixote *and Catholicism: Rereading Cervantine Spirituality*
Michael J. McGrath
PSRL 79

Four hundred years since its publication, Miguel de Cervantes' *Don Quixote* continues to inspire and to challenge the reader. The universal and timeless appeal of the novel, however, has distanced its hero from its author and its author from his own life and the time in which he lived. The discussion of the novel's Catholic identity, therefore, is based on a reading that returns Cervantes' hero to Cervantes' text and Cervantes to the events that most shaped his life. The authors and texts McGrath cites, as well as his arguments and interpretations, are mediated by his religious sensibility. Consequently, he proposes that his study represents one way of interpreting *Don Quixote* and a complement to other approaches. It is McGrath's assertion that the religiosity and spirituality of Cervantes's masterpiece illustrate that *Don Quixote* is inseparable from the teachings of Catholic orthodoxy. Furthermore, he argues that Cervantes's spirituality is as diverse as early modern Catholicism. McGrath does not believe that the novel is primarily a religious or even a serious text, and he considers his arguments through the lens of Cervantine irony, satire, and multiperspectivism. As a Roman Catholic who is a Hispanist, McGrath proposes to reclaim Cervantes's Catholicity from the interpretive tradition that ascribes a predominantly Erasmian reading of the novel. When the totality of biographical and sociohistorical events and influences that shaped Cervantes' religiosity are considered, the result is a new appreciation of the novel's moral didactic and spiritual orientation.

About the Author

Michael J. McGrath is a Professor of Spanish at Georgia Southern University and a Corresponding Fellow of the San Quirce Royal Academy of History and Art (Segovia, Spain). His research focuses on early modern Spanish life and literature, with special emphasis on cultural studies, the *comedia*, *Don Quijote*, and intellectual history. He is the author of more than 60 publications, including two books based on archival research, *La vida urbana en Segovia: Historia de una ciudad barroca en sus documentos* and *Teatro y fiesta en la ciudad de Segovia (siglos XVIII y XIX)*, editions of four of Miguel de Cervantes's *Novelas ejemplares* and plays by Pedro Calderón de la Barca, María de Zayas, Diego de San Pedro, articles that have appeared in the journals *Cervantes*, *Comedia Performance*, *Bulletin of Comediantes*, *Estudios Segovianos*, *ehumanista*, and *Romance Quarterly*, several book chapters, and over 20 book reviews. He has been the editor of Juan de la Cuesta Hispanic Monographs since 2008.

"*Don Quixote*, an example par excellence of multiperspectivism, fittingly lends itself to diverse interpretations. A lesson of *Don Quixote* is that, as with the dancer and the dance, the interpreter cannot be separated from the interpretation. Michael McGrath emphasizes precisely this point as he posits that Cervantes's novel solidly reflects the principles of Catholic theology. McGrath does not eliminate Erasmus from the picture, but he does remove the noted humanist as a guiding force of the commentary. Here, the aims of satire and irony are juxtaposed with a deep respect for Catholicism and its teachings. McGrath's personal faith and analytical skills serve him well. This is a thoughtful and well-argued study that will add to the critical dialogue on *Don Quixote* by accentuating a key ingredient of Spanish life, culture, history, and, lest we forget, fiction."
                                          Edward H. Friedman, Vanderbilt University

www.ingramcontent.com/pod-product-compliance
Lightning Source LLC
Chambersburg PA
CBHW061447300426
44114CB00014B/1868